Why do I feel so down ... When my faith should lift me up?

How to break the three links in the chain of emotional bondage

G.W. Mullen MD

Sovereign World

Sovereign World Ltd
PO Box 777
Tonbridge
Kent TN11 0ZS
England

ISBN 1 85240 246 6

This Sovereign World book is distributed in North America by Renew
Books, a ministry of Gospel Light, Ventura, California, USA. For a free
catalog of resources from Renew Books/Gospel Light, please contact your
Christian supplier or call 1-800-4-GOSPEL.

antiNomian vs.

Typeset by CRB Associates, Reepham, Norfolk.
Printed in the United States of America.

Dedication

This book is dedicated to my son Peter (9 years) and daughter Ruth (11 years). They (im)patiently endured the many months that Dad was preoccupied with 'that book'. It has not been at all difficult for them to appreciate that they are being raised by imperfect parents.

I want to particularly thank my wife Kathy who contributed one chapter and who has faithfully accompanied me in this journey to freedom.

I also want to thank my Pastors, Terry and Melissa Bone for their constant encouragement to keep on writing when it seemed I'd never see the end.

Kathy and I both want to thank our counsellor Sam DaSilva who made sense out of our confusion and walked us through 'the valley of the shadow of death.'

Contents

Foreword

According to the National Institute of Mental Health, 17.6 million Americans will suffer from depression in any given year. It is so prevalent that it has been called the common cold of psychological disorders. It creeps into the lives of all people regardless of age, sex, social or economic status. However, twice as many women struggle with depression as do men.

In America the number of doctor visits in which patients received medication for mental problems rose from 32.7 million to 45.6 million over the decade from 1985 to 1994. Visits in which depression was diagnosed almost doubled over the same ten years, from 11 million to 20.4 million. This is an incredible increase especially in light of the fact that only one-third of all those so afflicted will seek treatment.

The number of people diagnosed with anxiety disorders has also doubled. Struggles with fear, anxiety, and panic attacks have surpassed depression and alcoholism as the number one psychological disorder in America. We are experiencing a blues epidemic in an age of anxiety.

That is why I am so excited about this new book by Dr Grant Mullen who is by profession a medical doctor. Not all doctors are trained or even willing to look beyond their scientific discipline to seek a holistic cure for their patients. If all our psychological problems had a physical origin, then medication along with a balanced regime of nutrition, exercise and diet is the proper prescription. Medication can be helpful and in some cases essential in the treatment of depression and anxiety disorders. It is very difficult to process biblical truth in extreme cases of fear and anxiety until the physical symptoms have been reduced through medication. The alleviation of human suffering by legitimate medical means administered in the name of Jesus, is truly an act of mercy.

Such one-dimensional thinking, however, will not, provide an adequate answer. The medical profession openly acknowledges that most of their clients are sick for psychosomatic reasons. But you still wouldn't be biblically holistic if you only added cognitive and behavioural therapies along with medication, while ignoring the God of the universe, the god of this world, and the spiritual nature of mankind.

Dr Mullen offers a prescription for the body, soul, and spirit. We need both the church and the hospital, the pastoral counselor and the medical doctor. We are spiritual beings who possess physical bodies and live in a fallen world. You will delight in reading how Dr Mullen discovered, *that the whole world lies in the power of the evil one* (1 John 3:19). But more importantly you will be helped as he shares how you too can be physically, mentally and emotionally healthy.

He confronts two extreme views that cripple our chances of recovery. One extreme is to place all our hope in medication for resolving our emotional problems. The other extreme is to believe that taking any medication is a lack of faith in God. I am personally committed to helping people discover who they are in Christ and to live a liberated life in Him. That is why I encourage you to study this very readable book. You just may be set free in Christ.

Dr Neil T. Anderson

Introduction

Could this book possibly help me?

I know what you're thinking as you open to this page, 'Not another Christian book on emotional recovery. Could it ever help me?'

You are probably asking yourself if this book could ever assist you with the emotional struggles that you have lived with most of your life and never had victory over. Many of you have grown tired of all the Christian self-help books that promise to 'set you free' but have left you unchanged. You're ashamed to admit that you are no better after consuming so many books, tapes and seminars. You feel guilt, condemnation and shame that you are somehow to blame for your state of brokenness.

The Christian community (and society in general) has usually been reluctant to address emotional issues, since there has been such limited understanding of the nature of

Many Christians struggle their whole lives with emotional baggage.

emotional bondage. Those who have competence and experience in this area have often been shunned and marginalized by a skeptical church. They have been forced to become 'parachurch' organizations since the established churches were too afraid to make this ministry a regular part of their program. As a result, the life-giving ministry of those involved in emotional healing has only been available to those who sought for it outside the church.

It has been my observation that the church prefers not to discuss or think about emotional issues since it doesn't understand the problems nor does it have any idea what to do about them. The church of course, can't teach what it doesn't know so it avoids the subject. There is a general feeling that if you don't discuss the issue then it will go away. Emotional issues are too uncomfortable to be discussed or addressed in church or at home so the emotional dysfunction just keeps getting passed on to each generation. Emotions become an avoided subject like sexuality – or even financial planning. The result of this approach is easily observed in the anti-Christian rebellion by the teenagers of cold, rigid, religious families.

Why are emotions important?

> *'A happy heart makes the face cheerful, but heartache crushes the spirit.'* (Proverbs 15:13)

Emotions are one of the three fundamental God-given building blocks of our personalities. The other building blocks are intelligence and will. To function at the level of wholeness that God intends for us, we must be healthy in all three areas. If our emotions are damaged, we will not function at the level our intelligence or will would permit. If we have a defective foundation, we can never build a stable life on top of it.

It is not hard to see that when an extremely gifted and intelligent person has damaged emotions, they could have a lifetime of struggle and never reach their potential. Gifting, talent, ability, wealth, status, beauty, fame or even godly anointing cannot cover up or cure damaged emotions. If a person is emotionally unwell, it will be their 'Achilles heel,' an opportunity for Satan to limit or even destroy the use of their other abilities. This can be seen both in the secular and spiritual worlds since all humans have this characteristic in common. Anyone who has worked in a personnel department will know that emotional stability is every bit as important in the workplace as intelligence and skill. We often see in the media that a highly talented and gifted athlete, actor or even evangelist can ruin their career through emotional instability.

Our success in work, family and in ministry is dependent on our emotional health whether we want to admit it or not.

How I became interested in emotional health

When I first started out in medicine, my primary interest and training was in anesthesia, though I also did general practice. I was very interested in pain control through general and local anesthesia. In my general practice, I was surprised to discover that more people were suffering from emotional pain than from physical pain. I was also amazed to uncover the fact that to most people, the most painful moment in their lives was from emotional, not physical pain. Perhaps the greatest shock to me as a young physician was to see that so many Christians were in emotional pain. Their suffering seemed greater than those 'in the world' since they would not admit that they were in pain and were too ashamed to go for help. Their 'religion' which was intended to be a source of comfort and hope had become to them a barrier which prevented them from being honest enough to get help, for fear of being condemned and shamed by fellow believers. Christians didn't seem to know where to turn for assistance that they could trust.

I of course, was totally unprepared to treat emotional pain but I was drawn to this condition since it seemed like there were so few places that people could go for help. I was particularly interested in how to help Christians resolve their emotional suffering. This book is the result of seventeen years of observing the patterns of emotional illness and recovery. It is also a compilation of what I have learned from

Christians are ashamed to have emotional problems.

other Christian teachers and authors who have contributed greatly to my understanding of the spiritual dimensions of man. Most importantly however, it is the result of what I learned through personal experience in my own journey to emotional wholeness.

In this book I hope you will discover a broader, more integrated approach to emotional recovery which will bring hope and healing to those of you who are still struggling with your thoughts, feelings and emotions. As you read, God will show you the missing pieces to your emotional puzzle and your walk to freedom will be accelerated. Throughout the book I have placed anonymous testimonies from my patients which explains in their own words, their emotional struggles and path to freedom. I have also included short illustrative scenarios using fictitious names that are based on common situations that I see.

I am not an expert on every subject referred to in this book. There are many more qualified authors than I, who can provide more comprehensive discussions on these topics. My purpose is to show how the different teachings of these gifted Christians can be integrated with modern medicine to bring emotional recovery to larger numbers of people. In the 'Recommended reading' chapter, I have listed all the authors and books that I will be referring to. I encourage you to read them for yourselves.

The nature of man

Man is unique among all created things. He has a personal spirit which requires him to live in two realms, the natural and spiritual. The natural world is what he sees and the spiritual world is what he senses with his spirit. To be fully human according to God's design for man, we must be healthy and functioning in both worlds. This concept is very well explained in the book by Harold Eberle, *Spiritual Realities, Vol. 1.*

My purpose in this book is to show that thought and emotion are the only parts of us that exist in both worlds, natural and spiritual. Wholeness in this part of our being will always require healing in both the natural and spiritual aspects of thought and emotion. One cannot come to complete emotional wholeness if treatment is directed at only the natural or spiritual aspect of man. God wants to bring us to freedom in both realms. This book will outline both the natural and spiritual paths to wholeness.

From my observation, though I know this is controversial, there are three parts to man: body, soul and spirit.

The body is our physical nature, the part of us that relates to the natural or 'seen' world. As a result of the Fall of man, it is temporary, imperfect and subject to malfunction, degeneration and disease. It is the temporary container which our spirit briefly inhabits while on earth.

Our spirit is the eternal part of man. This is the true inner, unseen self which God places in us at conception. It is the part of us that relates to the unseen spirit world which includes both God and Satan.

Our soul, in my observation, is our personality which includes our mind, will and emotions. It is the part of us that relates to other humans. It is shaped by all of our accumulated life experiences. I like to think of it as being attached to a huge bag or drag-net into which all our life events go. These experiences both good and bad, shape our personalities and determine how we relate to others.

Before salvation, we are outside God's kingdom and in the domain of Satan. There he molds us into his image by wounding us in as many ways as possible. These accumulated wounds leave deep scars in our personalities which cause lifelong emotional bondage. The longer we live in Satan's kingdom, the greater will be our accumulated wounds and personality damage.

When we become Christians, our spirit immediately transfers ownership to God as we enter His kingdom. From this point on, we begin to have a relationship with God as He fills our spirit with His own. The Holy Spirit then begins the process of transforming us into God's image.

When we enter God's kingdom our body doesn't usually change much. I do know of some who have been miraculously healed of a chronic illness at the moment of salvation but most people notice no physical change. If we wore glasses before salvation, we usually wear them afterwards. Once in the Kingdom however, we are given the privilege of praying for divine healing. The body is still subject to the consequences of the Fall, which means it is still subject to disease and malfunction. The eventual transformation of our physical bodies will take place in heaven. Until then, we have to cope with somewhat unreliable physical containers for our eternal spirits.

The problem with our old nature

The most important question in this discussion is this, 'What happens to our soul or personality at the moment of salvation?' One way of looking at this question is to consider another one. How much must we change to qualify to become Christians? Well obviously we don't have to change at all. God, through the miracle of His grace takes us just the way we are so that He can clean us up and transform us into His image.

> *'But God demonstrates his own love for us in this: While we were still sinners, Christ died for us.'*   (Romans 5:8)

This means of course that we enter the Kingdom in a sorry state; broken, bleeding and wounded, with deeply damaged personalities from all the years that we have spent in Satan's kingdom. God accepts us as we are, damaged goods, 'factory seconds.'

It is possible then, to be a new Christian and still be bound in sinful habits and attitudes, with dysfunctional relation-ships, deep personality scars, addictions and compulsions. In other words, a new Christian can still have a very active and contaminated old nature which wreaks havoc in their mind even though their spirit now belongs to God. This old nature is metaphorically the bag that I referred to earlier which is part of our soul. Prior to salvation the bag is accumulating pain and scars that Satan is putting into it to mold us into his image. After salvation, we are still carrying the bag since it is so much part of our former or old nature. This bag will continue to hurt and paralyze us until the Holy Spirit so fills our life with God's new nature that the chain holding us to the bag of our old nature is cut.

> *'Do not conform any longer to the pattern of this world, but be transformed by the renewing of your mind. Then you will be able to test and approve what God's will is, his good, pleasing and perfect will.'* (Romans 12:2)

It is God's desire to free us from that bag of pain, clean us up and give us His new nature. He wants to empty the bag, heal all those wounds and scars and set us free from our sinful habits and thought patterns. God wants our new nature in Christ to control our soul and personality so that the old sinful nature is overcome and disposed of. These two natures are always in conflict.

> *'For the sinful nature desires what is contrary to the Spirit, and the Spirit what is contrary to the sinful nature. They are in conflict with each other, so that you do not do what you want.'* (Galatians 5:17)

This process of emptying the bag and healing the wounds is called sanctification, and it is accomplished through the actions of the Holy Spirit.

Where do you think the bag of our old nature is located? Where do you think this battle between our new and old natures takes place? Well, it's actually located between your

There is a lot of room between our ears to carry the bag of our old nature.

ears. There is a surprisingly large amount of space there for this battle to take place. You see, the battle is actually for your thoughts and for who will control them. As long as your old nature is unhealed and active, then your thoughts will be controlled and contaminated by your sinful and painful past. When the old nature is healed and cut away from you then your thoughts will be full of God's nature.

Your thoughts are really the rudders of your life. The spiritual force that controls your thoughts, will control your life. That is why there is such a battle between the forces of light and darkness to control your mind. Satan desperately wants to influence and control your thoughts by keeping your old nature alive and your new nature suppressed. God wants to set you free from that old nature so your mind will be free to think His thoughts and walk out of the bondage of your past into your new nature in Christ.

The bag of pain

Let's have a closer look at this bag which I call our old nature. What is it about this bag of pain that makes it so dangerous and disabling? If it's just a historical record of sin and injury how can it continue to hurt us after we are Christians?

Doesn't the Bible say that *'all things have become new'* (2 Corinthians 5:17)? After salvation can't we just turn ourselves in a new direction, say goodbye to the past and move on *'forgetting that which is behind'* (Philippians 3:13)? If our past is forgiven and 'covered by the blood' how can it be of any relevance to the present?

These are very common questions which I asked myself years ago when I began to get involved with emotional illness. I am still asked these questions by Christians who don't understand why people like me are involved in helping people find emotional freedom. They assume that at the moment of salvation everything is fixed and we just press on in victory. Anyone who stumbles along the way is dismissed as a weak, undisciplined, poorly motivated, disobedient and carnal Christian. These well-meaning Christians have created a climate of condemnation and shame which prevents Christians from admitting that they need help. The problems with the old nature are then suppressed and 'swept under the rug.' This of course guarantees that the person will remain struggling with their old nature and never come to the freedom that God intended. Satan loves this characteristic of Christians to shame and condemn each other. He encourages it at every opportunity. When Christians do his work for him, Satan couldn't be happier.

The reason that the bag of our old nature is so dangerous and disabling even after we have become Christians, is that the bag contains the chains of emotional bondage. Our souls become so contaminated while we are in Satan's kingdom that our emotions are damaged and are chained up so they can't be free to enjoy the blessings of our new life in Christ. These very heavy and encircling chains have to be broken for us to be free of our old nature and to have healthy emotions.

These chains of emotional bondage which tie us to our old nature do not automatically drop off at the moment of salvation. As I have already pointed out, we enter God's kingdom with this bag. It is God's intention to break our chains and set us free once we enter His kingdom. There is one condition of this process however, that can block a person from receiving the freedom that they are entitled to.

This process is voluntary.

Our old nature is Satan's playground, it will continue to hurt and bite us.

To come to freedom from our old nature and our emotional bondage, we have to want to be free and we have to allow God to break our chains. It is possible and surprisingly common to be a Christian your whole life and never be free, if you have not allowed God to break your chains.

The walled city

I like to think of the kingdom of God as resembling a huge walled city with one large gate. This gate is the entrance of salvation. At a far corner of the city is God's throne room. This is the place of greatest blessing, power, peace, anointing and the place where we can have the closest and most intimate relationship with God. The distance from the gate to the throne room is the path of sanctification. This is the path that God leads us along to find freedom from our emotional chains and old nature. It is God's intention that every new arrival at the gate be assisted down the path by the Holy Spirit who does the work of breaking our chains and setting us free. The problem is that each believer has the choice of whether or not they want to go on this journey to freedom.

It has been my observation that there are many Christians who huddle around the inside of the gate. Yes, they are saved and inside the walls of the Kingdom but they never progress past the entrance area. It is as if they are unaware that there is

Many abandon the path to emotional freedom.

a path to freedom which leads to a closer more liberating relationship with God. They never show any interest in progressing past the entrance. There they are, huddled as close to the gate as possible, not wanting to get too far away from the world they just left. They clutch tightly to the bag of the old nature, to which they are securely chained. They never lose their old ways of thinking, feeling and relating. They stay in their old sinful habits and attitudes. They remain bitter, angry, vengeful, dishonest, dysfunctional, fearful and unable to have satisfying relationships with anyone including God.

But they are saved.

God is calling to them to leave the gate, get on the path, walk with the Holy Spirit and allow Him to cut off the chains and release them from their old natures. The crowd at the gate doesn't seem to hear God's call. In fact, if one of them does ever recognize God's voice calling them to the throne room, the others try to talk him out of it and convince him that he didn't hear anything and to ever consider a change from his present state is just religious fanaticism. The bondage becomes so familiar to them that they consider it to be normal and they fear any change. The prospect of freedom to them is just a myth which is not worth pursuing.

Their state is much like a caterpillar who only knows crawling on leaves and refuses to enter the cocoon since he fears any changes to his familiar lifestyle. He is so frightened by the unfamiliarity of the prospect of flight, that he chooses to avoid it.

This crowd has become so established at the gate that they have built large towns all around the entrance area. These people deny that there is anything more to Christianity than to enter the gate. They get angry at anyone who points out that there is a path of change that leads to a much more satisfying relationship with God. They see no need for the Holy Spirit to do miraculous deeds to set believers free since they are so comfortable in their towns near the gate. They have even become so accustomed to the bag and chain of their old natures which torment and contaminate their minds continuously, that they have redesigned their religious clothing to make room for the huge bag underneath. In this way they have a wonderfully religious exterior covering a huge bag of sin and pain.

But they are saved.

They like these outfits so much that they make fun of the Christians on the pathway who no longer carry their bags and don't have such a large bulge under their religious

We have a choice, to stay at the gate or walk to freedom.

clothes. They accuse the believers on the path, of being too preoccupied with 'that touchy-feely, navel-gazing, inner healing, new age, religious extremism.'

Infant Christians

When believers are so attached to their old natures and the sin that always accompanies it, they will remain infant Christians. When you have a large number of infant Christians in a church, then that church is paralyzed in infancy and will never do the work that God has called it to until the members break free of their bonds. This is a surprisingly common state in the Christian world.

Satan is delighted to see 'the Church' immobilized by infant Christians so emotionally bound to their old natures that they can never move ahead with God. Satan's kingdom is never threatened by bound Christians. Satan will actively resist every step that a believer takes to break free of the bondage from the old nature which he placed on them. The old nature is his playground where he can reach into the bag of pain and hurl abusive, condemning and disturbing thoughts at unhealed Christians. Even though a believer is in God's kingdom, he can still be harassed by Satan, particularly if that believer is still chained to the old nature.

This conflict between the old and new nature can easily be

Our old nature becomes familiar and comfortable under our religious clothes.

illustrated by a Christian who is struggling with an old habit like alcohol or bitterness. These are characteristics from his old nature which Satan put into his bag to destroy him. After salvation he may still be struggling with these problems since the emotional root that caused the behavior is still unhealed. In this state, Satan can still overwhelm this believer with the urge to drink or hate. When God tries to activate the new nature and call the believer to greater closeness, Satan then turns up the urges and hatred so the believer feels so discouraged and ashamed that he turns back from God's call.

You can see from this illustration that the scars of our past will hold us back from God's plan for us until we are healed and set free. The longer we have spent in Satan's kingdom, the greater is the accumulated damage that we need healing from. We cannot heal ourselves by denying the reality of the chains. Ignoring the problem only guarantees that it will come back to hurt us again. The Holy Spirit is waiting to set you free from your chains once you become aware of them.

As we are healed, the bag empties, the chains fall off and we walk to emotional freedom. Satan then loses his influence on us since he no longer has the ammunition from your past to throw at you. When he tries to remind you of your old habits, you can just walk away confident in the love of God which surrounds and protects you. The fruit of the Spirit will then begin to appear in your life as you are set free. Your relationships with God and with others will be transformed.

The chain of emotional bondage

Let's take a closer look at the chain which binds us and makes us slaves to our old nature. This chain keeps us tied to unhealthy emotions so I call it the **chain of emotional bondage**. There are three giant links in this chain that must be broken if one is to come to emotional freedom.

The three links are:
- physical illnesses of thought control (chemical imbalances),
- the harassment of Satan (demonization), and
- personality injury (woundedness).

Physical illnesses of thought control refer to the medical

conditions doctors refer to as 'mood and psychotic disorders.' The most common disorders or 'chemical imbalances' are **depression, manic depression** and **schizophrenia**. In these conditions, one loses the ability to control one's thoughts due to brain chemistry deficiencies. These conditions require medical treatment and divine healing.

Demonization refers to the specific harassment of an individual by demonic forces. This can be experienced in a very general or in a very specific way depending on the degree of bondage a person is in.

Woundedness refers to every negative or damaging experience in a person's life that has hurt them and left a scar on their personality which restricts their emotional freedom.

In the secular world, the treatment of emotional bondage is primarily with the use of medications to improve thought control and 'cognitive therapy' which helps a person adjust his way of thinking to avoid painful and disturbing thought patterns. This method certainly helps a significant number of people.

In the Christian world, we have access to God's supernatural power to break us free of emotional bondage as well as the methods available to the general public. One would think then that our success rate in emotional recovery should be much higher than in the secular world. Sadly, it has been my observation that it is not the case. Why is that so?

How the Church has misunderstood the treatment of emotional bondage

In the Christian world, the treatment of emotional bondage has been a very divisive and controversial subject. As a result of the controversies, believers have divided up and polarized into primarily four ideological camps. Each camp has claimed at times to be the only path to emotional freedom. They have looked with suspicion and criticism on the other groups and even felt in competition with them.

Our Bible Schools have also been polarized into these camps. The graduating pastors then teach and practice this polarization with their parishioners. Is it any wonder that so few Christians reach emotional freedom?

Denial

In this camp the primary treatment method is denial, or the use of religious clichés. This group is primarily composed of very independent and religious males who feel that the best way to 'straighten out your feelings' is to use 'mind over matter.' They feel that feelings should always be 'subject to one's will', so if you are having an emotional problem, 'it's your own fault' and that you should just 'snap out of it' and 'get on with life.' To them, emotional problems are a sign of weakness and must never be admitted to. 'Real Christian men don't allow themselves to get depressed,' would be their unwritten motto. Women, in their eyes, are allowed to have such problems but only because they have not yet reached the level of enlightenment of their male brethren.

Physicians are to be avoided since they 'will only get you hooked on pills' which 'dull you to reality.' Counselors and therapists are dangerous too since they 'waste money' that could be 'going to our groceries' or to 'missions.' Therapists 'just get you dependent on them so they can have a steady income' and they just want you to 'wallow in your past.' Their best advice is to 'just get to the altar, pray it through and get on with your life' since 'the past is behind you,' 'you're a new creature in Christ, act like one!' They quickly get impatient with churches who focus on 'that touchy-feely, navel-gazing, inner healing, new age stuff.' 'Just take every thought captive, and be a man.'

Some in this group feel that all you need is 'more faith.' They teach that if you have enough faith you won't have any emotional or physical problems. Those who continue to struggle consider it to be their own fault.

In these groups there is a great deal of shame, bitterness and resentment which is submerged but expressed in other dysfunctional ways. Teenage rebellion is more common in these religious groups. No one reaches emotional freedom if they remain in this environment. Satan loves these groups since their old natures are alive and well and he keeps tormenting them with it. None will admit to a problem so they never get help. They are suspicious of anyone who addresses emotional issues in the church.

Medications

This camp, of which I was an active and evangelistic member, is the one that believes that virtually all emotional bondages are caused by physical illnesses or chemical imbalances. The treatment then is primarily physical or medical. It was my belief in those days that if everyone could get on the right medication, their mood would normalize and their emotional problems would resolve. I felt that everyone should be able to solve their own problems once the medications were working.

I too was suspicious of counseling or those who said prayer was the only answer.

Deliverance

In this group are very sincere and anointed believers who are familiar with the tools of Satan to harass believers and to keep them bound to the old nature. The extremists in their groups feel that medications and counseling are unnecessary. The total treatment is in the deliverance from the attack of evil spirits.

They are suspicious of physicians whose medications they feel only dull people out of spiritual reality and allow Satan to hide behind a drug-induced mental fog. They are also skeptical of counselors who 'miss the root issue' and don't do deliverance.

Inner healing

In this last group are most of the counselors who feel that emotional bondage is solely the result of personality wounds from the past. The 'inner healing' of these wounds will bring emotional freedom. Many of them feel medications are useless 'band aids' and that deliverance is unnecessary when the emotional roots are dealt with.

Satan has reveled in the polarization of Christians over the treatment of emotional bondage. There is no doubt that the latter three treatments have helped many. Each group has dramatic and factual success stories. The sad fact is though, that due to the polarization of treatments, most people have not come to the level of emotional freedom that

God intended for them since they have only received one of the three treatments that God wants us to use to find total freedom. A person may find freedom in one area but remain bound in the other two. This has led to a great deal of discouragement among Christians who wonder why they are not well after having some success in their chosen treatment path. The competitive polarization of treatments has confused believers so that they are reluctant or ashamed to try any of the other treatments. They then remain unhealed and struggling not knowing where to turn next.

What God has shown me in the past few years, is that to come completely free, we need to be ministering to emotionally broken believers in all three areas of bondage. The Body of Christ now must recognize the usefulness of medications, deliverance and inner healing as a combined treatment for all believers who struggle with their emotions. We are now beginning to see all three camps joining hands to see a far higher percentage of Christians come to emotional freedom.

In my opinion, the church should be a healing community. It should be rescuing men and women from Satan's kingdom and bringing them into an environment where they can be healed from the bondage and wounds that have accumulated while in darkness. The church should be 'on the cutting edge' of emotional healing using every method that God has given us to 'set the captives free.'

The greatest tool in evangelism, in my view, is not an attractive presentation, tract, speaker or song, but emotionally transformed, anointed Christians reaching out and offering hope and emotional peace to their communities.

The purpose of this book is to help you understand what emotional bondage is and to explain the fundamentals of the three treatment paths; medications, deliverance and inner healing. You will come to realize how they can all be integrated together and applied to the emotional healing of Christians.

By the end of this book I hope you will better understand not only how to begin your own journey to emotional freedom, but how to assist others in the same journey.

Now let's have a closer look at the three links in the chain of emotional bondage.

SECTION 1

Physical Causes of Emotional Bondage

Chapter 1

You mean I'm not going crazy?

'A man's spirit sustains him in sickness, but a crushed spirit who can bear?' (Proverbs 18:14)

The stigma

As I was growing up in the church, emotional or mental disorders in members were always spoken of in hushed whispers. It is understandable that any personal medical problem is confidential and should be spoken of with great sensitivity but there was another message communicated by the hushed whisper. The unspoken message was that emotional illness was a sign of spiritual and personal weakness and that strong Christians really shouldn't suffer from these conditions. In recent years I have even heard a denominational leader state that 'no Christian of good character will ever suffer from depression.' Another pastor and leader stated to me that 'if there was more repentance we could empty the mental hospitals.'

These careless statements by Christian leaders cause so much unnecessary suffering in Christians. These men are basically saying that emotional illness is the fault of the victim and that they should be able to get out of it themselves. This very damaging opinion is widespread in Christianity and has heaped condemnation and shame upon the most emotionally vulnerable in the body of Christ.

There are many who blame all emotional illness on willful sin or the activity of demons. There is no doubt as we will see later, that sin and demons play a role, but not all emotional disturbances can be blamed on spiritual causes.

This attitude, that emotional illness was not an acceptable

*The church has unintentionally put condemnation and
shame on depressed people.*

part of being a Christian, even made me suspect that a true
Christian could never become a psychiatrist. I just presumed
that if Christians weren't supposed to get this problem then
there would be no need for a Christian to treat the problem. I
had also picked up in the church the impression that
psychiatrists were anti-Christian and would try to rob you
of your faith. So then how could a Christian study to become
a person who blames faith for emotional illness and then
tries to remove faith as part of the treatment? This was so
ingrained in my thinking that even as a junior medical
student I was stunned to find out that there were Christian
psychiatrists who not only incorporated Christian values in
their treatments, but were willing to come to my University's
Christian Student Association and explain their work to us.

How I got involved in emotional illnesses

As I mentioned earlier, when I started practice I did family
medicine and anesthesia. I was totally untrained and unprepared to deal with the large number of people suffering
with emotional illnesses that came to my office so I referred
them to psychiatrists as I had been taught to do. Some
returned much improved on a new medicine but others were
totally defeated, feeling that their faith had failed them and

they were condemned to a life of psychiatric treatment. I saw so much emotional suffering in my patients and even in Christians, that I began to ask God how it was that this many sincere and well-meaning Christians could have such emotional pain.

During this time when my interest in emotional illness was beginning to awaken, God arranged for me to be given a book by Dr John White entitled *The Masks of Melancholy.* Here was a practicing Canadian psychiatrist who at the same time pastored an evangelical church! This to me was the ultimate paradox. How could two opposite positions exist in the same man. He was and remains a very respected Christian author and yet he was a psychiatrist.

In this book, Dr White explained how medical, spiritual and emotional issues all intertwined to cause emotional illness. When I completed this book it was like the lights went on in my mind and I began to understand the role of medical and spiritual treatments. At last I understood how to determine who could be helped by medications. For several years I used the book as required reading for any patient who wanted to see me about their depression.

Soon after this event I began to try some psychiatric medicines on people meeting the criteria I learned in the book. I thought it would be worth a try while they were waiting the many months before being able to see a psychiatrist. To my absolute astonishment (which I of course never showed to the patients) many began to improve. In my eagerness and disbelief, I questioned each of them very carefully as to what had changed in their mood, in what sequence and at what dose of medication. As a result of this process of treatment and inquiry I learned how to recognize and treat mood disorders. Word soon got around the Christian community that depressed believers were recovering at my clinic without any loss of faith. My mood disorders clinic was then born.

Within a few years of my entry into the field of psychiatry and more particularly, the treatment of Christians, I became aware that pastors and Christian counselors were as confused as I had been about the role of medical psychiatry in Christian emotional illness. I began to hear reports of pastors

resigning from ministry due to overwhelming discouragement. They clearly had become depressed and rather than go
for treatment, which they still considered as unbecoming a
Christian, they left the ministry in total burnout.

I was also hearing of pastors who resigned out of the
complete frustration of not being able to effectively help
the endless number of people coming to them for counseling. So many of their parishioners were not improving after
receiving the pastors' advice. The pastors then commonly
assumed that their 'anointing' or 'calling' had lifted or that
God was not as powerful as they had thought so there was no
longer any point in continuing in ministry.

I felt so sorry for these pastors that I began doing seminars
and even wrote a booklet on how pastors, counselors and
Christians in general could easily diagnose a mood disorder
and help a depressed person get medical treatment. With the
use of this information, a pastor or counselor can quickly
recognize the symptoms of medical illness and refer them for
treatment rather than become engulfed and discouraged by
endless discussions with a person they can't help. I have
included all the information from that booklet in this
volume.

Blurred vision and blurred thinking

In the first section of this book, we will examine the physical
causes of emotional illness. We will cover the basics of
psychiatric diagnosis and treatment so that you will be able
to tell who should see a doctor. I hope to remove all the
mystery, misunderstanding, confusion and stigma attached
to depression, manic depression, schizophrenia and attention deficit disorder.

Medical research in recent years has provided physicians
with very effective tools to treat these common conditions.
These treatments however, are not reaching the people who
need them because of the lack of awareness and misunderstanding of the general public.

The current situation is similar to the era when eye glasses
were first introduced. They were a very effective treatment for
blurred vision but they were not well received by the public

since people had no idea that they themselves had blurred vision and could be helped with glasses. Most had learned to live with their poor vision and ridiculed those who did wear glasses. I'm sure that there were those who said that 'if God wanted me to see better he would have made me that way, there's no need to wear those ugly things on my face.' In those days one could function quite well with poor vision since transportation was with horses and the animals always knew the way home even if the driver didn't.

Those who tried the glasses couldn't believe the improvement and wished that they had started wearing them years before. Their vision became normal but they had to live with the stigma attached to wearing glasses. The people around them didn't realize how much better the person's vision had become since blurred vision was an invisible handicap. It was easy and popular to criticize the ugly glasses.

Now we are dealing with problems of 'blurred' thinking, which are invisible to an observer. Even the sufferer doesn't know that he is not thinking as clearly as he should be. The victim is so accustomed to this disability that he doesn't know that he has a problem. He is then resistant to the suggestion that he could be helped and even ridicules those who do go for help. The church has been very guilty of criticizing and shaming those who go for psychiatric help since it has not understood the biological origin of 'blurred thinking.'

In those days people thought they could function well with poor vision.

Why would Christians need to understand brain chemistry?

Blurred thinking and blurred vision are equally important handicaps and both should be treated. There should be no stigma to either condition. Disorders of thought should not be over spiritualized any more than vision problems. For those of you who need glasses to read, how well does the Bible speak to you if you try to read it without your glasses? The Bible is silent if you can't see the words. Is this because you are spiritually dead? Has the Bible lost its power in this circumstance? Are you under spiritual attack if you can't see the page of scripture? Not at all. Do you need prophetic revelation or deliverance to get the Bible to speak to you again? No, you just have to put your glasses back on. To us it's just common sense.

I want you to think of chemical imbalances in the same way, except in this case the 'glasses' need to be swallowed to restore proper brain chemistry. If the thinking disability is left untreated it will be hard to read, worship, pray or have proper relationships. The disability will be personal, vocational and spiritual, but the treatment will initially be medical. I hope that after reading this book you will realize that it's just 'common sense' to recognize and treat blurred thinking. There should be no stigma at all to getting treated for these conditions. To ignore this problem is no different than refusing to wear your reading glasses and then not being able to read a Bible.

Satan loves mood disorders since he can so easily condemn Christians who suffer from them. When the condition is treated successfully, he loses his foothold on your thoughts. To ignore or refuse treatment for this condition is just like refusing to wear your glasses and voluntarily living with the consequences of poor vision. I hope that through this book the stigma to medical treatment will disappear and that these conditions will become as socially acceptable as vision disorders.

This section will allow anyone to 'measure' their thinking pattern and determine if there is any 'blurring' which could be corrected. This information of course, does not replace a proper evaluation by a physician or counselor but it will assist in the evaluation process.

Next we will find out how common these problems are.

Chapter 2

Has depression become an epidemic?

' "Meaningless! Meaningless!" says the Teacher. "Utterly meaningless! Everything is meaningless." '

(Ecclesiastes 1:2)

'I loathe my very life; therefore I will give free rein to my complaint and speak out in the bitterness of my soul.'

(Job 10:1)

'He wanted to die, and said, "It would be better for me to die than to live." '

(Jonah 4:8)

How common is depression?

Of all the different kinds of chemical imbalance mood disorders that we will discuss, **depression** is by far the most common.

Depression is one of the most undiagnosed and disabling medical conditions in society today. According to many studies, it costs the US economy approximately $27 billion annually in medical costs, lost productivity, unemployment, increased susceptibility to illness, suicide, family disruption, relationship failure, alcohol abuse and personal suffering. The Canadian costs are estimated at $5 billion annually.

Mental disorders cause a much broader degree of disability than most other medical conditions like back pain, diabetes and heart disease. A psychiatric condition affects all levels of functioning as compared to other diseases which only affect one organ system. Insurance companies are now very concerned at the staggering number of disability claims that are being submitted due to emotional disability. There are several corporations in Canada who realize that mental disability has become for them the most common cause of days off work due to illness. They have started prevention and early detection programs for their employees.

Depression is more disabling than most chronic illnesses. Even though there are now very effective treatments available, most people with depression remain undiagnosed and untreated due to lack of awareness and not accepting depression as a legitimate illness. The unnecessary suffering often continues for a lifetime, causing intense mental, emotional and physical anguish, disrupting all relationships both at home and work.

If a person acknowledges this condition and goes for help, they then must endure the unfair stigma of an uninformed public that presumes that depression is a character defect, lack of will power or a personal weakness. Not only does a depressed person have to cope with the illness but also with the scorn of society. No other chronic illness is treated so unfairly by the public.

Six to ten percent of the population is depressed at any given time. This very common condition is undiagnosed and untreated in eighty percent of its victims.

Depressed people have to endure misunderstanding.

The problem with the Y chromosome

Depression is more common in women due to poorly understood genetic factors. It is not because they are the 'weaker sex' or because emotional issues are 'women's problems.' There are some medical conditions that are more common to one sex or the other. Heart disease for example is more common in males for genetic reasons only. It has been estimated that ten to twenty percent of women will at some time in their lives have symptoms of chemical imbalance depression. The condition for the majority of them will usually be mild and remain untreated but that means that there are a very large number of untreated women who are not feeling as well as they could be.

The lifetime risk for men is a much more difficult statistic to estimate. When I first started treating depression, the lifetime risk for depression in men was four percent. The number has now climbed closer to ten percent in the past fifteen years. I'm not convinced that men are more depressed now than they were when I started practicing. I think the difference has come due to improved detection techniques for the symptoms of depression in men. It is much more difficult to diagnose depression in men and I have a theory as to why that is so.

We know that the difference between the sexes in the incidence of depression is due to genetic factors. The genetic difference between males and females is that males have a Y chromosome that females don't have. After many years of observation of men and through being one myself, I have come to the conclusion that the Y chromosome is likely made of 'denial!' It is extremely difficult to get a man to admit he is depressed or to accept treatment.

In my years of practice I have noticed a profound difference in how men and women suffer with depression. When a woman is depressed, she will usually come to my office and complain that there is something wrong with herself, that it is her fault and she wants help to fix the problem. When a man is depressed, if he comes to the office at all, which in itself is rare, he will say that there is something wrong, it's the fault of his wife and would I please fix her.

The Y chromosome is made of denial.

Instead of admitting to the problem, he will run from it, busy himself, watch TV or abuse alcohol to distract himself from the discomfort. It is very frustrating to try and get men into treatment for depression. It is even more difficult if they are serious Christians since they will always have a spiritual explanation for the problem that excuses them from medical treatment.

Depression is more common as people age and unfortunately the elderly assume that it is normal to be depressed and don't come for treatment. It is found in all races and social classes, even occurring in those who are not stressed and are otherwise completely well.

All disorders of mood are strongly inherited. If one parent has depression, there is a thirty percent risk that a child will also become depressed. If both parents are depressed the risk may rise to seventy-five percent.

Depression is not a benign illness. Fifteen percent of untreated depressed people will commit suicide and eighty percent of all those who commit suicide have a treatable mental illness. This means that there are a very large number of preventable suicide deaths.

At least ten percent (some researchers say twenty percent) of the population will suffer from a mood disorder at some time in their life. Most will not be treated because of the stigma attached to the diagnosis and treatment. Stigma is the single most important obstacle to treatment. Sufferers are afraid to report their symptoms due to the negative consequences which may come in their work and family as a result of their diagnosis.

Depression in the church

I have often been asked if depression was more or less common in Christians than in the general public. This is a very hard question to answer and to my knowledge there is no research available on this issue. I have however observed some trends in our churches.

It seems to me, though this is merely from personal observation, that there is a higher percentage of depressed people in evangelical churches than in the general population. This is not because Christianity makes you depressed. I think the explanation is that evangelical churches deliberately attract 'seekers.' Seekers are those who sense that there is something missing in their lives and they are seeking answers to their emptiness. This is the population who are most receptive to the gospel of hope that Christian churches provide. Our churches then fill with seekers who are searching for or who have found Christ. Depressed people are the most persistent seekers in the population. They know something is wrong but they are not sure what it is or where to look for a solution. It is easy to see how our churches could quickly fill with depressed seekers.

The most serious issue that church leaders must grapple with is, what happens to a depressed seeker after salvation? If the depression remains untreated or unhealed, as we will see later, the chemical imbalance will be a severe handicap to a maturing faith. It will be very hard to pray, worship or socialize while depressed. If a new believer with depression is not helped specifically with their depression, it is very likely that they will become discouraged in their walk with God and then give up and return to their previous lifestyle. The attrition rate for new converts suffering with depression is alarmingly high.

It seems to me that if churches would realize this, they

could become rescue centers for both the soul and the emotions. If new believers suffering with depression could be directed into a treatment program using the information in this book, far more of them would recover and discover an exciting walk with God. I have seen many find salvation through '12-step programs' where a person's emotional and spiritual needs have been dealt with in a supportive group environment. The effectiveness of Christian evangelism would be greatly increased if we took the message of spiritual and emotional hope to those who need it most.

The story of Ms L

I became a Christian at age twenty-seven and like most people, I had a lot of baggage to deal with. Emotionally I would go from being very 'hyper,' excited and happy to extremely angry, depressed and agitated in a matter of minutes. A simple comment or a mildly irritating situation would set me off into extreme reactions where everything was wrong, my whole life was awful and I could never do anything right. I cried frequently, with very little provocation, for happy or sad circumstances. I was very upset most of the time. I could never understand why I behaved the way I did.

When I became a Christian, I would find myself attacking those who tried to help me. I was totally ashamed of who I was and doubted a God who said he could love someone as disgusting as me.

My concentration level was short and ineffective. My thoughts were racing and I would focus constantly on the negative aspects of my life. There was little I felt I could do and while I hated my life at that time, I felt that I deserved my condition and that I couldn't expect anything better for myself. I had always been like that and I didn't know what change could look like.

When I was finally diagnosed with a chemical imbalance, I was again ashamed, fearful and felt I deserved to have a problem so much worse than other medical problems that I would now be labeled with. This brought on more self-loathing and general anger toward myself and God. I rejected those who tried to help me. I wanted to push everyone away.

I continued counseling during these times but I would

often give up since I didn't see much change although others would comment on the progress I was making. I was also very fearful that the medication would alter my personality and make me seem 'drugged up.' I also struggled with the fear of negative long-term effects of the medication on me and possible side effects that hadn't been discovered yet. In short, I was very suspicious.

I have been on medications since 1993 and I can say that things have improved. I still have days where I am reminded of my old self but at least now I realize who I am meant to be and that my emotions don't have to rule me. My concentration level is better and I find it easier to relate to God, and to spend time reading the Bible. I have grown in my Christian walk. I have had to work through problems with medication levels where I have tried to reduce the medicine and found that I didn't feel as well and had to return to it. Although this was a setback for me, I wouldn't want to return to the way I was functioning before.

I hold a firm belief that with the Holy Spirit's healing power and continued work through Christian counseling that I will be healed of the chemical imbalances that have dominated my life. My aim is to live without any medication. I am thankful that there are ways to control these imbalances so that I can continue to work through the issues that need to be addressed. I look forward to coming out on the other side where I can encourage those who have not yet started on this journey. I have set that as a personal standard and continue to seek God's daily help to see it become a reality.

I am grateful to the many Christians who have devoted their careers to helping people uncover this problem so that they can break through the clouds of stigma and shame.

Now let's examine the most common physical condition causing emotional bondage.

Chapter 3

What is depression?

'I have been allotted months of futility and nights of misery have been assigned to me. When I lie down I think, "How long before I get up?" The night drags on, and I toss till dawn. My days are swifter than a weaver's shuttle, and they come to an end without hope. Remember, O God, that my life is but a breath; my eyes will never see happiness again.'　(Job 7:3–7)

Isn't depression a normal part of life?

Sue was seventeen and in high school. She was struggling like everyone else her age to fit in and be accepted. This particular year she was not getting along with her friends and she had not been invited to any of their parties. Sue was feeling hurt and left out. She didn't want to go to church any more where she would see these friends. School was the only activity in her life that she enjoyed and her grades were excellent. Sue felt depressed.

Bob was thirty, a successful accountant until the last few years. He was finding it harder to do his usual work. He couldn't keep his mind on anything long enough to complete it. He was always tired. Bob was getting increasingly worried about insignificant things. Every pain he experienced made him wonder about cancer. He would lie awake at night, unable to stop worrying if he had made any errors in his work the previous day. Life was becoming a struggle and he was losing his will to continue the battle each day to survive. He just didn't seem interested in his work or family anymore. Bob felt depressed.

Both Bob and Sue felt depressed but there was a vast

difference between their situations. The general public does not correctly differentiate between normal and abnormal 'depression.' If we are going to help those who need it most, we must be able to tell who is suffering from the illness of depression.

Depression is by far the most common form of mental suffering. It is however, a poorly defined condition which means different things to different people. We must be able to distinguish between the transient 'depression' of someone unhappy about a recent disappointment (Sue) and the severe crushing despair of one who has for many years lost all interest in life (Bob). I choose to use the term 'discouragement' for temporary mood fluctuations which would be commonly referred to as the 'blues' and would never be considered an 'illness'. 'Depression' is reserved for prolonged disorders of mood which require professional help.

It is not always easy to distinguish between these two conditions and it requires considerable training and experience. There is presently no blood test or X-ray that will diagnose mental illness. Understanding what a person is thinking and feeling is the only way to separate these conditions. This difficulty in making the diagnosis has caused enormous difficulty in getting the right people into treatment.

Some day we might have a test for depression.

At this time we have no screening tool to use on the population to find all those that are depressed and need help. It is much easier to find people with vision impairment since the vision screening chart is widely available and well accepted by the public. Our ability to diagnose depression depends on a person's ability to describe what they are thinking to someone who understands illnesses of mood. This requires a significant level of insight, motivation and verbal skill. There are many sufferers who are just unable to communicate their thoughts and so they remain untreated. Since we have no test, we cannot prove that someone has a depressive illness. This allows skeptics to influence a depressed person not to accept treatment or to accept another explanation of their symptoms. The inability to measure mood causes the public to see psychiatric treatment as unreliable, unpredictable, 'hocus pocus' and to be avoided. It is a constant struggle for physicians to try to convince sufferers that there is a scientific and reliable treatment for something that can not be measured scientifically.

I will try to describe the differences between true depression and what I call discouragement.

Discouragement is transient with an obvious cause and the person is still able to enjoy other unrelated activities. It resolves with time and supportive counseling. A discouraged person can still be hopeful, with good thought control and concentration. In our example, Sue had recently felt badly about her circumstances but she still did well at school which requires great concentration. She met the criteria for normal discouragement over life events.

Depression is usually very prolonged with unrelenting symptoms. It is often, though not always characterized by sadness. There is an inability to enjoy activities and all interests fade. There is general hopelessness and a lack of ability to control or steer thoughts. This is a much more disabling condition than discouragement. Bob was truly depressed. He had been suffering for years, his concentration and thought control was worsening. He was losing interest in all of life. Bob needed medical treatment and counseling. Sue likely only needed a friend or at the most, counseling.

What causes depression? Can't they just 'snap out of it?'

The brain is divided into regions or 'control centers' that direct every activity of the body. I have attempted to illustrate these regions in Figure 1. These control centers work independently of conscious thought to automatically regulate your body. For example, your pupil size is adjusted continuously by one of these control centers, yet you have no control over it whatsoever.

In the movement control center, nerve cells communicate with each other and with muscle cells to create movement. This process is initiated by a thought of intention to move a limb. The nerve cells in the movement intention region of the brain send a command to the nerves cells which connect to the muscles to carry out the movement. If there is any kind of nerve damage or chemical imbalance in the movement control nerves, there will be no transmitted signal nor will there be movement. Nothing will move even though there may be a very strong intentional thought to move the limb. This is the situation after a stroke. The intention to move is there but nothing moves due a nerve injury.

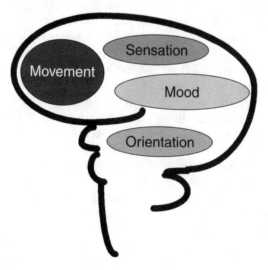

Figure 1 Brain control regions.

How far can you go without a steering wheel?

You only have voluntary control of your limbs if all your nerve cells are working correctly to give you that control in response to a thought of intention. If any nerves in the chain of command are not functioning correctly, nothing moves regardless of the intensity of the intention.

This situation can be illustrated if you consider a high-performance sports car fueled and ready to go. The highly skilled driver takes his seat, pulls out his maps and waves to the crowd who is encouraging him on. The conditions for driving are perfect. When the driver attempts to pull out of the driveway he discovers that the steering wheel is not connected to the wheels. How far is he going now?

In this scenario, there are very strong intentions but nothing happens since there is an internal invisible problem that takes control of the vehicle away from the driver.

It is important to realize that forming a thought is as physical an event as blinking an eye or moving your arm. Nerve cells in the brain allow you to form thoughts in the same way that they permit movement. We only have full control of our thoughts when all the nerve cells are working properly to give us that control. This process is subject to malfunction like any other part of the body. We can lose voluntary control of our thoughts if we have an internal

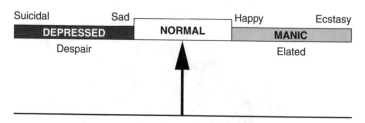

Figure 2 The mood control center should maintain mood in the normal range regardless of circumstances.

neurological malfunction or an imbalance of nerve transmitter chemicals even though we may have the best of intentions to control our thoughts.

The mood control center which is illustrated in Figures 1 and 2, is a place in the brain where thought content and thought speed is regulated. This center controls what you think about and how fast you think about it. It therefore controls mood and concentration. We don't know where it is located in the brain since it is more of a function than a location.

If your nerve cells are working correctly in this location, your mood and concentration will always be kept within the normal range. It is impossible to measure mood but we define normal mood as being relaxed, content, feeling in control, concentrating normally, being clear-headed and coping with stress. I'm not sure that I know anyone this normal; they would likely stick out from the population and be very dull. When the control center is functioning well, your mood will always eventually return to the normal range regardless of the degree of negative stress which would be depressing or positive stress which would be exhilarating. It works much like a top or gyroscope which will always return to the vertical position as long as it is spinning.

There are very specific chemical substances called neuro transmitters which are produced by brain cells to regulate these control functions. If anything happens to disrupt the production of these chemicals, then the control center will malfunction and mood will fluctuate outside of the normal range and you will lose the ability to control your thoughts. If for example, there is a chemical imbalance, you would find

The ability to control thoughts is lost.

your thoughts going much faster and it would be harder to control what you were thinking about. If something positive happened, your thoughts could race uncontrollably in excitement or if something bad happened they could race with depressive thoughts. You would lose the ability to put brakes on the thoughts.

It is now well established that mental illnesses are usually the result of an imbalance in the chemicals associated with mood control. This tendency to malfunction is usually inherited. Symptoms may just appear without reason or depression may come as a result of stressful circumstances that bring out the inherited tendency to have a mood disorder. As a result of the discovery of the above facts, depression is now seen as a physical illness needing and responding to medical treatment.

Due to the genetic nature of the condition, a triggering stress is not always needed. Sometimes depression just develops over years with no obvious cause. There is no doubt however, that stress can trigger a depressive illness in someone who already has the genetic potential for depression. If there is very strong genetic potential, then it will take very little stress to trigger an illness and symptoms may appear at an early age. If the genetic link is weaker, then more stress is needed to cause disability and the condition may not appear until late in life if at all.

The treatment of depression is the same whether or not it was triggered by stress. If the chemical imbalance is present, it can be treated regardless of the cause. Think of it this way. If someone breaks their leg, they will need a cast. It doesn't matter if it was caused by a fall or a car accident, the treatment of the resulting disability is the same.

When the chemical imbalance is corrected, the person is then better able to deal with their stresses since their thought control has been restored.

How does a depressed person feel?

Depression has a very wide variety of symptoms and each individual shows a different pattern. Generally speaking, these people have usually been sad for prolonged periods without obvious cause. The onset of depressive symptoms is usually very slow and insidious so a person doesn't realize that they are slowly sliding into depression. They just gradually adjust to an ever-worsening mood and assume that they are reacting normally to life's circumstances. The onset of depression is often during the teen years but at that time the symptoms may dismissed as just an 'adolescent phase' (see Chapter 4).

In my clinic, after someone has recovered from depression, I always ask them when was the last time they had felt as well

Depression is very disabling.

as they did after treatment. The answer is commonly, 'I have never felt this well in my life' or 'not for at least twenty years.' This was a shock to me in my early years but it illustrated how gradually the condition takes hold and how people just get used to being depressed.

Depressed people lose interest in most activities of life which previously gave them pleasure. They feel defeated, useless, hopeless, unable to pray, punished by God, and unworthy of anyone's love or God's forgiveness. They may feel that God has left them or is no longer listening to them due to unknowingly committing the 'unpardonable sin.' They consider themselves to be a failure as a Christian and as a person. Plagued by guilt, they condemn themselves for not being able to 'snap out of it.' Some have increased irritability and will attack everyone around them as the likely cause for their unhappiness. They find it hard to relax or ever feel content. There is a diminished interest in sex or any kind of intimacy.

Depressed people often have great difficulty falling asleep due to persistent and uncontrollable racing of unpleasant thoughts or worries through their mind. Many will awaken at 4 am and will be unable to fall asleep again because of the same racing of thoughts. Others oversleep and use it as an escape from an unpleasant reality.

Concentration on work, pleasure or reading becomes impossible while struggling with the continuous stream of unpleasant and depressing thoughts which cannot be kept out of the mind and become like a tormenting audio tape that can't be shut off. In this state they become the victim of their thoughts rather than the initiator and controller of thoughts. When reading they will see the words but have to reread the sentence many times before understanding what was said. It is hard for them to keep their minds on anything. Memory seems to fail and it becomes very difficult to finish any project due to fatigue or lack of interest.

Fatigue becomes overwhelming in eighty percent of depressed people. Daily responsibilities which were previously easy and pleasant are seen as enormous undertakings. Everything becomes such an effort that all activities are avoided. A depressed person also finds it very hard to make decisions since their self-confidence is so low and concentration is so impaired. Anxiety becomes a continuous thought pattern which cannot be turned off. The depressed person will worry about everything, even tiny details of life which never before attracted their attention. Fifty percent of depressed people can't stop worrying. Intense fear and worry may induce unusual behavior patterns like repetitive hand washing to rid themselves of a sensation of being dirty. This is also known as **obsessive compulsive disorder (OCD)**, which we will discuss in Chapter 8.

There may be a preoccupation with body symptoms and frequent visits to doctors with complaints that can never be diagnosed or treated. Chronic pain is often present and it hides the underlying depression. Unfortunately, medical treatment is then directed at the pain so the mood remains untreated and the emotional disability continues undetected. Sixty percent of chronic pain patients have a medical depression but they may hide behind the legitimacy of pain to prevent the detection of a less socially acceptable condition. Depression causing pain was even described in the Bible by David:

> *'Because of your wrath there is no health in my body; my bones have no soundness because of my sin. My guilt has overwhelmed me like a burden too heavy to bear. My wounds fester and are loathsome because of my sinful folly. I am bowed down and brought very low; all day long I go about mourning. My back is filled with searing pain; there is no health in my body. I am feeble and utterly crushed; I groan in anguish of heart. All my longings lie open before you, O Lord; my sighing is not hidden from you. My heart pounds, my strength fails me; even the light has gone from my eyes. My friends and companions avoid me because of my wounds; my neighbors stay far away.'* (Psalm 38:3–11)

Socialization is difficult during depression and it becomes very uncomfortable to attend church. Depressed people find that they don't get anything out of church services and often complain that they 'aren't being fed.' They have multiple complaints about the pastor or members. It is very common for them to change churches frequently in search of a congregation that will fill their needs.

Crying becomes a frequent event. There is a tendency to blame others, especially spouse, family members or God for their state of unhappiness.

All of the above symptoms by themselves are common and do not always indicate a mental illness. When however, a number of these signs are present continuously for over two months, then treatable illness must be suspected. A more complete list of the symptoms of depression can be found in Chapter 12.

Depression affects every part of our ability to think and feel. It clouds our personality and changes how we interpret events and how we relate to others. It magnifies physical pain, disrupts relationships, blocks communication and changes our eating and sleeping patterns. It also affects everyone around us in a negative way. There are very few illnesses known that cut such a broad path of devastation and disability. It is a very common condition but it often goes undiagnosed since there is no confirmatory test and it can be masked by chronic pain, fatigue and burnout.

One common type of depression only occurs during the winter months. It is called **seasonal affective disorder** or **SAD**. In this depression, a person can be totally symptom free in the summer but will notice a drop in mood every fall. During the winter months the symptoms are identical to conventional depression but they remit spontaneously in the spring. These sufferers may only need medications during the winter months. Light therapy is also effective in some people. It involves sitting in front of a special type of lamp for several hours daily in place of taking medications.

It has been my observation that most of those who have come to my clinic suspecting that they had SAD did in fact have depression symptoms year round but were only aware of them in the winters. They responded best to continuous year round treatment rather than winter only medications.

Dysthymia

Most cases of depression are mild. If you refer to Figure 3, the arrow is usually just slightly into the black zone. When symptoms are mild, most people ignore them and are never

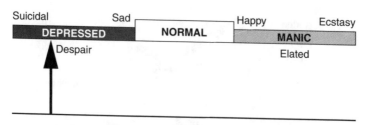

Figure 3 Chemical imbalance prevents the mood control center from restoring normal mood so thoughts slide into depression.

treated so it leaves them chronically emotionally disabled but unaware of it. Researchers estimate that at least six percent of the population are chronically unhappy, in a state of mild depression. This state of mild depression has now been termed **dysthymia**. People with this form of depression are very susceptible to becoming severely depressed with advancing years or increasing stress. Dysthymics often suffer from chronic vague physical symptoms that don't easily fit medical symptom models like persisting headache, abdominal pain, poor sleep, fatigue and poor appetite. They can't be easily diagnosed or treated since their problems are so ill defined. Dysthymics also have chronic poor relationships.

Once again we can draw a comparison to vision abnormalities. Most short-sighted people have only mild symptoms, very few ever need a 'white cane' which indicates blindness. We commonly, however, prescribe glasses to the mildly impaired since we know it will help them with reading and driving and improve their quality of life. The same should be the case in mood disorders. Mildly depressed people should also be treated since their disability is definitely interfering with their lives and relationships. Unfortunately, this group is the hardest to detect and the most difficult to convince to get help. Mild depression and dysthymia responds to the same treatment as severe depression. A symptom checklist for dysthymia can be found in Chapter 12. With any of those checklists, you will be able to diagnose yourself or a loved one and know if medical treatment is needed. These kinds of depression are broadly referred to as **unipolar depressions** (see Figure 4).

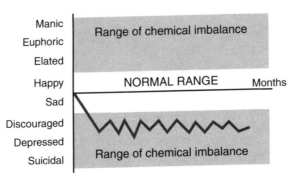

Figure 4   *Unipolar depression. The onset of depression is insidious and can continue undetected for a lifetime.*

The story of Mrs M

Why Lord? Why do I feel this way, act this way, speak this way, treat others this way? I am not me anymore! The real me is lost somewhere and a stranger has taken over. Oh God, please help me, I hate myself! What kind of Christian am I? Maybe I'm not even a Christian at all. If this is a spiritual battle Lord, I'm not winning. My husband and children would be better off without me than to have to continue living with who I have become. What's wrong with me Lord? I'm powerless and am so very tired of the struggle.

Have you ever found yourself thinking these thoughts, believing you were truly on the verge of going crazy? I have many times during my life. I lost interest in living. I didn't feel worthy of the gift of life. I felt defeated, useless, hopeless, unworthy of anyone's love or forgiveness, including God's. I was full of guilt and self-condemnation always thinking that I should be able to snap out of this. I was irritable and blamed others for how I felt. I screamed at my husband and children over the simplest things.

The ministry of music that God had blessed me with was suddenly meaningless. All the music within me had disappeared. Sleep was something I longed for night after night. I would just lie awake tossing and turning, full of worries and feeling that something horrid was about to happen. My concentration was so poor that prayer and devotions became impossible. This made me feel even more guilty.

I would forget things, do weird things, say things that didn't make sense. I couldn't make decisions and would even come to tears trying to decide what to make for supper. I was so tired that my housework was ignored and my home looked awful.

I had crying bouts as well as times when I felt empty and incapable of any emotion. I hated myself and others. My faith in God was at an all time low and I had no faith at all in people. I felt so alone. Maybe you do too. The good news is that you're not alone and you're not going crazy.

God graciously led me to a Christian doctor who diagnosed a chemical imbalance. He prescribed medication to restore my brain chemistry so that my thoughts and feelings came under control again. With the help of a counselor, I am now dealing with the wounds that I have suffered as a result of this mood disorder. I must learn to forgive myself and my other relatives with the same imbalance for all that has happened over the years.

I am thankful that God has given me an answer and that now, with His help, I can move on to enjoy life and really live as He intended. A friend's comment the other day meant so much to me. She said, 'The person that I grew to know and love is back once again and I'm so glad.'

If I could hold your hand and look into your pain-filled eyes, I'd tell you to go and get help, there is hope! You can begin to live again or maybe start living for the first time.

Next we'll examine how depression disrupts so many areas of our lives.

Chapter 4

How can a medical problem disrupt society?

'He came to a broom tree, sat down under it and prayed that he might die. "I have had enough, LORD," he said. "Take my life; I am no better than my ancestors." '
(1 Kings 19:4)

'For sighing comes to me instead of food; my groans pour out like water.'
(Job 3:24)

'Where then is my hope? Who can see any hope for me?'
(Job 17:15)

In my opinion, there is no other medical problem found in humans that can cause such severe disruption in a person's life and the lives of those around them. Depression affects virtually all activities and relationships and it is found in all levels of society. In this chapter we will see some common situations that are greatly disrupted by depression.

Does depression affect marriage?

Dave and Mary (fictitious characters) married in their early twenties and had a wonderful relationship for many years. Over the past five years however, Dave had become increasingly sad and worried. He had lost interest in his career, in going to church and in socializing. He blamed it on becoming forty and the financial pressures he lived under. In the past year he lost interest in his own children, he blamed God for the state of his life and he rarely talked to Mary. This year he told Mary that he was no longer in love with her and that they should consider separation. Mary was shocked, devastated and didn't know what to do.

Dave was suffering from a gradual onset of depression which was steadily worsening. He didn't recognize that he was ill since he had learned to live with it for so long. He found many sources of stress on which to blame his deteriorating mood so he thought his response was reasonable and logical. His depression was disrupting his work, his spiritual life and marriage. If he didn't get help his marriage was finished.

Depression and all mood disorders disrupt relationships both inside and outside the home. Marriages are severely strained by the temper, irritability, fatigue and apathy found in a depressed spouse. Twenty percent of all marriages are unhappy. In fifty percent of those unhappy couples, one or both spouses have a mood disorder. In my clinic, one of the most common causes of marriage failure is a mood disorder in a spouse. It is so important to get depressed people treated so that marriages can be saved.

Isn't adolescent depression just a normal phase of life?

Virginia's parents just couldn't understand how their daughter had changed. She had been such a nice quiet girl up until age twelve. She had done well in primary school even though she was very shy and seemed to worry excessively. Now that she was in high school she had become angry, irritable, rebellious and was skipping classes. The slightest thing could set off her very bad temper. She spent too much time alone in her room listening to music. What had gone wrong? Her parents wondered if this was just part of being a teenager but it was disrupting their entire home life.

Virginia was depressed.

Depression and other mood disorders are very common in the teen years and it is estimated that up to twenty percent of teens have depressive symptoms. The rate of suicide in adolescents has risen two hundred percent in the past ten years so it is now the third leading cause of death in that age group. Depression is not a normal developmental phase that will pass. Adolescent mood disorders cause serious disabilities in academic progress and personality development.

Most adult mood disorders begin in adolescence but they are not detected due to the public perception that it is normal for teens to have emotional instability and that 'it's just a phase.' Frequently it will be assumed that a depressed irritable teen merely has 'normal youthful rebellion' and then will not be considered to have a treatable illness. This is tragic. Depressed teens will respond to medications as well as adults do, so they are suffering needlessly. Without treatment, they may have developmental, academic and social problems with destructive lifelong consequences.

The teen years are when **attention deficit disorder (ADD)** children (see Chapter 11) begin to develop mood instability so it is very important to treat them. The symptoms of adolescent depression are the same as in adults, with perhaps a greater degree of irritability, defiance, lack of interest in school and low self-esteem. Depressed teens lose the ability to enjoy activities, they change their eating habits, complain of constant fatigue and become worried or withdrawn. They may also show antisocial behavior with stealing, fighting and trouble with the law. Depressed teens have few friends since they are considered socially undesirable. Many will turn to drugs and alcohol to calm their minds from the constant stream of unpleasant negative thoughts. Addictions are very common in this condition. Families with depressed adolescents are often in constant turmoil and conflict due to the irritability of the teenager.

Adolescent depression is also strongly inherited. Fifty percent of children with depressed parents will also become depressed. In my experience teens respond to the same medications that are used in adults and with the same rate of success. It is very hard however, to convince a teenager or their parents that medications are needed. As a result, the vast majority of adolescent mood disorders remain undiagnosed and untreated, causing years of unnecessary disability and in some cases death. In Chapter 12 you will find a checklist of depressive symptoms common to adolescents. If you see these symptoms in a teenager, they need help quickly.

Does menopause or premenstrual syndrome cause depression?

Premenstrual syndrome (PMS) is a very common condition that occurs seven to fourteen days prior to the onset of a menstrual period due to the hormonal change that takes place during that interval. It has both physical and psychological symptoms that usually clear when the period starts. Up to to ten percent of women have PMS mood changes severe enough to greatly interfere with their lives. Many women become profoundly depressed during the PMS days. No one is certain why this is so, but some researchers have suspected that changing estrogen levels may affect the serotonin levels in the brain which control mood.

Menopause has always been blamed for causing depression and has been unkindly referred to as 'mental pause.' This is not so. It is not mandatory to become emotionally unstable at menopause.

There is no question that mood is affected by the hormonal fluctuations of menopause and of normal menstrual periods. These fluctuations won't however, actually cause a chemical depression. In my observation, menopause and PMS tend to magnify the symptoms of a pre-existing underlying depression. If for example, a woman has been suffering with a mild undiagnosed depression or dysthymia for many years, the hormonal change at menopause or during her PMS days, may magnify her depressive symptoms to the point where she wants treatment. The menopause or menstrual cycle was not the actual cause of the depression but it aggravated the condition enough to expose it.

When women go to their doctors complaining of menopausal and depressive symptoms, they usually get treated for only the menopausal symptoms or cyclic bloating and the underlying depression is missed. It is important to treat both the menopausal and depression symptoms separately. They are both legitimate biochemical, treatable conditions. Both menopausal and PMS depressions respond well to antidepressants.

There are other circumstances taking place in a menopausal woman's life that can aggravate her mood and which have nothing to do with her hormonal status. She likely has teenagers who may be already exhibiting symptoms of mild depression which they inherited from her. This will greatly increase her stress levels.

She may also be married to a man who is himself struggling with an undiagnosed depression and being a man, would never go for help. He would far rather blame his emotions on his wife's menopause. A woman in menopause is always a convenient target for a depressed man in denial who is going through is own 'mid-life crisis.'

Is it normal for the elderly to be depressed?

Depression is very common in the later years but it is usually missed and the symptoms wrongly attributed to normal aging. Society has come to expect depression to occur in later years and so it is ignored. This is much like the neglect of adolescent depression since it too has been considered normal for that age group.

The incidence of depression increases with age. It is presumed that this is caused by a decline in the level of nerve cell chemicals. This decline seems to be much worse if another unrelated chronic illness is present. Up to thirty percent of stroke victims will become chemically depressed. There is also an increasing level of stress and number of losses in later years which could precipitate depression. The rate of successful suicide reaches its peak in the elderly age group.

Depression can be easily confused with senility and can be found along with senility. It is important to treat depression as an independent condition since it will respond to treatment at any age.

The elderly should be treated for depression in the same aggressive way as those in other age groups. They will respond to medications too. It is important to be watching for depression in the elderly since their quality of life and that of their care-taking relatives can be greatly improved with proper treatment of such a common condition. There is also strong evidence that a depressed mood will predispose one or more physical illnesses. After a heart attack for example, the risk of another attack is much greater in those who are depressed.

Why do people commit suicide?

Depression is a potentially fatal illness and unfortunately, suicide is common. Up to twenty percent of depressed people will attempt suicide. Some researchers estimate that fifteen percent of untreated depressed people will successfully kill themselves.

When people consider or plan suicide it's because they become overwhelmed with hopelessness and see death as the only escape from the torment of their present reality. Depressed people are much more likely to commit suicide if they are abusing drugs or alcohol, if they have another serious illness, if they have recently experienced a major loss in their lives or are under significant stress. People who have previously attempted suicide are more likely to commit suicide at a later date.

Many who attempt or talk about suicide are actually calling out for help. It is at this point that we should take the threat seriously and guide them into treatment. It is wrong and dangerous to ignore them believing that 'it's only a cry for help, they won't do it.' Many lives will be saved if we could intervene at this stage.

If you are concerned about the risk of suicide in someone you love, watch for any of these classical warning signs. A person's mood may rapidly decline so that they are preoccupied with hopelessness and despair. Watch for reckless behavior that is out of character, where they no longer care about consequences. Some will become more socially withdrawn, lose interest in activities or friends, stop eating and give away important possessions. The most obvious signs would be a rewritten will, insurance application or openly discussing death. If you see these signs, the person is in need of urgent medical assistance. Don't ignore them!

If someone has recently attempted suicide, they will need a great deal of love and support since they suffer from an added burden of guilt and shame on top of the pre-existing depression.

I often get asked about the activity of evil spirits at the time of a suicide attempt. It is my observation that mental illness alone can cause one to be so tormented that suicide is seen as the only way out. As I will discuss in a later chapter, Satan loves depression and all mental illnesses. When you have poor or weak control of your thoughts, Satan will want to insert his thoughts into your mind. When your mood is low and you are preoccupied with negative thoughts, he may plant thoughts of suicide into your mind to convince you that it is worth considering. In this way he takes advantage of the illness to try to cause suicide. I have also however, known patients to get demonic suicidal thoughts when they are not depressed at all. So as you can see, Satan can be very active at the time of suicide but not all suicide attempts are of a demonic origin. It has been my experience that if a person's mood disorder can be successfully treated medically, their vulnerability to demonic thought insertion is greatly reduced.

Can antidepressants help anorexia nervosa, chronic fatigue, fibromyalgia and alcoholism?

A person suffering from **anorexia** or any other eating disorder is obsessed with unwanted continuous negative thoughts of being too fat. They will be unable to stop worrying about their weight so dieting becomes a compulsion that can't be stopped. Fasting to the point of starvation may take place since the thoughts won't quit and the person can never be satisfied that an acceptable weight has been achieved.

Thirty to fifty percent of those with anorexia also suffer from mood disorders since both conditions are caused by a chemical imbalance that allows the mind to race with negative thoughts. Antidepressants can correct the imbalance and restore normal mood and thought control. When the obsessional thoughts stop, the person can then relax about their weight and resume a normal eating pattern. Counseling is also necessary with all of these disorders since there are major emotional issues associated with eating disorders.

The list of symptoms which define **chronic fatigue syndrome** have considerable overlap with those of depression. Antidepressants can help with the depressive symptoms of the syndrome so that considerable relief can be obtained.

Fibromyalgia is a condition which among other things, involves chronic muscle pain, sleep disturbance and depression. It is known that sixty percent of those with chronic pain will also have a chemical imbalance depression. The depression can be a result of the chronic pain, or the pain can be a result of chronic depression.

Fibromyalgia will often improve with the use of antidepressants which can improve sleep, relax muscles and give some pain relief. The benefits can be seen even without depressive symptoms being present.

Alcoholism is a very complex disorder with many causes. One reason why people drink to excess is that it dulls their minds to the repetitive tormenting thoughts from a depressive illness. If the depression can be removed with antidepressants, then the drive to drink will be reduced.

It is easy to see that antidepressants have very wide uses in any condition where unwanted thoughts disrupt concentration or behavior.

The story of Mrs J

Before I came for treatment I was such a mess. I could not concentrate on anything. I used to love reading but unless I had total silence, I would read and reread the same sentence and not understand it.

I was so frustrated, I would throw the book down and give up, my mind was like a movie projector, it would not stop even when I was sleeping. I would wake up with my mind full of all these little things to worry about that didn't even happen. I was ashamed to tell anyone for fear of being 'put away.'

More people kept asking me what was wrong. I used to say 'nothing' or 'I'm tired,' I didn't know what was wrong. I was happy one day telling jokes and then crash the next day into a depression. I would lock my door, not answer the phone, put the blinds down and just sit and stare, hoping no one would come to my door.

I had this consistent black cloud above my head that was so heavy. Sometimes I would feel under the cloud for six weeks, then it might lift for a week and I would be able to pray again. During my dark days I could not pray and I felt so hopeless. I often felt that there was no use to go on living this way but I would then remember my family and think to myself that if I did something drastic, they would suffer, not me. I would feel such guilt for having these thoughts.

One day a friend took me for medical help. It was a hard choice to make since I was very afraid of what the doctor might say. It was then that I met Dr Mullen. He understood all about me and I felt quite at ease to tell him how I felt.

After taking medicine for about a week, I couldn't believe I felt normal. I could read, my mood was stable, I could cope with all sorts of things that I used to overreact to. Spiritually I was back on track. I had hope again. I hadn't felt this good about myself in years.

Later I had a deliverance experience from something horrible in my past, twenty years ago. It was hindering my spirit. After this was dealt with I was at last free and haven't looked back since.

Since taking medications, I am more confident with my walk with God and much closer to Him. Since the deliverance, my medications have been reduced slightly. Maybe I will be able to come off them but you can still be on medications after deliverance. God gives us common sense so we must use it.

My advice to someone who feels this way is not to be ashamed. It is not your fault, you can't control this yourself, it will not get better without treatment, don't waste another precious moment in darkness when you can be well. You haven't lost your faith, it is still there, when treatment starts to work everything will fall into place. Treatment has not always been smooth, the doctor had to adjust my medications many times depending on how I was feeling.

I now feel like a new person. I have always taken my medication even though many times I thought of throwing it all away. I just remember what it was like to be out of control and I never want to be that way again.

I can think now, read and cope with situations that used to overwhelm me. Make that first step and you will be so glad you did. The results are wonderful. I am a manic depressive and without medical help and Jesus, I could not have written this testimony or coped with my life. I give all the glory to God.

(*Note*: In the year since this letter was written, she has gradually come off all her medications under my supervision and has remained free of depression. It is very possible that her deliverance experience cured her manic depression.)

Next, we will examine the unique way that depression affects Christians.

Chapter 5

How does depression affect Christians?

'A cheerful heart is good medicine, but a crushed spirit dries up the bones.' (Proverbs 17:22)

Depression disrupts all relationships including your relationship with God. A depressed Christian will feel that they have lost the joy of their salvation and that they no longer feel God's presence. God will seem farther away, silent and unreachable. It will be very difficult to pray and do devotions since both of these acts require concentration which is disrupted by depression. The victim will be unable to participate fully in worship services since they feel dead inside. At this point many assume that God is punishing them or that they have committed the unpardonable sin. A Christian will then suffer even greater depressive pain since not only do they feel cut off from people but also from God, their last resort for help.

Disorders of mood, particularly depression, are the only medical illnesses that I know of, with spiritual symptoms. Unfortunately, when the church sees spiritual symptoms, it presumes there is a spiritual cause to the problem and that the solution must be spiritual. When well-meaning Christian friends find out how depressed the person is, they will suggest a greater commitment to prayer and Bible study as a treatment for the condition. This of course, is impossible, since both acts require a great deal of concentration which depression always interferes with. Unfortunately, this inability to pray and study will indicate to the friends that the depressed person must have a spiritual problem, a lack of faith or that they don't really want to get well. Self-help books and tapes will then be tried along with perhaps pastoral counseling. These methods only work when a person has total thought control which allows them to change their thinking patterns. When Christian self-help methods fail, the depressed believer feels so spiritually dead and hopeless that they may give up Christianity completely.

Another source of confusion for Christians is over the question, 'Is depression genetic or generational?' The medical viewpoint is that the tendency to have a mood disorder is inherited genetically because the problem runs in families. The spiritual view is that since it runs in families, it must be a generational curse of demonic origin. In my opinion both views are partially correct and both problems should be addressed.

I have previously explained that mood disorders are the only conditions that exist in both realms, physical and spiritual. There is no doubt that the chemical imbalance is a physical condition that is biologically inherited. It should be treated medically. I also believe that Satan loves to harass those with mood disorders and he attacks families with depression since they are more vulnerable. This attack needs to be dealt with spiritually. These two viewpoints are actually quite compatible and there should no longer be any conflict between their proponents. As I have mentioned before, treatments should be combined if we are going to get the best results for the greatest number of people.

A depressed Christian has additional guilt added to their depression since they usually condemn themselves for not snapping out of it. They will assume that they have a spiritual weakness or a character flaw. Pastors may have taught them that a true Christian will never get depressed and that it is a sign of defeat, disobedience and unbelief, so they feel increasingly guilty. It will be harder to attend church since socialization is very difficult and they feel like hypocrites for not being able to pray, worship or read the Bible. When concentration is so impaired, they get little out of sermons so they tend to change churches frequently since they 'are not being fed' or the church 'isn't meeting their needs.' Depression is particularly painful for Christians and there is much unnecessary suffering due to their wrong understanding of

Depressed Christians often feel beaten up by the church.

mental conditions. The correct response is to recognize that there is a medical illness present and get them treatment so that their spiritual life can recover.

When so many Christians are suffering from depression and not improving with spiritual treatments, it is very discouraging for the pastors who are trying to help these people. That leads us to the next question.

How does depression affect pastors?

In the August 1998 edition of Dr James Dobson's letter from *Focus on the Family*, he stated,

> 'Our surveys indicated that eighty percent of pastors and eighty four percent of their spouses were discouraged or were dealing with depression. More that forty percent of pastors and forty seven percent of their spouses reported that they were suffering from burnout, frantic schedules and unrealistic expectations. We estimated that approximately one thousand five hundred pastors left their assignments each month due to moral failure, spiritual burnout or contention within their local congregations.'

I have been called upon to treat a number of depressed pastors. In the opinion of Dr Dobson and myself, pastors are commonly a very discouraged lot. There are a number of reasons for this. To begin with, since they have been called to be the extensions of God's hands to society, they become targets for the attack of Satan. Discouragement is perhaps the most effective tool that Satan uses against the clergy. Pastors become very discouraged if they see few results from their ministry. If pastors are trying to counsel people with mood disorders who should be seeing a physician, then they are likely to fail. This makes them feel useless as a pastor and even question the power of God or their 'calling.' Most pastors are human, regardless of their own view of themselves, so they are just as susceptible to human disorders as anyone else. They too can suffer from depressive illnesses.

An untreated depressed pastor can cause serious damage to a church and to his own ministry. His negative outlook will contaminate all his relationships and his sermons. A cloud of condemnation and frustration will settle over the church. He will likely label his symptoms as 'burnout' and may blame it on the congregation, his spouse or superiors. Most often he will blame himself for sliding into a spiritual valley where prayer and Bible study becomes very difficult due to the poor concentration that comes with depression. When the condition doesn't improve using the usual scriptural methods for drawing closer to God, he then will presume that he is too far from God to be helped and that his 'call' or 'anointing'

Pastors get depressed too.

has lifted. Pastors are very reluctant to seek help from fellow ministers due to embarrassment, so they suffer in isolation.

If there is mood instability, they may act impulsively and slip into sin. This will then put them under discipline. They will likely leave the ministry in personal disgrace. This sequence of events can be easily prevented if depression is recognized and treated early.

Traditionally, churches criticize and then expel any leader who seems to be slipping in their attitude or performance. I would like to encourage all Christians to be watching for any signs of depression in their leaders. Instead of criticizing them, offer to support and help them get treated. If treatment can be started early, a pastor may not even need to be away from his pulpit before he returns to full function.

Chapter 6

What's so wrong about feeling great?

Joan was a committed Christian who wanted to grow spiritually. She would often go to conferences since the worship and teaching would be exhilarating. On this occasion she was away for several days. The conference was exceptionally good and the services ran late into the night and started early in the morning. She found herself too excited to sleep. Each day of the meetings her energy would increase as would her passion for worship. She became loud, opinionated, irritable, excessively spiritual and even disruptive in the services. By the end of the conference she had to be hospitalized because she couldn't slow down or control herself. What went wrong?

What is manic depression?

Depression is the most frequent form of mood disorder. The manic depressive or what is now termed 'bipolar' mood disorder is the next most common. It is characterized by wide mood fluctuations ranging from deep depression and despair to extreme happiness, euphoria and mania (see Figure 5).

During a depressed phase, **bipolar depression** is indistinguishable from **unipolar depression**. If a person is having their first episode of depression, it is not possible to tell which type of depression is present. About thirty percent of people having their first episode of depression are in fact bipolar but the swinging mood pattern has not yet emerged.

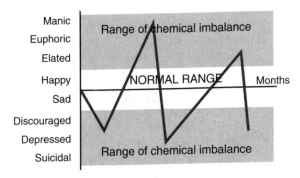

Figure 5   *Bipolar illness causes wide mood swings into both ranges of abnormal mood.*

During a manic phase a person will talk excessively and loudly with words pouring out in an animated continuous stream, interspersed with wit and humour. They will be unable to sit still or relax and there is continuous agitation. They will be distractible, changing topics rapidly, never totally finishing one thought and over-committing themselves to any task. Being the 'life of the party,' they show endless energy, developing grandiose plans based on gross over-estimations of their own ability. Their thoughts are continuously racing with exciting plans or jobs to do which demand immediate attention. When opposed they may show intense rage and irritability. They have poor judgment especially when spending money. They need very little sleep and consider rest and eating to be a waste of time only for the weak. Lack of sleep can trigger a manic phase and then continuing lack of sleep will fuel and intensify a manic episode as with Joan, illustrated above. During this phase they may act totally out of character and impulsively take risks of a sexual, personal, or financial nature. During a 'high' they are very reluctant to seek treatment since they feel so great and powerful. Manic episodes are often followed by periods of profound depression which are triggered by the slightest disappointment. A complete list of symptoms will be found in Chapter 12.

Milder mood swings can also be found in bipolar illness. This condition is called **cyclothymic mood disorder**. There

People with mania are full of energy and ideas.

is still a fluctuating mood with racing thoughts but the elevated mood symptoms are not as intense as the ones listed above. In this milder condition, the times of mood elevation can be very productive and entertaining. I have noticed that many actors, entertainers and evangelists have this mood pattern since it gives them the confidence to be in front of audiences. Unfortunately, the times of mood elevation are still followed by depressions.

The usual age of onset of bipolar depression is in late adolescence and the early twenties, the same as in other mood disorders. It is usually not recognized until symptoms have been present for on average ten years. In the years preceding diagnosis there is usually unpredictable mood and behavior with marked irritability. This is commonly seen during the adolescent prelude to being diagnosed, when this behavior is called 'a normal phase.' Those with bipolar mood disorder are very prone to abuse alcohol and street drugs as a way of self-medicating their confused and tormenting thoughts.

Bipolar mood swings can easily become so severe that they slip into what is known as 'psychosis.' We will discuss psychosis in more detail in the chapter on **schizophrenia**. Psychotic thinking means that a person has lost touch with reality. It can happen at the extremes of depression or elation. A person in psychosis may hear voices when there is no one around, may feel that they are being watched or followed by strangers, or may feel that others can read their minds. They may also develop strange delusional beliefs that they have superhuman abilities. When psychotic thinking is present, it is impossible to distinguish the condition from schizophrenia. What I do in my clinic to separate the two conditions is that I ask what their mood was like in the few days leading up to the psychotic episode. If there was depression or elation then the cause was likely a mood disorder, otherwise schizophrenia would be the probable cause.

Bipolar mood disorder responds well to treatment as we will discuss later.

The story of Mrs E

I suffered with mood swings for about forty-five years. I never had a full-blown manic episode but I was certainly aware of distinct mood swings. Sometimes I would talk loud and fast, sleep poorly and then crash into depression. During my entire life, I was embarrassed, frustrated or confused about my problem. Occasionally people would mention my condition but I had no answers for them. I am a counselor and often refer clients to physicians for a diagnosis. I promised myself that the next time I had a severe mood elevation, I would go to the doctor.

For many years I observed the behavior of some of my relatives who had mood swings but none of them sought medical attention. Due to my family history, I was easily diagnosed and prescribed lithium. I have side effects but I like the results of lithium so much that I do not plan to go off it after more than three years. The benefits of taking the medications are:

1. No more mood swings.
2. I am more peaceful, relaxed and I talk slower.
3. I have a more intimate relationship with God and have grown much faster spiritually.
4. I can listen and relate to people better.
5. I am more organized, make better decisions and solve problems faster.
6. I have more self-control so I rarely get fearful in crowds, no longer feel helpless and have more stable relationships. My marriage has improved.

7. I have more self-esteem, greater credibility with others and more confidence in my work.
8. I am more alert, creative and with greater energy.

Now we need to examine a very misunderstood condition.

Chapter 7

When reality seems so far away

'Immediately what had been said about Nebuchadnezzar was fulfilled. He was driven away from people and ate grass like cattle. His body was drenched with the dew of heaven until his hair grew like the feathers of an eagle and his nails like the claws of a bird. At the end of that time, I, Nebuchadnezzar, raised my eyes toward heaven, and my sanity was restored. Then I praised the Most High; I honored and glorified him who lives forever. His dominion is an eternal dominion; his kingdom endures from generation to generation.' (Daniel 4:33–34)

Mrs L was a patient in hospital that I was asked to see because she was thinking strangely. She was very quiet, withdrawn and suspicious of me. When I asked her what was the reason that she was in hospital, she replied, 'I'm rotting inside because I was standing too close to wallpaper that was peeling off the wall.' She had clearly lost contact with reality but I needed to know how firmly convinced of her delusion she was. I asked her if this had ever happened before. She answered, 'Yes it had but she had acted quickly and saved her own life.' 'And how did you do that?' I responded. She showed me a twelve-inch scar across her neck. 'When the poison was beginning to move towards my head, I cut my neck to let the poison out and saved my life!' She was clearly quite convinced of her diagnosis and of the treatment she needed. I cringed as I thought of the doctors who had to close such an enormous life-threatening neck wound, while she was so proud of her life-saving procedure. Mrs L was schizophrenic and demonstrating psychotic delusional thinking.

What is schizophrenia?

Schizophrenia is a very misunderstood condition and it is not 'split personality.' It is a 'psychotic' disorder, rather than a mood disorder, which means that there is a loss of contact with reality. It is caused by a different type of chemical imbalance than a mood disorder. Nebuchadnezzar appeared to have suffered from a psychosis in the scripture reference above. Schizophrenia is a thought disorder where one loses the ability to tell what is real and what is imaginary. If you refer back to my diagram in Figure 1, this disorder is a chemical imbalance in the orientation part of the brain but it can also affect the mood control center to cause mood symptoms as well.

Schizophrenia usually begins in young adults like the other mood disorders. It affects two percent of the population which makes it more common and far more disabling than diabetes. Like the mood disorders, it tends to be a recurring condition.

Schizophrenics often feel that they are being watched, followed or persecuted. They may hear voices and see things that no one else can. They often have peculiar beliefs that

Schizophrenics often think they are being watched or followed.

have no basis in reality and their thoughts seem very scattered and disorganized. They are commonly very withdrawn, emotionless and suspicious. A more complete list of symptoms will be found in Chapter 12. I have no idea if Nebuchadnezzar had schizophrenia but he did demonstrate many symptoms compatible with psychosis in Daniel 4.

Schizophrenia is a more difficult condition to treat than the mood disorders and the medications, called antipsychotics, tend to have more side effects. Antidepressants and mood stabilizers can also be used in schizophrenia if there are many depressive thoughts or wide mood swings along with the psychosis. Antipsychotics are also used in mood disorders when the person is having symptoms of psychosis along with their mood symptoms.

Christians often get very confused over this condition. In my experience I have heard schizophrenia blamed on previous teen drug abuse when they must have 'fried their brains,' or more commonly blamed on demons since the person is hearing voices and is spiritually confused. There is no doubt that schizophrenia is a real and common physical illness. Satan of course, loves any condition where you lose the ability to control your thoughts, which includes mental illnesses and any drug or alcohol impairment. He inserts disturbing thoughts into a schizophrenic mind no differently than he does into a depressed person. We must be very compassionate and supportive to schizophrenics and their families to keep the sufferer encouraged and in treatment to prevent relapses.

There are very helpful support groups for patients and families to encourage and inform those who suffer with this condition.

The story of Mr K

Thank you in the name of our Lord for your medical treatment and spiritual ministry to us and our son. This is the first year since he was diagnosed schizophrenic that he has not been hospitalized. This is because his chemical imbalance has been properly diagnosed and he is on the right medications.

You have no idea how our lives have been disrupted by this illness. Now at last it is controlled and he is no longer out of control on the streets or chained to a hospital bed as that used to be the case. I know that he has an appointed time and when that time comes, he will be totally free. In the meantime, thank God that we have medications. I believe that one day the Lord will restore what we have lost. I sincerely thank you for the hope that you have brought to our lives.

Chapter 8

I can't stop worrying, what's wrong with me?

*'Terror will seize them, pain and anguish will grip them;
they will writhe like a woman in labor. They will look
aghast at each other, their faces aflame.'* (Isaiah 13:8)

*'When Saul saw the Philistine army, he was afraid;
terror filled his heart.'* (1 Samuel 28:5)

*'He too shared in their humanity so that by his death he
might destroy him who holds the power of death, that is
the devil and free those who all their lives were held in
slavery by their fear of death.'* (Hebrews 2:14–15)

Anxiety disorders are conditions that interfere with your
ability to control or stop a sense of continuous worry or fear.
They are very common and have the same incidence and
lifetime risk as the mood disorders. Anxiety disorders are
commonly found with depression since the continuous
anxious thoughts are just another form of negative clutter
and racing thoughts that can't be shut off. In my opinion,
anxiety appears to be a subtype of the depressive mood
disorder since they both have negative thoughts that
can't be controlled and they both respond to the same
medications.

There are several types of anxiety disorders. Panic disorder
is the most severe and disabling of these conditions. In this
disorder, panic attacks will start with no obvious trigger.
There will be sudden unexplained terror and a sense of
impending doom. There will be many physical symptoms
that occur simultaneously like a pounding heart, sweating,
chest pain and light-headedness. Phobic disorder is when a

Anxious thoughts often can't be stopped.

person will become very fearful or even panic over a well-defined object or situation like heights, snakes or crowds. General anxiety disorder is when a person is worried all the time about everything.

Obsessive compulsive disorder

Obsessive compulsive disorder (OCD) is quite a common disabling anxiety disorder. Three percent of the population will suffer from it at some time in their lives. It is more common than schizophrenia or manic depression but it is well concealed and rarely diagnosed.

Obsessional thoughts are recurrent, intrusive, unwanted ideas, images, impulses or worries that are often senseless but can't be shut off. They will often take the form of swear words, repetitive phrases, violent thoughts which are totally out of character or feelings of being dirty or contaminated. This is very disturbing for the victim who feels powerless to control the thoughts. The anxiety associated with OCD can be overwhelming.

Compulsions are repetitive unnecessary acts done in response to the obsessional thoughts. They are intended to neutralize the fear or discomfort that comes with the obsessional thoughts. These acts are purposeless, time-consuming and unwanted. They are very disruptive to relationships and to one's performance at home or work. The acts usually involve excessive touching, checking, cleaning, washing, counting or note-taking. The victim hates doing it but must continue the act until they get a sense of completion which may require a large number of repetitions. During the compulsion there is never a sense that the action has been completed correctly. Some have described it like an itch that won't go away until it is scratched a certain way and a certain number of times.

The most common obsessions are fear of contamination by dirt or germs, fear of harm to self or others, fear of illness, fear of sexual thoughts and fear of committing sins. The most common repetitive rituals to suppress the fearful thoughts are repetitive cleaning, recitation of a phrase or number, touching, checking of locks, excessive orderliness and hoarding. It is not uncommon for someone with OCD to wash their hands thirty times a day to stop the fear of contamination.

Anxiety and depression are often so intertwined that they are indistinguishable. In my clinic I have not found it necessary to separate the conditions. They both have negative thoughts that can't be shut off and they both respond to the same antidepressants which are designed to restore thought control.

Next, we'll discuss how to escape from the prison of mood disorders.

Chapter 9

You mean I have to take pills?

'I waited patiently for the LORD; he turned to me and heard my cry. He lifted me out of the slimy pit, out of the mud and mire; he set my feet on a rock and gave me a firm place to stand. He put a new song in my mouth, a hymn of praise to our God.' (Psalm 40:1–3)

It's an illness, treat it!

It is important to realize that since depression is an illness, it cannot be fought alone by the patient. It can't be wished away. It needs specific medical treatment to correct the imbalance just like insulin is used to treat diabetes. The most important first step is for the patient to accept the diagnosis and consent to treatment. Even mild chemical depressions can be cleared with medications so there is no need to wait until one is suicidal to begin treatment.

There are many impediments to treatment. Patients and their families are often afraid of mental health professionals and so won't come for help. They refuse to accept the diagnosis due to the stigma and stereotypes surrounding mental illnesses and psychiatric treatment. We will see in the next chapter how Christians use religious reasons to avoid treatment.

What do the drugs do?

The medical treatment of mood disorders involves the use of drugs which are extremely effective in restoring the normal balance of neurotransmitter chemicals. For depression, there are nearly twenty medications called antidepressants. They

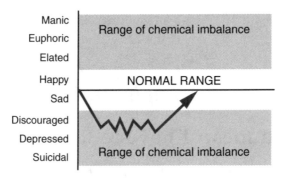

Figure 6   *Antidepressants will slowly raise mood by restoring concentration and brain chemical balance.*

restore brain serotonin levels and correct the imbalance. Concentration, mood and thought control will then be restored and the racing thoughts will stop (see Figure 6). For bipolar or manic depressives, the mood stabilizing drugs like lithium, valproic acid, or carbamazapine are used to eliminate and prevent mood swings (see Figure 7). Some bipolar patients will need to take a combination of stabilizers and antidepressants to prevent both depression and mood swings. If we use the vision analogy again, this is like wearing bifocals, a lens for distance and one for reading.

Most of these medicines have been around for many years and have an excellent track record for long-term safety. They

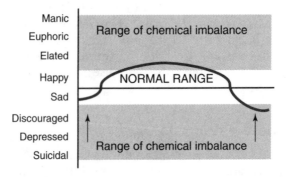

Figure 7   *Lithium and other mood stabilizers will normalize mood through restoring brain chemical balance and flattening mood swings.*

are not habit-forming and do not include tranquilizers. They are not 'uppers' or 'happy pills,' they only restore normal mood and the ability to control one's thoughts. They do not create an artificial high nor artificial personality and have no effect at all on a person with normal mood.

It is not possible to know in advance which antidepressant medication will work for any given person. Many may have to be tried before finding the right one. The benefit of a pill can take six weeks to feel, which is frustratingly slow. I warn everyone that it may take six to eight months to find the right medication that will give maximum benefit with the least side effects. This process is similar to trying to find the right key to open a lock. Many keys may have to be tried before the lock opens. During this waiting period the person needs lots of encouragement to continue trying to find the right medicine.

Once the correct medicine is found, one must stay on it for at least six months after the end of depressive symptoms. This long period lessens the chance of relapse after the

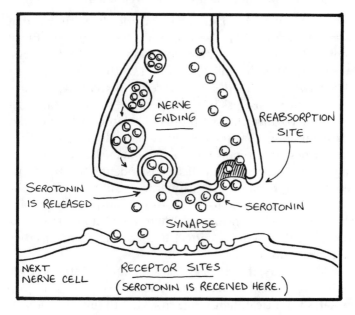

Before treatment, serotonin levels are low.

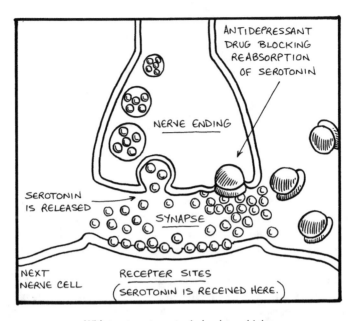

With treatment serotonin levels are higher.

medications have been stopped. Statistics have shown that after one episode of depressive illness, fifty percent of recovered people will suffer from another episode within two years. After having two episodes, the risk of relapse within two years increases to seventy percent. After three episodes the relapse risk is ninety percent. It's important that patients recognize the symptoms of relapse early and start treatment as soon as possible. It is generally recommended that the best way to prevent or reduce the risk of relapse is to stay on antidepressant medications indefinitely. For those people who remain on treatment, medications must be considered equivalent to eyeglasses, insulin or heart pills which must be taken for life. These medications are not a crutch but they actually correct the problem as long as they are taken continuously.

Unfortunately, the chances that someone will stay on their medications for the correct time period are very low. The drop out rates from treatment range from ten to seventy percent. This is certainly true in my clinic. The majority of patients will drop out of treatment after three visits to the clinic. The reasons for these bad statistics are many. Often the patient does not accept the reality of the illness and won't take the medications. In other cases friends and family encourage them to stop treatment or the side effects are intolerable. In any event there are many people who should be in treatment but refuse. It is estimated that only twenty percent of the mood disorder population is receiving treatment.

While I was preparing this book I came across a newspaper article which described the use of antidepressants in animals. It appears that chemical imbalances are found in many mammals. In this article, it explained how veterinarians in the Calgary, Alberta Zoo were using Prozac to help a polar bear stop its 'neurotic pacing.' The improvement was dramatic so they are doing a study on the use of anti-depressants in animals. We will have to wait and see how pet owners will cope with the stigma of their animals being on mood-altering drugs.

You mean I can't drink coffee?

One very important fact which is often overlooked in the treatment of depression is the disruptive role of caffeine and other 'over the counter' substances. It has been my observation over the years that caffeine directly opposes the action of antidepressants and mood stabilizers. This is true of all 'stimulants' like ginseng, decongestants and many other 'natural' products designed to 'pick you up' or help you lose weight. In each case the stimulant increases the repetitive disturbing thoughts that the medications are trying to subdue. Caffeine and other stimulants work directly against the medications. I have been astonished at how much my patients improve when they eliminate caffeine and stimulants from their diets. In some cases I have been able to reduce their doses once the aggravating substance has been removed. I have also noticed that a frustrating tendency for anti-depressants to lose their effectiveness over time is reduced if caffeine is eliminated. Caffeine comes in many products including pain killers, coffee, tea, colas and chocolate. Whenever there is an unexpected decline in the mood of one of my patients, I always look for something they may be consuming that is causing a drug interaction with their medications.

Are tranquilizers ever used?

In many cases tranquilizers are used to temporarily relieve the torment of repetitive anxious thoughts. They do not correct the underlying imbalance but cover it over for a short time. These medicines have generic names that commonly end with the letters '...pam,' for example 'diazapam.' Tranquilizers are useful in the short-term treatment of an acute episode of anxiety or mood disturbance. They are commonly used for immediate symptom relief while waiting the several weeks it takes for an antidepressant to take effect. Since tranquilizers can be habit forming, they are usually tapered off as the antidepressant corrects the underlying problem.

Antipsychotic medications are used to stop psychotic symptoms which can occur with severe depression, mania or schizophrenia. They can be combined with antidepressants and stabilizers when necessary.

What is 'shock treatment?'

Shock treatment is more properly known as **electro-convulsive therapy** (ECT). It was the original treatment for depression but is now rarely used due to the effectiveness of medications.

ECT is the application of an electric shock to one side of the brain to induce a seizure while the person is safely under general anesthesia. The seizure causes a rapid release of all the nerve cell chemicals which are used to regulate brain function. Some of those chemicals are the ones deficient in depression. The sudden release helps correct the chemical imbalance and restores normal mood. Usually up to ten treatments are required to get the chemicals up to the necessary levels to restore mood. Antidepressant medications are often used to maintain the recovery after ECT.

ECT is now generally used only in those who do not respond to medications. It is a safe and rapidly effective treatment. I have had suicidal patients recover dramatically within two weeks of having ECT after failing to improve on medications. Please don't ever discourage someone from accepting this form of treatment since it could save their lives.

What about the families?

One very often overlooked part of the treatment of depression is the support that is needed for the families of depressed people. These families are living under severe relationship stress and need to understand the illness and how it is treated. They must be helped with the guilt that they carry for having this problem in their family.

Personal and family counseling is a very important part of the treatment. There are usually many scars to heal as a result of psychological trauma and conflict. Counseling works best after the depressed person has regained control of their thoughts and concentration. Friends and counselors can be very helpful in supporting the person while they are waiting for the medications to work.

Support groups are now widely available for those suffering with emotional disorders. I have found them to be extremely helpful in providing education to the patient and their families. Perhaps their greatest value however, is to provide encouragement to the sufferer to persist with treatment until they have recovered.

What can you do?

If you are a friend or loved one of someone suffering from a mental illness you can play a pivotal role in your loved one's recovery. The most important way you can help is by encouraging the person to get help and to stay in treatment even during the frustrating weeks needed to find the right medications. You can be a constant encouragement for them to go on. You can keep reminding them that this is a medical problem, that it's not their fault. Prayer is a very important part of recovery. It is also very helpful if you can take them to counseling, prayer for the sick or deliverance ministry. We are to pray constantly for physical healing of these conditions. In the last few years I have seen a number of my patients supernaturally healed from their imbalances through the prayers of believers.

The treatment of depression and any emotional bondage involves treating all three links in the chain. Medications are one of the links, counseling, inner healing and deliverance are the remaining links that we will examine later in this book. All those involved in treatment should work together and support the efforts of the others. Competition between treatment modalities is unhealthy and has caused many to remain in their chains since they did not participate in the other treatments.

With correct treatment, a supportive family and church, a depressed person can become relaxed, content, optimistic and in full control of their thoughts and behaviors.

The story of Mr L

I have suffered for a long time with depression and ADD. Four years ago I went on medication for both and began to see healing begin. In all the years of counseling, the truth never reached the need. God used medication to remove the veil of confusion off my mind. The Word of God, His Spirit and godly guidance penetrated the veil and suddenly the confusion lifted and God put into practice all the seeds He had sown in me. What freedom and release to be able to recognize choices instead of being chained to reactions. The healing process was able to wash over me and take root and God changed me.

I thank God in faith for His creation of my body and chemical make-up. I pray for healing but I stand in acceptance of what He has for me now. I thank God daily for the development of Prozac and Ritalin. This is the route God has provided for my healing at the present time. I praise Him.

Next we will look at why, in my experience, Christians are so difficult to treat.

Chapter 10

Why are Christians so difficult to treat?

'He has blinded their eyes and deadened their hearts, so they can neither see with their eyes, nor understand with their hearts, nor turn and I would heal them.'

(John 12:40)

Can a Christian take drugs?

Mental health problems are poorly understood by the public at large as we have already discussed. The Christian population is not only equally uninformed but we have created our own explanation for the cause and treatments of mental illnesses. It is assumed that since spiritual symptoms are present, then there must be a spiritual cause and that a spiritual treatment will always work. A depressed person is usually offered a large number of Christian self-help books and tapes which give many easy answers to depression. These books often imply or even state openly that a good Christian should never be overwhelmed by depression and that a spiritual solution will always work. Medications and psychiatric treatment are often ridiculed as unnecessary except for the spiritually weak or those disobedient to God's instructions.

When these spiritual treatments don't work, the depressed person blames himself for inadequate faith or motivation. Christians don't realize that depression is the only medical condition with spiritual symptoms. The root cause is medical not spiritual.

Christians assume that they are in full control of their thoughts but this is not so when a mood disorder is present.

I WANT TO DIE
I CAN'T GO ON
I CAN'T PRAY
I MUST HAVE SINNED
GOD IS PUNISHING ME
I'M ANGRY
I'M SAD

Christians feel overwhelmed by shame and condemnation.

One's ability to control thoughts depends on how well the brain cells are functioning to give you that control. It is much like the control of a car. One only has full control if the steering wheel is properly connected under the hood. In mood disorders, the problem is not with the will of the person but with the nerve cells 'under the hood.'

Christians are very reluctant to seek medical help with their moods since they perceive that this is an admission that they 'don't have enough faith in God' or that 'the Cross isn't enough.' This is sometimes reinforced by well-meaning friends or pastors who intensify their guilt. It is also thought that no medical treatment could ever help a spiritual problem so it would be an insult to God to accept such treatment. Christians often have the opinion that after you are saved then your past is all 'under the blood' so it should no longer have any affect on you, 'just pick yourself up and get going' they say. If you do continue to have emotional problems as a result of your past life or chemical imbalance, you will feel shamed and condemned by Christians since you obviously don't have enough faith to 'live in the freedom of forgiveness.' The fact of the matter is that chemical imbalances can affect all humans, saved or not and you can't just wish it away with greater faith. Our past will continue to affect our emotions until we have gone through a healing process. Our pain and wounds do not just go away with salvation.

I had one patient who had been successfully treated with

medications but after a weekend seminar at her church, decided that she was to 'claim' her healing and stop the pills as an act of faith. Soon after stopping her medications, all the depressive symptoms returned and she was plunged once again into despair and emotional instability. When this was reported to me, she insisted that she was still 'healed' but that these were lying symptoms that had to be 'rebuked.' She would not consider returning to the medications since that would be an insult to God. She never returned. I hope that Satan's stronghold of shame and guilt did not keep her out of treatment. It's tragic to think that she may be suffering unnecessary mental torment for religious reasons.

Everywhere I go speaking on this subject, I am overwhelmed by the number of Christians who are using religious arguments to refuse treatment. Many who are taking medications seem paralyzed by guilt, shame and self-condemnation for accepting medical help. I have met many depressed pastors and evangelists who fear the loss of their ministry position if someone should find out that they take antidepressants. Satan loves this state of affairs. As long as he can use religious arguments to get Christians to believe his lie

Christians are often kept from treatment by religious arguments.

that they should never consider medical treatment, then he can have easy access to the minds of depressed Christians. Those who do take the treatment and recover are no threat to Satan if he can get them overwhelmed by guilt and shame.

Christians need to understand that treatment won't undermine their faith nor override their will. Antidepressants are not 'mood altering drugs' nor are they addicting. It is quite permissible for Christians to take them. Medications are a part of the recovery process along with counseling, praying for healing and personal devotions. A properly treated person will find inner healing and deliverance easier and more effective if they have regained control of their thoughts through medications.

The reasons why Christians have reacted so strongly against psychiatric treatment are rooted in the Church's strong reaction to the humanistic teachings of Freud which excluded the spiritual nature of man. The church feels that the drug treatment of emotional illness is another humanistic, anti-spiritual treatment which is a logical extension of the teachings of Freud. The church doesn't realize that the teachings of Freud have been largely abandoned by psychiatrists and that medications are seen as a way of improving a person's thought control, not a way of controlling a patient's thoughts. The church has also been unaware that a racing, cluttered, depressed mind has great difficulty making any progress with deliverance or inner healing. Successful medical treatment should accelerate emotional healing, not prevent it.

Another argument used by Christians to discourage the use of medications is that when you are on them you become so artificially happy that you no longer face the pain of reality and avoid the inner healing that is necessary for complete emotional wholeness. Christians must realize that antidepressants only give people improved thought control, they do not create artificial happiness. A well-treated person is far better able to face the tough issues after treatment since they will no longer be overwhelmed and paralyzed by life stresses.

There is one Christian criticism that I have found occasionally to be true. I have seen some people so amazed and relieved by the dramatic improvement in their mood obtained through medications, that they no longer have any motivation to proceed with inner healing and deliverance. They stop their emotional healing process after the medical recovery since they feel so much better than they used to. These people are in fact lulled into the false sense of security that they are emotionally free merely by regaining thought control. I try very hard to point out that medical recovery is only the first step in the three-step process of emotional healing.

It is my hope that with the information in this book, anyone will be able to understand depression well enough to know when to recommend that a person seek medical help and to then support the person in the treatment process. Pastors get worn down by the endless counseling required by medically depressed people who rarely show improvement. Using these tools, a pastor, counselor or friend can know when to refer someone to a physician. He can help the victim understand that this is just another treatable illness. This will give the person a better recovery and will encourage the pastor/counselor rather than exhaust him.

The church should become a place of healing and recovery rather than of condemnation, shame and denial. As Christians, we should be able to offer hope to the depressed. With the information presented here, you can outline a pathway of recovery for the broken. We need to give permission for the depressed to admit their struggles and then have someone come alongside them to walk them through recovery. As long as the church remains silent about these issues, many will give up on Christianity, live tormented lives and some will commit suicide needlessly.

We all agree that the 'Great Commission' instructs us to rescue men from the bondage of sin. Would it not also be reasonable for the church to help people break free from the captivity of their minds?

The story of Mrs P

I'm glad that when I was born again no one told me that all my problems would be gone. I found myself struggling with mood swings. It seemed that one day I would be so up that I would want to save the world but the next day I would be in severe depression. All I ever wanted was to find a balance after my eight-year struggle with mood swings.

I went to a seminar where Dr Mullen was speaking. He talked about mood disorders, mood swings and depression. As I compared myself to what he was describing, I couldn't deny that maybe part of my problem could be medical. You see, I was one who didn't believe in going to a doctor for medication. I never believed that God could also bring healing through doctors or medicines.

I went to see Dr Mullen to find out if I really did have an imbalance. After he confirmed my suspicions, I was given medications. After the first week, I noticed that my relationship to my boss was changing. He didn't irritate me as much as he used to. I also noticed that my moods were no longer swinging. I found that for the first time in my life I felt balanced. Even my thoughts were no longer negative but actually positive.

After two weeks of treatment, the Lord kept speaking to me and saying that He wanted to spend time with me. Joy filled my heart that the Father really loved me. You see, before this time, my mind was never secure in my relationship with God or with others. Negative thoughts ruled me. Now positive thoughts have filled my mind which has set me free in my relationships. Thank God that He works in ways that we don't expect and that we may not even accept.

In the next chapter we will discuss one of the most controversial topics in the public press and in psychiatry.

Chapter 11

I can't concentrate

'For God is not a God of disorder but of peace.'
(1 Corinthians 14:33)

Why is this so controversial?

Attention deficit disorder (ADD) has become one of the most controversial and emotionally charged subjects in medicine, education and child rearing. The public and even the medical profession are divided into several groups. One group says that ADD really doesn't exist, it's just bad parenting, bad environment, poor social skills and not enough discipline. This group feels that medical treatment is not only unnecessary but it is a cruel way of suppressing a child and excusing the parent or teacher from their child rearing or teaching responsibilities. Another group feels that ADD is a common physical handicap that needs to be treated medically just like poor vision is treated in children. Yet another group feels that it should only be treated with natural herbs, vitamins and diets.

Just as in every other area of psychiatry, the root cause of the controversy is our inability to measure mood, thought speed and concentration. We have no reliable, objective test to tell if a person has ADD or any other mental health condition. Whenever something cannot be proven, it will be the subject of speculation. Once again we rely on a checklist of symptoms that when present, indicate a high likelihood that a chemical imbalance is present. There are many in medicine and in the public who cannot accept that a checklist of symptoms is sufficient grounds to initiate drug treatment in a child or adult.

I hope this chapter will introduce you to this subject and clear up much of the confusion surrounding such a common handicap.

What is ADD?

Attention deficit disorder simply means that a person has a chronic inability to concentrate or focus their mind. It usually presents in one of two ways, with hyperactivity (**ADHD**) or without. This is the most common thinking problem in children and it is estimated that six percent of children suffer from it. It is a leading cause of school failure and under-achievement. At least fifty percent of the affected children will never be diagnosed or treated so that they remain disabled, often for life.

The normal brain seems to have filters or gates which allow you to block useless information or stimuli that could distract you from an intended task. In ADD the filters are so weak that the child is bombarded with useless and irrelevant thoughts which are continuously distracting them from learning and remembering. It is very much like being in a small room with many loudspeakers all shouting instructions

They are constantly being distracted by too many thoughts.

and not being able to tell which voice is the important one. The child finds that their brain tells them too many things at once and they don't know how to process all the commands. For example, as you read this page, you are likely not aware of the street noises or even the buzz of the lights or fans in your room until I draw your attention to them. Your thoughts are focused on what you are reading. In ADD a person's thoughts are going so fast that they are not able to concentrate on the page and the environmental noises are just as important as what they are reading. The brain can not prioritize what the most important stimulus is at any moment. The street noise becomes as important as the page and the mind is distracted to the noise so the reading is never completed. That is why distractibility is such an important symptom in ADD.

ADD is a severe handicap to learning and is often found in addition to learning disabilities. When new information is learned by a person with normal concentration, it is stored in the memory at a location where it can be easily retrieved for future use. You might say the information is filed in a drawer labeled with the appropriate subject so when it is needed, the memory can be easily retrieved since it is well marked. In ADD there is no such filing system. New information just seems to be tossed over the shoulder into a pile of memories. It is virtually impossible to retrieve the information even though you know it's in there somewhere.

This inability to concentrate is caused by an inherited chemical imbalance in the brain, just like the one which causes adult mood disorders. Children have the same racing of thoughts but they are less likely to have the mood symptoms. Their thought clutter is of a more random nature where the adult pattern has more anxious and depressing thoughts. It is very common to find both ADD and mood disorders clustering in families since they are closely related conditions which are both inherited.

There are many symptoms of ADD and not every affected child will have all of them. Children may have any of the following symptoms: not finishing what they start, fidgety, distractible, hearing but not listening, unable to concentrate on school work, making noises in class, falling grades, acting like they are driven by a motor, unable to sit still, loud, always talking and impulsive. They are excitable, unable to share, impatient and demanding of their own way with wide mood swings. In a classroom they appear to be daydreaming or disruptive, unable to apply themselves to a task and easily confused by details. They rarely follow instructions and have exceedingly short memories. There is usually considerable moodiness with extreme emotional responses to events. The irritability, impulsiveness and immaturity make it hard for them to make or keep friends so they become socially isolated. This causes great frustration which leads to impulsive and socially inappropriate behavior.

They usually have poor grades since school is such a struggle. They need constant supervision and assistance to complete a task or learn a skill. They are often in trouble with authorities and are automatically blamed for anything that goes wrong. These pressures cause the child to lose all self-esteem and feel rejected. They become sullen and withdrawn as they get older. In this way ADD is often seen with depression, anxiety and learning disabilities. Twenty-five percent of learning disabled children also have ADD.

These children are usually of normal intelligence but they are unable to perform and make use of their abilities. This condition is much like having a high performance sports car ready to go inside a garage but having no driveway to get it on the road. There's great potential but no performance.

How can ADD be treated?

Fifty to eighty percent of ADD children are never diagnosed or treated. For those who are identified, the treatment involves a multifaceted approach. I have not found dietary restrictions to be consistently helpful but medications are extremely useful. As in adult mood disorders, the drugs will correct the chemical imbalance and restore normal thought speed and sequence. There are many medications that are helpful including stimulants and antidepressants. Many drugs may need to be tried before the right combination is found, though eighty percent of children will respond to stimulants like methylphenidate (Ritalin). The medications will reduce impulsivity and hyperactivity by slowing down the speed of their thoughts. At a more normal thought speed, it is easier to control thoughts and behavior. Concentration, learning, self-confidence and mood will improve as thought control increases. Treatment can release a child from the prison of thought bombardment so that he is able to choose his own thoughts at his own speed and focus his attention at will.

Parents are generally very reluctant to accept the diagnosis or give pills to their children for this condition. This is very understandable since no one wants to see their child on medications. The fact is however, that with medications the child will be happier and calmer with better performance and self-esteem. This will greatly improve home life and family relationships. I encourage parents to consider methylphenidate (Ritalin) to be equivalent to eyeglasses or insulin which no parent would deny their child. It must be understood that ADD is a medical problem with behavioral symptoms which will respond to treatment.

Physicians who treat ADD with medications are widely criticized for medicating children needlessly. Having seen the family disruption, educational failures and the personality injury to those children who have not been treated, it is my opinion that it is more dangerous and unfair to deny treatment to an ADD child than to give them medications. When I am in doubt of the diagnosis, I choose to err on the side of offering hope and treatment, than to tell a parent there is nothing that can be done for their child. The risks of medications are very low but the consequences of missing the diagnosis and leaving a child untreated to face the long-term disability of ADD are enormous.

The education professionals can be very helpful in tailoring a program for the affected child. Limiting distractions in a classroom and seating the child at the front of the class can be very helpful. Giving instructions frequently and in clear simple terms will help these children respond better. Firm and consistent discipline is necessary though rarely effective if used alone. ADD children need lots of praise and encouragement for the tasks that they do well. Self-esteem must be preserved.

Parents are usually exasperated and very embarrassed by

their children's behavior which they seem to have no control over. We must reach out to these parents and try to assist them, rather than join the many friends and neighbours who condemn them for poor parenting. Individual and family counseling is very helpful for these troubled families and individuals. Support groups like **Children and Adults with Attention Deficit Disorder** (CHADD) can be a lifeline of help for parents struggling to cope and understand. There are many helpful parenting strategies which can be learned in support groups. Medications are but one of many helpful interventions in ADD.

What happens if you don't treat ADD?

Mr B was twenty-one years old when he first came to my office. Throughout junior grade school he had been fidgety, disorganized, concentrating poorly, and with low grades so he was diagnosed with a learning disability. He was in university when I met him. He was sent to see me by the school counselor who suspected ADD.

As an adult, he continued to have the same difficulty and symptoms that he had as a child. What was new however, was his mood swings. Since his teens he described recurring episodes when his mood would be very elevated with high energy, ambition, optimism, impulsivity and racing thoughts of great plans and ideas. These episodes would be followed by a plunge into despair, low energy, low ambition and racing negative depressing thoughts.

Mr B was demonstrating a very typical life history of ADD symptoms as a child which continued into adulthood. After adolescence he developed symptoms of what was clearly bipolar mood disorder along with the ADD.

He was treated with mood stabilizers and his grades went from a failing average to a 'B' average within a few months. His moods stabilized and he became a consistently pleasant, happy person, delighted with his new academic success. He still had a learning disability but it was much easier to deal with. With the use of mood stabilizers, both his symptoms of ADD and mood disorder were resolved since they were caused by the same chemical imbalance.

It used to be thought that ADD ended in adolescence. It is now known that in forty to sixty percent of cases, the condition continues on into adulthood.

When children with ADD go untreated, they may become sullen with low self-esteem, withdrawn, irritable, rebellious and conditioned for failure. They then associate with other kids with the same disability since they are rejected by their peers who can't tolerate their impulsive behavior. In their teens they may become rebellious, defiant and often have trouble with the law. When experimenting with drugs and alcohol, they notice for the first time that they are able to relax and concentrate until the drink wears off. They then continue to drink because it is the first time in their lives that they have been able to have control of their thoughts. There is a very high incidence of drug and alcohol addiction among untreated ADD and mood disordered adults. Chronic use of these substances will actually make the chemical imbalance worse.

With age, the hyperactive symptoms decline but the mood symptoms increase so there is a very high incidence of depression, anxiety and mood swings added to the inability to concentrate. Untreated ADD may lead to a lifetime of blame, shame, failure, anger, social isolation, restlessness, underemployment, relationship failure, drug and alcohol abuse and mood disorder. They lead disorganized lives, forgetful, chronically late, poor time managers, frequently change jobs, homes and spouses. They have severe interpersonal problems due to impulsiveness and intolerance of the opinions of others. This condition affects every aspect of life and personality. I consider it urgent to treat anyone suspected of ADD as soon as the diagnosis is made.

Adults with ADD are often discovered when they bring their own children in for an ADD assessment. At that time the parent may recognize that they too have had the same symptoms their whole life.

Adults can be treated with methylphenidate (Ritalin) but more often with antidepressants and mood stabilizers. Counseling is very important for the adult with ADD since there is usually so much emotional hurt and scarring to overcome before progress can be made.

Treatment will make these people more relaxed, tolerant, dependable, confident, happy with good self-control and self-esteem.

Mark Lowry is a Christian entertainer who has written a fascinating autobiography of his life with ADD. I highly recommend his book *Out of Control* to anyone who has this condition. He considers ADD to be a gift which God can use since there are positive attributes that come with this diagnosis. These people are more creative, higher in energy and passion and with a greater sense of humour. The world would be a very dull place without the ADD population. The challenge is to improve the concentration and channel the energy and creativity.

ADD is a very large subject that can never be adequately covered in a small book like this one. There are many very helpful books that have been written on the subject and the Internet is full of information. I encourage you to read further into this subject if you recognize yourself or a loved one in the symptom list.

The story of Mr T

As a result of prayer for help with my marriage, my wife found herself talking to someone about an entirely different topic and this person was holding a book. He referred to this book and the fact that he had just been diagnosed with attention deficit disorder (ADD) and he was reading about it. As this person was trying to explain a bit of this to my wife, he used the word 'chaos' as a way to describe his house and his life. Chaos was a word that really spoke to my wife as that is how she described our house. She immediately thought, 'Could my husband have ADD?' and this thought was burned into her mind for the rest of the day. I already had an appointment with my doctor for a different matter on the next day. That prompted my wife to gather some material quickly and talk to me that night. With the pamphlets in her hand she cautiously approached me to discuss ADD. My response was 'no way.' Yes I knew that something was wrong and I was working on it with the Lord, but I didn't have ADD and I wasn't going to take medication for the rest of my life. I was very angry.

The Lord prompted me to sneak a peak at the pamphlets that night, so the next day at my doctor's I asked him if I could have ADD? He said no, I was just being human. Usually I would have been happy with this answer but this time I wanted another opinion since I was almost convinced from the pamphlets that I might have ADD. My doctor didn't know who to send me too but eventually we found Dr Mullen. He diagnosed me with ADD and mood swings and started medication. Since that time I have been calmer, more confident and have become much closer to God. I am now even helping a friend recognize that he needs treatment too.

In the next chapter you will find the lists of symptoms which are usually found with chemical imbalances.

Chapter 12

Symptom checklists

Compare yourself to the symptoms listed below. If you see yourself being described, you should take this list to your physician and discuss it with him.

Depression or anxiety

At least five of the following symptoms need to be present every day for at least two weeks and that there is no other personal situation (like grief) or medical condition that may be causing the symptoms like drugs or low thyroid:

1. Persistent sad, anxious, or 'empty' mood, most of the time, most days.
2. Feelings of hopelessness, pessimism and low self-esteem.
3. Feelings of guilt, worthlessness, helplessness.
4. Loss of interest or pleasure in hobbies and activities that were once enjoyed, including sex.
5. Insomnia, early-morning awakening or oversleeping.
6. Loss of appetite and/or weight loss or overeating and weight gain.
7. Decreased energy, fatigue, feeling 'slowed down' or agitation that can't be controlled.
8. Procrastination, since simple tasks seem harder.
9. Thoughts of death or suicide, suicide attempts, constant feelings of 'life isn't worth living like this.'
10. Restlessness, irritability, bad-tempered, never relaxed or content.
11. Difficulty concentrating, remembering and making decisions due to persistent uncontrollable cluttering of

down, sad, negative thoughts that can't be kept out of the mind.

Other common symptoms of depression are:

12. Persistent physical symptoms that do not respond to treatment, such as headaches, digestive disorders, and chronic pain.
13. Continuous anxiety which can't be turned off. Uncontrollable worry about small things, including physical health.
14. Social isolation or withdrawal due to increasing difficulty making small talk.
15. Other relatives with depression, alcoholism or nervous breakdowns.
16. In children, look for increased irritability, persisting complaints of physical problems, agitation and unwarranted anxiety or panic, or social withdrawal.

Adolescent depression

1. Depressed mood or irritability that may lead to anti-social or rebellious behavior.
2. Unstable mood that changes rapidly even with insignificant events.
3. Poor concentration, drop in school performance, skipping school.
4. Loss of interest in school or friends, social withdrawal even from family.
5. Inability to stop worrying.
6. Inability to sleep or always oversleeping to escape.
7. Over or undereating.
8. Too much restless energy or always overtired.
9. Inability to enjoy things that they used to find pleasurable.
10. Many physical complaints like muscle pains, headaches, abdominal pains.
11. Feeling picked on or that everyone is against them.
12. Inappropriate guilt, shame and blame.
13. Increased use of street drugs or alcohol to self- medicate.
14. Loss of interest in own appearance and personal hygiene.

Dysthymia

Dysthymia is a milder form of depression that is just as treatable as depression and with the same medications.

1. Depressed mood most of the time for most days for at least two years with at least two of the following:
2. Poor appetite or overeating.
3. Insomnia or oversleeping.
4. Low energy, always tired.
5. Low self-esteem.
6. Poor concentration and difficulty making decisions.
7. Feeling hopeless.
8. These symptoms interfere with social or vocational function.

Obsessive compulsive disorder

1. Recurring intrusive and persisting, disturbing thoughts which cause anxiety and distress.
2. The thoughts are unrelated to actual events.
3. The person tries to stop the thoughts with another thought or action.
4. The person is aware that the thoughts are untrue and from his own mind.
5. Repetitive meaningless behaviors (hand-washing, ordering, checking) or thought rituals (praying, counting, repetitions) that they must do to neutralize the unwanted disturbing thoughts.
6. The thoughts and resulting actions are time-consuming, disruptive and embarrassing to the person but they have no control over them.

Mania or hypomania (mild mania), indicating bipolar disorder

1. Exaggerated elation, rapid unpredictable mood changes.
2. Irritability, impatience with others who can't keep up with them.

3. Inability to sleep, not needing sleep, too busy to sleep and not being tired the next day.
4. Big plans, inflated self-esteem, exaggerated self-importance, impulsive overspending.
5. Increased talking, louder and faster and can't stop.
6. Racing and jumbled thoughts, changing topics rapidly, no one can keep up.
7. Poor concentration, distractibility.
8. Increased sexual desire, uninhibited, acting out of character or promiscuous.
9. Markedly increased energy, 'can't be stopped,' erratic aggressive driving.
10. Poor judgment, no insight, refusing treatment, blaming others.
11. Inappropriate high-risk social behavior, brash, telling people off, overreaction to events, misinterpreting events, distortion of meaning of ordinary remarks.
12. Lasts hours to days, usually ending with a crash into profound depression.
13. Not caused by street drugs like 'speed' or cocaine.

Attention deficit disorder

Without hyperactivity

ADD may be mild, moderate or severe so these symptoms may only be present mildly. As in the other mood disorders, everyone is affected differently.

One needs six or more of these symptoms daily for over six months:

1. Racing cluttered thoughts causing constant thought distractions and making them very susceptible to any distraction.
2. No attention to details, lots of careless errors.
3. Inability to complete tasks since they can't pay attention long enough to remember or follow instructions.
4. Hearing but not listening even when spoken to directly.
5. Unable to concentrate on school work unless with one to one attention.
6. Making purposeless noises to fill any silence.

7. Falling grades, disruptive in class, defiant of authority, disorganized.
8. Daydreaming, losing things, forgetful.
9. Sometimes shy and withdrawn.

With hyperactivity

1. Fidgets and squirms.
2. Can't remain seated in classroom.
3. Excessive running and climbing when inappropriate.
4. Can't do anything quietly.
5. Always in motion as if 'driven by a motor.'
6. Can't stop talking.
7. Blurts out answers before question is completed.
8. Unable to wait a turn and easily frustrated.
9. Often interrupting and intruding, impulsive and disruptive.
10. Difficulty making or keeping friends, unable to share, demanding their own way, impatient, poor losers and generally socially immature.
11. Exaggerated emotional response to both good and bad events with wide mood swings.

There will often be a family history of ADD, depression, other mood disorders or alcoholism in relatives of an ADD child.

Adult ADD

1. Chronic forgetfulness.
2. Problems with time and money management.
3. Disorganized lifestyle.
4. Frequent moves or job changes.
5. Periodic depression, mood swings or anxiety as in the mood disorders above.
6. Chronic patterns of under achievement.
7. Feelings of restlessness.
8. Impulsive behavior.
9. Tendency toward substance abuse.
10. Low self-esteem.
11. May be over/under reactive.

12. Easily frustrated.
13. Difficulty concentrating
14. Difficulty maintaining relationships
15. Often labeled as lazy, immature, daydreamers, quitters, having a bad attitude.

Schizophrenia or any psychotic breakdown

1. Emotionally flat and withdrawn or very excited, hostile or grandiose.
2. Poor verbal communication, disorganized, unconnected thoughts.
3. Delusional thinking, believing something to be true which is outside the realm of reason and for which there is no real evidence, often religious.
4. Seeing things not visible to others or hearing things not audible to others.
5. Feelings of being watched or followed by other individuals or organizations.
6. There are many complex symptoms in psychotic illnesses needing professional assessment. Basically, during a psychotic episode a person loses touch with reality and is unable to function in their normal life activities. If you see this symptom, the person needs urgent medical attention.

The information contained in this chapter is for educational purposes only and does not replace the medical evaluation of a physician.

These checklists are adapted from *The American Psychiatric Association: Diagnostic and Statistical Manual of Mental Disorders*, Fourth Edition. Washington, DC: American Psychiatric Association, 1994.

Chapter 13

Section 1 conclusion

*'You turned my wailing into dancing; you removed my
sackcloth and clothed me with joy.'* (Psalm 30:11)

It is important for the public to realize that a person with
depression, mania, anxiety and attention deficit is helplessly
in the grip of a condition that they can't control. Don't give
these people simple 'pat' answers on how to overcome their
problems by becoming more spiritual or listening to worship
tapes (that is a part of the recovery process, not the whole
solution). To expect people to recover with these suggestions
is no different than to tell someone to 'go home and get
taller.' It just increases the burden of shame and guilt that a
depressed person is already struggling with.

These conditions are legitimate physical problems with
medical treatments just like diabetes or any other chronic
illness. It is unfair the way these people are treated with fear,
suspicion, hushed embarrassment and condemnation. Most
of these people can be totally controlled with medication and
returned to a normal productive life. Christians must realize
that these are very common treatable physical illnesses which
can affect anyone through no fault of their own.

Our communities and churches are full of hurting people
looking for answers to life's struggles. Many of them will
have mood disorders needing treatment. They are hurt when
friends or pastors declare that depression is a sign of weakness or deficient faith. A depressed person should never be
told to 'snap out of it' any more than a diabetic should
be told to 'smarten up and stop using insulin.'

Many are suffering needlessly from depression and other
mood disorders. They are unaware that treatment is available

and acceptable for Christians. Through public education, more depressed people will realize their need for treatment and they will no longer see themselves as social outcasts. People with mood disorders need to be encouraged to recognize the problem and get help.

This book can help a person diagnose the kind of disorder they have and discover what treatments are available. The symptom checklists in Chapter 12 summarize the symptoms of chemical imbalance of mood control. If you are wondering if you or a family member are suffering from a mood disorder, then just compare yourself with the symptoms in the checklist. If you have a number of the symptoms, then take the list to a physician and discuss how you are feeling so that a treatment plan can be started.

The story of Mrs N

As I was entering menopause, my mood and concentration began to change. My mind seemed to lose control of its thoughts. I was like a car engine that wouldn't turn off. My thoughts were cluttered and racing all the time. Sometimes I was very positive and energetic, other times depressed and wanting to die. My memory was so bad that I would even leave things to burn on the stove. I had a very hot, unpredictable temper. My moods were just like a yo-yo, going up and down all the time.

I really suffered spiritually. I was lying, swearing, couldn't pray and the Bible was just too hard to read. I got nothing from sermons. It seemed like nothing could sink into my head. I knew there was something wrong.

I knew I had reached bottom when I threw my Bible across the room and cursed. I cried out to God to help me and He heard me. There I was, lost, broken, suicidal, out in the desert of my mind with no energy or will left, when a friend suggested I go and see Dr Mullen. This was hard for me to do since I had always been in pride and denial.

Dr Mullen gave me medications and one month later my head cleared and I felt a light turn on inside me. The engine in my mind finally stopped. I then entered Christian counseling which was very helpful to heal the hurts of my past and deliver me from the attack of Satan. God has now turned my life around 180 degrees. I now have a clear mind, stable moods, I can concentrate. This is the first time I have been consistently happy since I was nine years old.

It has been two years since I started medications. God has now equipped me to reach out to others and give them hope when they are in that dark valley.

In the next section of the book, we will look at the second link in the **chain of emotional bondage**, the harassment of Satan.

SECTION 2

The Harassment of Satan

Chapter 14

The attack of Satan

*'Be self-controlled and alert. Your enemy the devil prowls
around like a roaring lion looking for someone to devour.'*
(1 Peter 5:8)

If we ignore Satan, won't he just go away?

The whole matter of Satan's kingdom and how he attacks
humans is a vast subject which is highly controversial. Satan
has conveniently urged Christians in Western cultures to
ignore, avoid and even fear the subject. He has so successfully
marginalized those who teach or minister in this area, that
the Christian community prefers not to address this issue
and will even criticize those who do. It is generally felt that
demonic issues are a problem only in the developing world
within animistic cultures so that only missionaries need to
discuss such topics. Physicians are reluctant to discuss such
issues for fear of appearing to be non-scientific or to be
stooping to the level of mysticism. Satan loves this situation
since it allows him to continue his work unhindered by
Christians who deny the reality of his influence.

I am in no way an expert on Satan's kingdom or his
activities. I have however, encountered him on enough
occasions to know that he is real and active. In this section
of the book I want to introduce you to the subject and show
you how Satan takes advantage of our vulnerabilities. Later, I
will explain why we have authority over Satan and how we
are to use it.

I am so grateful for the authors who have written such
helpful books on the subject to assist people like myself
to understand what can't be seen but can certainly be

The church often marginalizes those who teach deliverance.

experienced. In this section, I will be drawing from the works of Neil Anderson, Dean Sherman and Peter Horrobin. Their very helpful books are listed in my bibliography section at the conclusion of this book. I strongly encourage you to read them.

I come from a conservative evangelical background where the activity of Satan was rarely discussed. I just assumed that Satan was harassing the people still in his kingdom and that primarily he was working in developing world countries like Africa where there were witch doctors. Deliverance ministries or those who taught about demons were considered 'fringey' or extreme. It was more convenient and comfortable to ignore the subject assuming that it would just 'go away.' It was generally taught that Christians just couldn't have problems in those areas so it was best not to talk about it. I realize now that this whole attitude was based on the fear of Satan by Christians who didn't know their authority in Christ.

How I became involved

When I started treating mental illness in my office, I had the mind-set that emotional illnesses nearly always had a physical cause which could be treated with medications. Though I was a Christian, I didn't see a very important role for counseling and deliverance was only for the fanatic fringe groups.

As I interviewed more and more people with mood disorders, I heard stories of strange phenomena. They would report visual or auditory experiences yet they did not have a psychotic illness and were totally sane. I became so intrigued with these unexplainable events that I began to routinely ask all new patients about such experiences as part of my psychiatric interview. I was not prepared for what I uncovered.

To my absolute amazement, the more people I asked, the more reports I would get of unexplained supernatural events that had never been reported due to the fear of being considered insane. The events were usually frightening and involved hearing from or speaking to a spirit. The events would vary from hearing strange laughter coming from 'Heavy Metal' rock music posters, to having spirit beings walk into the living room right out of the television program that was being watched. Children were not exempt from these frightening experiences. Many told me how they had difficulty falling asleep due to the arrival of frightening spirits which would appear in their bedrooms every night to threaten them.

It became very clear to me that occult spiritual activity was far more common than most people thought. The only reason why we have not been aware of it is because it is not socially acceptable in Western society to discuss these events. In the developing world, such occult events are commonplace and even expected, so they are discussed openly.

As I was learning more about these occult events and how they affected my patients, I noticed some clear patterns. There was no doubt that those who deliberately dabbled in the occult had more spirit visitors and their lives were more terrorized by voices and visitations. The occult dabbling could have been considered by some to be quite 'innocent.' I have seen many children who were never the same again after playing 'Ouija' or performing common schoolyard rituals during school recess where they would chant to call up a spirit, thinking it was just a game. I have seen others who consulted a fortune-teller hired to entertain at a birthday party. From that moment they were filled with fear and strange mental voices.

The other common route that triggered occult experiences was reading or watching entertainment which contained themes and personalities which were evil. I have been absolutely astonished at the number of patients who have had demonic visits after exposing themselves to pornography, violent or occult entertainment. I was also uncovering the fact that the children of these people, who did not actually watch the event, were also being terrorized by the same spirits that the parents had allowed into the house through entertainment which they thought was harmless.

The story of Mrs K

I spent several years inquiring about these supernatural occult events in my patients before the day that I met Mrs K. This woman came to see me about a long-standing depression. She was very vague and nervous during the early part of the interview. After a few minutes of superficial small talk and preliminary questions she said to me 'I'm having trouble listening to you since there are three people talking to me continuously in my mind.' Well, this was a new experience for me. She was clearly not schizophrenic so I knew that this was not a psychotic illness causing her to hear voices. She was totally sane, though depressed.

I wasn't sure what to do but I wondered if she was having one of those occult experiences that I had spent so many hours inquiring about. This interference was going to make the interview very difficult, so I paused and made some simple notes in my chart to buy time. In my heart I said to God, 'I don't know what's going on here. If this woman is hearing from evil spirits, in the name of Jesus could you please shut them up so I can finish this interview.'

When I then looked up from my notes she looked at me with an intensity that I had not seen in her before and said 'What did you just do?' I explained that I had just noted her last statement in my chart. She would not be put off by that answer and persisted, 'No, you did something else.' I was confused by this time and again stated that I had only been writing in her chart and what made her think that I had done anything else. Her answer changed the course of my spiritual and professional life when she stated, 'You did something, since the voices stopped for the first time in twenty years. They are now hiding and they are afraid of you. What did you do?!'

Well I can tell you that I was the most surprised person in the room. Why did they stop, who were they afraid of and why? My mind was suddenly opened to the fact that yes indeed, she was sane and she was being tormented by the voices of demons. They stopped speaking to her because when I prayed, the authority of Christ filled the room and they were afraid of the power of the Holy Spirit who is within every believer. From that moment I realized that I was in the front line of a war that I wasn't previously aware of and didn't know anything about. My learning experiences soon became far more intense, as I will explain in later chapters.

I thought I was being helpful

Having interviewed so many people with occult experiences, I became somewhat efficient at exposing demonic activity in my patients both Christian and secular. I found it surprising though, that this skill often did not accelerate their recovery from depression. Unfortunately, quite the opposite occurred. I noticed that the majority of people who were having occult experiences never returned for their second visit. The few that did return told me harrowing tales of dramatically increased demonic attacks, harassment and threats after their visit to my office. The spirits were furious that I had exposed them and that the person had admitted to their presence. The patients were usually threatened with their lives or that of their loved ones if they ever saw me again. Since my patients were already suffering with depression, anxiety and mood swings, this increased mental torment was enough to make them give up on medical treatment, particularly from someone as dangerous as me.

My office became a battle ground.

One morning in my office, I had two Christian women with back-to-back appointments. They did not know each other. During both interviews when it came to the point that I asked about occult activity, their heads jerked off to the side so that they were looking over their shoulders and their jaws were tightly closed. Through clenched teeth they both were able to whisper 'They won't let me answer that question, they've grabbed my face and are twisting my head.' This was quite a shock and surprise for me particularly when it happened twice in one morning. It illustrated to me how vigorously Satan will resist detection. It also taught me to pray prayers of protection every time I enter my office since it is a battle zone.

I find Neil Anderson's book *The Bondage Breaker* an extremely effective tool to help understand demonic bondage and to expel Satan from one's life. I recommend it to my patients. The book is so powerful that Satan will oppose attempts to read it. One of my patients went into a bookstore to buy it and after browsing and handling many books, they were physically unable to touch the book and purchase it. They described a tight band surrounding their body and arms which was felt only when looking at that book. They did not buy it and dropped out of treatment since the harassment became so intense. Another patient was a new believer, just starting her journey to freedom and was reading *The Bondage Breaker* in bed beside her common-law husband. Without warning and without any preceding conversation, he flew into an uncontrollable rage, lost the ability to speak clearly and viciously attacked her. Police had to be called and he was jailed. It's a powerful book!

I began to wonder why was Satan so upset with people coming to see me. I was not in a deliverance ministry but he considered me to be a major threat. My only role was to treat depression with medications. It slowly became clearer to me why Satan was so threatened by the medical treatment of mood disorders.

Why Satan loves mood disorders and hates doctors who treat them

Spiritual warfare or conflict is a very real issue, especially in depressed Christians. The loss of concentration and the cluttering of negative thoughts make a person particularly vulnerable to occult influences.

When a person's mind is filled with negative discouraging thoughts which can't be shut off, then it is very easy for Satan to insert even more condemning thoughts or suggestions in among the person's own thoughts. The depressed person is unable to detect the intrusion of lies, condemnation or misinterpretations from an evil source and just assumes that the thoughts are their own. The inserted thoughts are intended to magnify the pain of depression and to separate the victim from supportive friends, counselors and most of all, from God. When concentration is impaired by depression, it is very difficult to *'take every thought captive'* (2 Corinthians 10:5) and block the intrusion of dark thoughts.

This state is like having a house with no doors or windows covering the holes in the walls. The house is always filling with dirt or debris that is blowing by. It is impossible to keep the house clean. When a mind is racing and cluttered, there is very little defense against evil, disturbing thoughts that are directed against that person. These thoughts will just 'blow in' and fill part of the house. A poorly protected mind will accumulate many unwanted negative thoughts, especially the kind which separate a person from God.

When a person recovers from depression, it is like putting glass and doors over all the holes to keep out unwanted thoughts. In this way, thought control is restored and any thoughts of an evil origin are quickly detected and disposed of. The mind can then be kept clean since the entry points are controlled and monitored.

In my experience, the first step in the process of deliverance or becoming free from the harassment of evil, is to treat any depression that may be present. When thought control and concentration is restored, then believers can use their authority over Satan and he will flee.

Some patients, like the ones I've spoken of, have such severe oppression that they are unable to keep appointments or take their medication. These ones need some deliverance just to get them into my office to begin treatment.

There are many who feel that the cause of depression is always demonic. As you can see from all the preceding chapters, I don't believe that. In my experience, most depressive illnesses are caused by physical chemical imbalances which Satan takes advantage of. It is in the 'taking advantage of' that people skilled in deliverance, sense the power of darkness and assume that deliverance is the primary treatment. I of course, endorse deliverance as a very essential tool in setting people free from the chains of emotional bondage. When the harassment of Satan can be removed, a person can more rapidly come to wholeness. Deliverance remains a part of the treatment as much as medications and inner healing are parts of the treatment process. That all being true, I have still had patients who met all my criteria for a mood disorder, who improved with treatment (which confirmed the diagnosis) but who after deliverance were totally symptom free and didn't need any further medications. In these situations I have to assume that the chemical imbalance was of a demonic origin, presumably spirits of infirmity who induced the imbalance. The condition responded to treatment since the imbalance really did exist but the root cause had not been dealt with until deliverance was performed.

More commonly, after deliverance, people with mood disorders make a significant improvement but still require some medication though often much less. I have seen severe uncontrollable people with bipolar illness become very stable and easy to control after deliverance though still needing some medication. What I have learned from these patients is that in most cases, the demonic influence will magnify a pre-existing mood disorder and take advantage of it. The best treatment of course, will always be a combination of medications, deliverance and inner healing.

The story of Mrs P

I met Mrs P more that two years ago. She was a middle-aged married Christian who had been depressed most of her life. She had survived two suicide attempts and had been hospitalized many times for depression. Her past was filled with severe emotional wounding and drug addiction.

I was able to adjust her medications to improve her mood and stop the swings but she still was generally struggling with her life. She hungered for God and faithfully attended church and sought out times of prayer ministry. On one occasion she was at the front of her church receiving prayer ministry when she flew into a severe demonic manifestation. She felt evil pouring out of her for quite some time. At the conclusion of this ministry time the improvement in her mood was dramatic. She wondered if she had been healed of her depression. I reduced her medications but within a month some depressive symptoms reappeared but they were far milder and easier to control than in the past. It appeared to me that her biological depression had been magnified by the demonic oppression. When this influence was broken her chemical imbalance improved to some extent so her medications could be reduced.

Within a year she was at a time of prayer ministry and she again had an experience where she felt something leave her but it was far less dramatic. Again there was a significant improvement in her mood. Again I slowly reduced her medication to see if her chemical imbalance had changed. To our absolute delight, she was able to gradually come off all her medications without any return in symptoms. Now, a year later, she is still free of depression, on no medications and walking confidently in the Spirit, helping others who are suffering from depression.

I have several other cases where people have been totally healed of their chemical imbalances after deliverance. In these cases, I believe that the cause of their imbalance was likely demonic.

I have been quite surprised to find that even non-Christians have reported a reduction in the intensity of demonic harassment after recovering from a mood disorder. This always confused me since they have no spiritual protection from Satan while they live in his kingdom. The only way I can explain this observation is that when thought control is restored, there is less vulnerability to demonic attack even in a non-believer. Racing uncontrolled thoughts will always be Satan's playground and correcting that condition will always reduce the number of ways that Satan can attack.

Why are deliverance ministries suspicious of medications?

It has been my observation that those involved in deliverance ministries are often very suspicious and skeptical of the role of medications. There are several good reasons why this point of view has evolved.

Medications are usually prescribed by non-Christian physicians who deny the reality of the spiritual realm, feel that physical causes can explain all emotional problems and that medications are the only answer. Medications are then perceived as anti-spiritual or a substitute for spiritual treatment since they came from a secular source. As a Christian physician I hope to remove the cynicism towards medications by showing how they can be incorporated into a broader treatment plan.

Medicines have also been accused of covering up spiritual symptoms and preventing a person from realizing that there is a spiritual issue. Medicines have been blamed for keeping people so drowsy and emotionally numb that they ignore the other issues that need healing. There is some truth in this last accusation. If a person is on tranquilizers, it is possible for them to be so sedated that they do become emotionless and their minds are too foggy to participate in deliverance or inner healing. Tranquilizers can of course become drugs of abuse and be just as bad as alcohol. I use tranquilizers very sparingly to try and avoid this situation. Antidepressants are totally different. They are not habit forming but they may be sedating. There is a definite risk that antidepressants can make a person feel so much better in the natural realm, that they ignore the spiritual or personal issues that also need healing. It appears that they are so relieved with the improvement from medications that they feel well enough to ignore the other aspects of recovery. This is a true risk so in my clinic we continue to emphasize the 'three links' throughout the recovery process. In most cases fortunately, when a person's mind clears, they are very anxious to get on with the other aspects of healing.

Another criticism of mental health physicians is that we give anti psychotic medications to those who are hearing demonic voices, mistaking them for schizophrenic symptoms. These medications are so powerful that a person can become so sedated and passive that they can't participate in deliverance or inner healing. This accusation is true. I have met patients who were totally sane but because they admitted hearing voices, they were presumed to be psychotic and were given powerful medications that did not help the underlying problem. This often happens because physicians are trained that anyone who sees or hears things that others don't see or hear is psychotic needing those stronger medications. There is no diagnostic category in medicine for supernatural phenomenon. In the story of Ms K above, she was hearing voices but was not psychotic. If I hadn't been aware that there was possibly a spiritual issue, I could have easily put her on such medications and she would have never recovered to the degree that she has today. It is often not easy however, to tell if voices are demonic or as a result of chemical imbalance. This is especially true with schizophrenics who could be hearing voices from their illness and from spiritual sources. In my opinion, when in doubt, treat both conditions medically and spiritually.

Next we will look at how Satan attacks humans.

Chapter 15

Am I really in a war?

'But I am afraid that just as Eve was deceived by the serpent's cunning, your minds may somehow be led astray from your sincere and pure devotion to Christ.'
(2 Corinthians 11:3)

'Put on the full armor of God so that you can take your stand against the devil's schemes. For our struggle is not against flesh and blood, but against the rulers, against the authorities, against the powers of this dark world and against the spiritual forces of evil in the heavenly realms. Therefore put on the full armor of God, so that when the day of evil comes, you may be able to stand your ground, and after you have done everything, to stand.'
(Ephesians 6:11–13)

It's not difficult to understand that Satan's primary purpose is to oppose the purposes of God by attacking and controlling man. We can easily accept that anyone who chooses to remain in Satan's kingdom will be subject to his control and attack. Where we have difficulty, is in understanding how Satan attacks Christians who are not resident in his kingdom. This has been a huge stumbling block for Christians in Western cultures as I have mentioned before. All my life I have listened to Christians arguing about this matter. As a result of my experiences which I outlined in the last chapter, I have come to the conclusions which are explained in this book. I realize that my positions could be considered by some to be controversial but I don't know how else to explain and understand the spiritual events that I witness on a regular basis.

Can a Christian be attacked?

In the introduction to this book I explained how we all enter God's kingdom carrying a bag of 'old nature,' which contains our painful past and all its wounds. That bag was designed and shaped by Satan so you could be molded into his image. He did this by wounding you through damaging relationships which we'll discuss in the last section of the book. The wounds hurt and left you with emotional scars which continue to hurt you until you allow Jesus to heal them. In these bad memories, Satan has planted lies that you believe since they were based on the wounding event. For example, if you were let down or hurt by your father, Satan would then plant the lie that 'no man can be trusted,' or that 'God is no better than your father, you can't trust God either.' Satan knows that if he can get you to believe a lie, then he can control your behavior whether you are inside his kingdom or God's. He has been lying to humans since the Garden of Eden so he knows how predictably humans fall for lies.

One of the most common ways that Satan attacks Christians is by filling their minds with lies based on negative events of the past. As long as we have an unhealed old nature, we are vulnerable to attack with lies. There are an infinite number of lies that control peoples' minds and

Satan loves to attack our minds.

behaviors. Here are some of the most common and damaging lies that I have come across that torment Christians' minds:
- You are worthless, hopeless and can never change.
- It's all right to sin if no one knows about it.
- You're unforgivable, God will never accept you, you've run out of chances.
- You must look out for yourself, God can't be trusted to protect your interests. Keep worrying about your life, fight your way to your goals.
- You can't forgive them.

Demonic attachment

To greatly reinforce and magnify a lie, Satan will sometimes assign a demonic spirit to a person to keep the lie very active in a person's mind so they remain in emotional and mental bondage. The lie is also designed to lead them into greater bondage by encouraging sinful behavior. When this happens we refer to it as a demonic 'attachment' since the spirit is specifically assigned to a person and to a lie which it continually reinforces.

There are many ways that people become susceptible to demonic attachment. The most obvious behavior which invites a demonic spirit to attach to a person is occult pursuits. As I mentioned earlier, playing with the occult through games, rituals, fortune tellers or witchcraft will open the door wide to demonic attachment. Any willful and repetitive sin or sinful thought pattern could open the door to allow Satan to assign a demonic spirit to attach to that sinful behavior or thought to reinforce it and make it unstoppable. Satan loves to reinforce sinful actions or thought patterns of lust, rage, bitterness, worthlessness, suicide or any negative emotion. He wants to keep these thoughts or actions alive, threatening and persistent. In so doing, Satan forges a chain or stronghold that holds you to the sin or thought.

Another way that we can come under the chain of demonic influence is through what we call 'generational' sin or curses. In this situation, the sin of an ancestor has invited Satan into the family and given him legal rights to

attack the subsequent generations. The Bible refers to this in
Exodus 20:5:

> *'You shall not bow down to them or worship them; for I, the
> LORD your God, am a jealous God, punishing the children for
> the sin of the fathers to the third and fourth generation of
> those who hate me.'*

It is very easy to see in the natural realm how the sins of
parents will have consequences on their children. I have had
several dramatic illustrations of how bondage in a parent
creates bondage in children.

On one occasion I was the member of a ministry team
praying for a family with teenage children who were present
in the room. As the parents would confess sin and repent, we
watched how after each repentance, one of the teens would
cough, retch and show obvious signs of demonic activity as
the curses were being lifted off the children by the repentance of the parent. On another occasion I was asked to pray
for a child's bondage in the presence of the Christian mother.
As I prayed for the child's freedom, the child remained
motionless but the mother went into coughing spasm as
she 'felt something coming out.' Though I can't really
explain what's going on, it's clear to me that there is a
spiritual bond between generations that can be for good or
evil. This complex subject is discussed in the books by Peter
Horrobin which are listed in the 'Recommended reading'
chapter.

When we become Christians, we enter the kingdom carrying our bag of wounds, lies and the demonic spirits that are
attached to the lies. The bag stays attached to believers until
they choose to release it through the process of emotional
healing. This means that it is very possible for Christians to
be in God's kingdom and spend their lifetime harassed by
wounds, lies and the spirits attached to them. This is a very
unfortunate event that God wants to rescue you from. The
whole purpose of this book is to help you get free of your bag
of emotional pain and walk to freedom.

Another way to understand how Christians can have
problems with demonic spirits is to think of the process of
buying a house. On the closing date you are presented with

the deed to the house which indicates full ownership. The house is now completely yours but is it totally cleaned and decorated to your specifications? No, of course not. After you move in you start the process of cleaning and decorating.

When we become Christians, Jesus takes complete ownership of our lives but you enter the Kingdom broken, filthy and carrying that bag of pain and perhaps demons. God then starts the process of cleaning you up and emptying the bag. You can choose to work with God and accelerate the process or you can choose to resist Him and remain in emotional bondage.

The story of Mrs F

Mrs F was a strong Christian involved in overseas missions. I met her during a healing conference when she came forward for prayer. She explained that for the previous twelve years, since a car accident, she had been in constant neck and spine pain. She also knew that quite apart from the pain, she was being tormented by demonic spirits. (I was unable to ask at the time how she knew she was being tormented.)

I had often seen Pastor John Arnott of the Toronto Airport Christian Fellowship pray for those with spinal injuries. He would lead them in a prayer forgiving those who had caused the accident (including themselves) and then would pray for healing. I was amazed how many people improved after such a prayer. I felt Mrs F needed to pray such a prayer forgiving those who had caused the accident which had caused her so much pain. I did not address the demonic issue at all since there were so many waiting for prayer that evening. After she had prayed forgiveness, I then prayed a simple prayer for healing and the power of God came over her and she rested on the floor.

Six weeks later I received the following letter.

Dear Dr Mullen,

I recently attended the conference during which time I received prayer for healing my herniated disc, spinal injuries and demonic attack. Since that evening I have been able to

walk straight, pain free and without any more attacks! I don't
know yet how to express what I feel after twelve years of
dealing with the physical pain and the emotional turmoil
since the accident. I am so grateful. I know God is the healer.
There is not a day that I do not marvel at what He has done
for me. The cleansing from demonic attack is fantastic, the
physical healing is just icing on the cake. I have already been
able to help a friend come free of phobias by showing them
how to forgive.

Mrs F was delivered from a demonic attack and chronic
pain by a simple act of forgiveness and a healing prayer. She
was a fine Christian involved in full-time ministry but she
had unresolved emotional issues of unforgiveness that Satan
used against her to attack her mind and body.

How can you tell when you are being attacked?

There are an infinite number of ways that Satan attacks
people. I have grouped the types of attacks that I have
observed into a few very broad categories. These categories
are not to be used as hard and fast rules by which to measure
people's experiences. They are just guidelines to give you
clues to what may be causing your particular problem.

The lowest level of attack is what I call 'the harassment of
all believers.' This is the constant hassle that we all have as
we serve God in a fallen world. It can take the form of
difficult relationships, health problems, occasional struggle
with thoughts and disappointments. I have had these kinds
of experiences show up as a period of six months of unexplained insomnia that immediately corrected after the prayer
of a friend who discerned the attack and broke it in prayer. At
other times Satan has tried to intimidate me by filling my
mind with lies, misunderstandings or fears which were very
upsetting. We all need to be aware of this level of attack since
it's a constant reminder that we are in a war and that God has
given us all the weapons we need.

The next level of attack is when there is a demonic
attachment which continually fills your mind with unwanted
sickening, disturbing, shocking thoughts that are totally out

of character and thoughts that you would never choose to have. When this type of attack is combined with a depressive illness, the results can be devastating since the person is unable to control their thoughts due to the illness.

These thoughts may have a loud, shouting characteristic to them even though they are heard only in the mind. They may have a gruff, low-toned 'male' voice which you recognize as not being your usual 'thought voice' that you have when you are thinking to yourself. The 'thought voice' could be the voice of a relative or friend but the content of the words is not just a replayed memory of that person but a new disturbing thought never before heard from that individual.

Many have told me that these 'thought voices' are usually critical, sneering, mocking, laughing and even commanding of an action. They commonly negate every good thought that enters your mind through perhaps a sermon or conversation with a friend or therapist. The 'voice' may continually tempt you to sin or remind you of events that would push you into sin or danger.

As the intensity of attack increases, the 'thought voices' can become audible and the spirits can become visible particularly at night before falling asleep. I have had several patients who were even physically assaulted by spirits but would never admit this to anyone for fear of being thought to be crazy. They were all very surprised when I asked them specifically about such events and then didn't put them in hospital. These events are not uncommon but can't be easily discussed in our society. In the developing world they are considered to be a normal part of life.

Those of you with medical training will quickly see that there is a great overlap in the symptoms of demonic harassment from the last paragraph and the auditory and visual hallucinations of schizophrenia or psychotic thinking. When someone is in a psychotic episode, I personally feel that I am unable to tell to what extent their symptoms are medical or spiritual. In this situation I choose to treat them medically on an urgent basis and then see what their thinking is like after the psychotic episode has resolved. The demonic attacks that I have listed in the previous paragraph are only of diagnostic value in someone who has no other signs of psychotic illness.

In other words, if a person is otherwise completely sane but seeing and hearing from spirits then I strongly suspect demonic attack.

You can be free!

2 Corinthians 10:3–5 states:

> 'For though we live in the world, we do not wage war as the world does. The weapons we fight with are not the weapons of the world. On the contrary, they have divine power to demolish strongholds. We demolish arguments and every pretension that sets itself up against the knowledge of God, and we take captive every thought to make it obedient to Christ.'

Through Jesus' death and resurrection Satan has been disarmed and we are able to break free of the chains that he has placed on us. Through a process of repentance and forgiveness, we can restore our spiritual armour, remove the legal grounds that Satan has used to harass us and break

You can be free!

free. This process is clearly described in the books by Neil Anderson, particularly *The Bondage Breaker.*

The story of Mr D

Mr D has been a patient of mine for many years. He was a very wounded person who came to Christ but gave up on Christianity when he experienced further wounding in the church. He had a serious depressive mood disorder which was very difficult to treat. I always felt so useless during his visits since his mood showed so little improvement even with a very large variety of medications. The following are excerpts from an exchange of letters we made nearly two years ago after he had moved far away and was unable to see me on a regular basis.

> Dear Dr Mullen,
>
> I have read the emotional healing books that you recommended and since then I have been overwhelmed by negative and hopeless thoughts and feelings. Although I know where this is coming from (Satan), I cannot overcome this on my own. I am truly in a battle that I feel I'm losing. As I read the books I kept sinking further into despair, hopelessness and anger. It brought all kinds of memories to the surface but instead of being able to release and forgive the person who hurt me, I just felt the pain. I kept thinking, 'Where is God in all this pain?' I guess I'm just waiting to die or for Jesus to come and rescue me.

I responded:

> Dear Mr D,
>
> I'm glad you were able to do as much reading as you did. The pain you are feeling is a result of feeling exposed and therefore very uncomfortable. This pain of exposure is actually part of the healing process as we come to recognize exactly what we have been running from and how it began.
> You are correct that Satan wants to prevent you from reading the books and becoming whole. He wants you to

become so overwhelmed by the pain that you are paralyzed. Yes, you must ask God to protect you from the attack of the enemy while you are in the process of healing. Satan wants to aggravate your wounds while God wants to expose and heal them. You are **not alone** in this process. The Holy Spirit has led you to those books and His arms are around you while you are discovering the sources of your pain. He will also lead you to your healing as you finish reading them. You would also do well to read *The Bondage Breaker* by Neil Anderson. It would help you push off Satan's attack.

Yes the memories will stir up anger. Recognizing this is part of the process. You must however continue to forgive and continuously give the 'diseased' thoughts (as Leanne Payne says in her books) to Jesus as He hangs on the cross in your mind, wounded and bleeding for your pain. He died to take your pain and thoughts away. Keep giving them to Him. This is the only effort needed on your part, to keep giving it to Jesus and talking to Him. It would be very wise to also see a Christian counselor who can walk you through the process much faster. When you are doing the process with someone else, it is easier to overcome the waves of lies that Satan throws at you to distract you off course.

One month later he replied:

Dear Dr Mullen,

This letter is going to be a true 180 degree turn from my last one. I received your letter and it was the beginning of a change in me.

I decided to follow your advice and read *The Bondage Breaker* and what a blessing it has been to me. That book has turned my life around. I have followed every prayer, confession and have turned everything over to God to take care of for me. I now know that I am special to Him and no matter what happens, He loves me. I always knew that in my head but I could not get it into my heart. It is there now and every day I commit myself to believe Him and not Satan's lies. I have confessed my sin and committed myself to walk in the Spirit and show the Spirit's fruits. I have also released others by forgiving them for offenses against me. My attitude has completely changed. I see people in a different light so I can offer them encouragement and understanding instead of condemnation. This is so simple, why didn't I get this long ago? I allowed myself to be deceived by the devil just like Anderson says. It's like a light has been turned on in my head, like stepping out of a dark room into the sunlight and feeling the warmth of God's love.

So with all this happening, can you doubt that there is a God and that He is working in our lives every day, especially mine?

Mr D still takes his medications for depression but there has been a total transformation of his life since the hold of demonic lies on him was broken. This change took place within a four-week period and without any counseling. It was just God and him. This case illustrates the power of Christ's authority to break us free of the chains of lies and oppression that we carry. *The Bondage Breaker* is such an easy to use tool to break free of lies and of demonic oppression.

The ox-cart and the rocket

In the Introduction to this book I gave you the picture of the kingdom of God as a walled city. Those who entered the gate were given a choice. They could remain at the gate holding onto their wounds, pain and old nature or they could accept the Holy Spirit's invitation to move down the path of sanctification to the throne room.

It has been my observation that the process of sanctification which is also the process of inner healing and breaking free of emotional bondage, has been painfully slow. I liken it to being in an ox-cart laden down with a huge bag of your old nature along with all the chains and wounds that go with it. As the cart slowly rolls along the path, the chains gradually fall off, the wounds are healed and the bag dissolves. This is a wonderful but slow process.

It is always easy to talk about reaching emotional freedom and breaking free of demonic harassment. Many of you have heard this message many times but have not experienced the freedom that the speaker or author has promised. I want to encourage you, because in 1 Corinthians 4:20 it states:

> *'For the kingdom of God is not a matter of talk but of power.'*

We have all heard a lot of talk in our churches but have rarely seen New Testament power. The good news is that we are currently living in a time of unprecedented anointing for emotional healing. God is at this time pouring out His love and refining fire to free us of our chains. This book is a direct result of this outpouring which I have both witnessed and experienced.

This outpouring is almost like Jesus sending an angel sitting on a rocket, up alongside our ox-carts! He is beckoning us to leave the ox-cart and join Him on the rocket where we can be quickly transported to the throne room without our bag and chains. I have witnessed many of my patients, friends, my wife and finally myself getting onto that rocket and experiencing the most transforming power of the Holy Spirit to break emotional chains. This touch of God allows

Jesus seems to be offering us a faster way to freedom.

people to repent, forgive and to walk to freedom at a speed that I have never witnessed before in all my years of psychiatry.

I want to encourage you to ask God again to set you free. Seek out a Christian counselor, attend prayer ministry, visit a doctor if necessary but set out again to find your freedom. The fact that you are reading this book means that you want to see a change in your life. God does too! Open your mind and heart to let God change you.

To push Satan out of our minds, we need to know our spiritual weapons. We need to learn the best kept secret in Christianity. Keep reading!

Chapter 16

The best kept secret
in Christianity

*'We do, however, speak a message of wisdom among the
mature, but not the wisdom of this age or of the rulers of
this age, who are coming to nothing. No, we speak of
God's secret wisdom, a wisdom that has been hidden
and that God destined for our glory before time began.
However, as it is written: "No eye has seen, no ear has
heard, no mind has conceived what God has prepared for
those who love him" but God has revealed it to us by his
Spirit.'* (1 Corinthians 2:6–7, 9–10)

*'His intent was that now, through the church, the
manifold wisdom of God should be made known to
the rulers and authorities in the heavenly realms, according to his eternal purpose which he accomplished in
Christ Jesus our Lord.'* (Ephesians 3:10)

About six years ago I was interviewing a woman in her
hospital room. She was severely depressed and was not
responding to medications. As I was asking her questions
about her thoughts, she suddenly developed a 'glazed' look
and I knew that she was no longer able to hear me. She
seemed to be frozen in her own thoughts while staring into
the distance. Moments later she spoke in a mechanical
unnatural voice and said 'Leave her alone, she's ours!'
I'll finish the story later, but I can assure you that at
that moment, my interest in spiritual authority increased
dramatically.

In previous chapters I explained how oblivious I was to
Satan's activities throughout my life. I didn't know anything

about spiritual authority. I didn't seem to need it and I never heard anything about it in my church. Like so many others, I presumed spiritual authority was for missionaries in under-developed countries. After the above experience and many other similar experiences since then, I have learned that the best kept secret in Christianity is that every believer has authority over Satan regardless of how you feel. In my opinion this is one of the greatest treasures of 'God's secret wisdom' that is being revealed to us and that He 'has prepared for those who love Him.'

In Matthew 28:18–19 Jesus says,

> *'All authority in heaven and on earth has been given to me. Therefore go and make disciples of all nations, baptizing them in the name of the Father and of the Son and of the Holy Spirit.'*

Here we see the extent of Jesus' authority and that this authority is foundational to the process of evangelizing the world. This authority is clearly for the use of all believers to extend God's kingdom.

What authority are we referring to?

I never understood the believer's authority until I read Dean Sherman's excellent book, *Spiritual Warfare*. The following explanation is what I learned from that book. I encourage you to read Sherman's writings for yourself since they so clearly explain such a complex subject. His book is listed in my 'Recommended reading' list.

When Satan was still an angel in the courts of heaven, he became jealous of God. He wanted to be like God and to have more power and authority: *'I will make myself like the most high'* (Isaiah 14:14). As a result of his rebellion he was cast down to earth with no authority.

When man was created, God permanently delegated a small part of His authority to man so that he could rule the earth (Psalm 8:6). This limited authority belonged to man as long as man continued to obey God. It was conditional. Man was also given a free will so that he could decide if he wanted to obey God.

When Satan saw this new creature, he realized that man had more authority than he had. He also understood that man held authority only to the extent that he chose to obey God. Satan then saw an opportunity to steal man's authority by convincing man to disobey God and in so doing, disqualify himself from authority.

This is of course what happened. Satan convinced man to believe a lie and then to sin. The authority was then lost and Satan stole it in a spiritually legal transaction much like the theft of Esau's birthright by Jacob. Satan had won a huge prize. He could now strike back at God, attack man and disrupt the creation. He now had man's authority over creation and over man himself.

This stolen authority is only over man and it is exercised through men who Satan controls to do his will. He only has authority over man as long as man chooses to stay in rebellion and sin which places him in Satan's kingdom. In other words, man stays under Satan's authority as long as he chooses to live apart from God. Man is the instrument of Satan's authority, to the extent that Satan controls his thoughts and actions. That is why Satan so vigorously resists any attempt to improve man's thought control through medical treatment or counseling. It is then obvious that Satan loses his authority when man chooses to repent of sin and rebellion and return to God's kingdom.

At the time when Adam was being expelled from Eden, God spoke to Satan in Genesis 3:15:

> 'I will put enmity between you and the woman, and between your offspring and hers; he will crush your head, and you will strike his heel.'

This meant that a human would come who would 'crush his head' and defeat him. Satan then turned all his attention to destroying mankind so that this man would never appear. He successfully corrupted nearly the entire race to the extent that God had to send a flood to destroy all but Noah's family. God's plan however, was not hindered.

A few generations later Satan heard God promise to Abraham that one of his descendants would be a blessing to all people (Acts 3:25). This told Satan that the man he feared would come from the nation of Israel. The attack was then focused on Israel through war, moral corruption and idolatry. Satan wanted to both physically destroy them and keep them spiritually bound in rebellion. God's plan however, was not hindered.   *religion*

Generations later the birth of Jesus was announced in the heavens so Satan knew that the man had finally appeared. He then arranged the massacre of babies to try and kill Jesus. God's plan however, was not hindered.

Satan tried to attack Jesus using the same trick that worked so well on Adam. He tempted Jesus to believe a lie and then to sin, which would have put Jesus under Satan's authority and removed the threat. Satan even offered Jesus a part of the authority that had been stolen from Adam. God's plan however, was not hindered, since Jesus could not be distracted from His mission.

Jesus survived all attempts to kill or tempt Him throughout His ministry. When the time came, He then voluntarily

reBEllion
reLIgion

Jesus survived all attempts to destroy or corrupt Him. BeCause HE only wanted 2 do the WiLL of the FATHER, GOD.

submitted himself to Satan to be humiliated, tortured and killed. Satan of course, thought he had finally won as he vented his fury of revenge against Jesus. After Jesus died, Satan experienced a cataclysmic shock as Jesus entered Satan's kingdom:

> *'And having disarmed the powers and authorities, he made a public spectacle of them, triumphing over them by the cross.'*
> (Colossians 2:15)

Jesus disarmed Satan and then took back the keys of authority that Satan had stolen from man.

> *'I am the Living One; I was dead, and behold I am alive for ever and ever! And I hold the keys of death and Hades.'*
> (Revelation 1:18)

The authority that had been lost by a sinful man who disqualified himself was then won back by a sinless man who was fully qualified to defeat Satan. Jesus then handed the keys of authority back to man as described in Matthew 16:19:

> *'I will give you the keys of the kingdom of heaven; whatever you bind on earth will be bound in heaven, and whatever you loose on earth will be loosed in heaven.'*

This authority is now available to every believer in God's kingdom. When we leave Satan's kingdom, he loses all authority over us and we come to freedom in Christ. Satan of course, does not want you to know this and he will go to any extent to prevent you from knowing or acting on your authority.

Why then is the world still in such a mess?

Man has authority over Satan only when he is in Christ's kingdom. Satan still has authority over men in his kingdom who choose to remain in sin and rebellion against God. Satan loses his authority over man when an individual enters God's kingdom through repentance. Since there is no shortage of men living in spiritual darkness, Satan continues to wreak havoc on the earth through men whom he controls. Satan has infiltrated every level and organization in all societies through his control over the thoughts and decisions of men. Satan has very effectively infiltrated the Christian church using spirits of religion who distort the truth and cause believers to attack each other. He is always challenging God's authority and attacking Christians by using his favorite weapons, lies, fear and intimidation. In this way he causes believers to back down from standing against him and using the restored authority. When we are unaware of our authority or how we are being attacked, we will be easily defeated.

Satan wants to keep us blinded, paralyzed and confused so that we never use our authority against him nor realize who we are in Christ. The most effective way to paralyze a Christian is to magnify the characteristics of the old nature so that the lies and events of our past, controls, suppresses and distracts us from our new nature which is in Christ. This is a battle for our minds and emotions. Satan makes very good use of the 3 links in the chain of emotional bondage. He knows that when he magnifies depression, demonic attachments or the emotional wounds of our past, we will be prevented from moving forward in faith and authority. That's why it is so important to break the three links in the chain of emotional bondage, so that they can no longer be used against us.

The beggar and the battle

A Christian who does not know and use his authority is like a beggar who has millions of dollars in the bank that he is unaware of. These disadvantaged believers are living in spiritual poverty when in fact, they have unlimited access to all the resources of God. It's like having a credit card with unlimited credit, no payments required but never accessing it. We have to learn how to make withdrawals!

Satan knows that if we can be distracted away from our authority, we will never use it. Satan has done this very effectively by distracting the church into becoming an inward looking organization preoccupied with its own problems rather than an outward looking rescue center.

Dean Sherman in his excellent book *Spiritual Warfare* gives this very helpful illustration which I will paraphrase and expand on. Sherman describes the spiritual war on the earth as resembling a soccer or football match. The two teams are the church and Satan's demons. Satan has a very experienced and organized team who know humans well. They are highly focused on their mission to control the world and destroy mankind. They line up on the field in battle formation ready to score points.

The church, on the other hand, crowds around the opposite end of the field oblivious to the fact that they are in a war. Most of them have never seen the enemy and many don't believe an enemy even exists. There is no battle strategy and no unanimity of purpose. Instead of battle formation, the church forms little groups of people with similar interests, ideas and worship styles. They put all their energy into maintaining the appearance of their group as they march in circles looking at each other and criticizing the group next to it. On the sports field, the church is going in circles while the game is in progress and Satan's team is continuously scoring points.

To maintain the paralysis of the church during the game, Satan's players will regularly bump into one of the Christians

The church often seems oblivious of the unseen battle that they are in.

without being seen. The Christian will then quickly turn around to see where the attack came from. Seeing no one, he will accuse the closest person to him in his circle as being the culprit. This infuriates the accused so they begin to squabble. Inevitably one will storm out of that circle and join another. As this process is repeated, the church team becomes a crowd of angry, bitter people who are continuously changing groups but always marching in circles and losing the game.

How are we to use our authority?

The church is unaware of the unseen battle that it is in. Instead of battling with each other and with other churches, it is time that Christians became aware of the life and death war that we are all in to push back Satan's kingdom.

To understand this war, you must first realize that the unseen spiritual realm is more real than the world that we can touch and see. The seen world is temporary, the spiritual world is permanent. Our bodies are the containers of our spirits for a short time before we begin our life in eternity. Everything that surrounds us now will eventually disappear. Man's physical existence on earth is only a tiny blip in the time line of eternity, even though it's a rather important blip to us. Eventually, all that will remain of our present existence is our spirit in the spiritual realm. There is an unseen battle for the spirits of man between the kingdoms of light and darkness. The outcome of this battle will determine the eternal destiny of the souls of man. The stakes could not be higher.

Man is the primary instrument in this battle and his spirit is the prize. Satan uses man to exert his authority and accomplish his purposes of destroying man, imprisoning his spirit and opposing God's plan. God uses man to push back Satan's kingdom and reclaim lives, one at a time.

> *'For he has rescued us from the dominion of darkness and brought us into the kingdom of the Son₁he loves.'* Light
> (Colossians 1:13)

When we enter God's kingdom, Satan loses all authority over us. We then in fact, have authority over him and he is subject to us! We are central to this battle and we cannot remain neutral. We are in the battle whether we want to be or not.

It is absolutely critical to realize that our battle is against Satan, **not people**. Ephesians 6:12 states:

> *'For our struggle is not against flesh and blood, but against the rulers, against the authorities, against the powers of this dark world and against the spiritual forces of evil in the heavenly realms.'*

We must never fight people, only the forces that make people behave the way they do. Our authority is not over people, it is over Satan and his kingdom. We must never use our authority to control or dominate people. Our authority gives us the legal right and the Holy Spirit gives us the power to carry out God's will on earth to reclaim lost men. We have all the power and tools that we need to successfully wage the war. As it says in Ephesians 2:6:

> *'And God raised us up with Christ and seated us with him in the heavenly realms in Christ Jesus.'*

Since we are raised and seated with Christ, it means that we share in the power and authority of His resurrection. What else could we need!

The battle is over our heads in the unseen world and that's where we must keep it. Satan wins as soon as we fight people. He wants to lure us into fighting people which will distract us from the real battle with him. People are only pawns and victims of Satan's control. We can never hurt Satan's kingdom by fighting people.

There are many excellent books that I have already referred to, which explain in greater detail how to wage spiritual war for the freedom of individuals, organizations and even nations. I will just mention here some of the basic principles of warfare.

The key to warfare is to discover and experience God's love for each one of us and for mankind. When you have an intimate Father–child relationship with God, it is not hard to feel His heart for us and for lost humanity everywhere. The closer we get to God's heart, the more we will experience His

love, power and authority. We must get to the place where
God so fills our thinking and being that Satan becomes an
insignificant irritant. Knowing God is far more important
and effective than knowing all the practices of the occult
world. As Dean Sherman often says in his *Spiritual Warfare*
videos,

> 'We are to be impressed by God and aware of Satan, not
> impressed by Satan and aware of God.'

Remember that Satan is a created being on the level of angels,
he is not a god. He is not omnipresent nor omniscient and
only took one-third of the angels with him.

Believers have been given all the weapons we need for this
battle. One very powerful weapon is worship. It is through
worship that we come into the presence of God where all
authority rests. In worship, we sense the love of God for us
and for others. In worship, we will often hear the voice of
God directing us to do His will. Satan hates worship. He will
flee from worshipers. What weapon could be easier for a
Christian to use than worship?

Another weapon is the Word of God which is the truth
that breaks the power of Satan's lies. Satan hates truth and
flees from it. Then we have the name and blood of Jesus
which bought our authority. Jesus blood carries authority
and strikes terror into demons.

One of my patients who was often overcome by evil spirits
once told me that when she was overcome, she could see
what the demon was seeing and hear their conversations. She
told me that when they were in the presence of Christians,
the demons saw Christians as covered in Jesus' blood. This
filled them with fear and made them want to find the nearest
exit.

The power behind our authority is the Holy Spirit. The
Holy Spirit is released as we pray and He carries out the will of
the Father. Prayer is the most powerful and effective force to
push Satan back from his plan to control the earth. Satan is
already defeated and he knows it. He however, will hold his
ground until we push him back with God's power and
authority. As someone once said to me, 'The gates of Hell
will not fall down spontaneously, we must knock them

'I didn't know that I could release the most powerful weapon in the universe.'

down.' Remember, Israel had to clear the promised land themselves even though it was already theirs. God waits for us to use His power and authority to push back Satan.

We have overwhelming firepower to wage this war. Our authority is a legal reality regardless of how we feel. Satan knows our authority and he will flee when we use our weapons. Every believer can be victorious and the 'Gates of Hell' cannot stop us. This authority is not just for pastors, evangelists or 'full-time staff.' It's for lay people like us. Remember, Satan is threatened by every believer who knows his power and authority. As Dean Sherman says:

> 'Our victory is not in question, but who shares in that victory is.'

Let's get practical

Many Christians would intellectually agree with everything I have stated in this chapter but they have no power or

authority operating in their lives. They live in defeat, being
pushed around by Satan's control of their thoughts. It isn't
enough to have head knowledge of our authority, it must
become our lifestyle. accent=stress upon ascent=Build upon.
advance. Suc-
-cession

As I have previously explained, I knew nothing of the
kingdom of darkness nor of my authority in my early adult
years. That day when in my office the voices stopped because
they were afraid of me was a total shock and surprise. It did
however, start me on a journey to learn my authority.

Not long after the office episode referred to above, I was
speaking to a woman in a hospital room. As I mentioned at
the beginning of this chapter, a voice came from her stating,
'Leave her alone, she's ours!' It did not take much discern-
ment to realize that I was no longer speaking to my patient
and that an evil supernatural force had pushed her aside to
directly intimidate me. To be quite honest, it was being very
successful at that moment.

This was my first direct encounter with a demon.

I can assure you that I felt no authority whatsoever. Every
hair on my skin stood at attention as I was engulfed by fear
and intimidation. What was I to do now? I reminded myself
that I was a fully qualified physician in a hospital and that I
was trained in how to handle emergencies. I had authority in
that institution to direct personnel to deal with emergencies.
This was certainly an emergency but one that I had never
been trained to handle. I considered calling for nursing
assistance which would have been readily available. How
could I explain the situation to her? I considered calling a
psychiatric physician for assistance but I knew he would not
have been trained for this either. Seconds ticked by as I sat
alone in overwhelming fear with this strange voice. What
could happen? Would the furniture start to fly around?
What if someone walked in? This was not 'my finest hour'
but perhaps my longest minute.

I then concluded that this would only be resolved spiritually and that there was no one to call. Even my pastor at that
time, had no experience in this area. It was just me, God and
the voice. I then quickly reviewed my lifetime of church
attendance to remember everything I had learned about
dealing with demons. This didn't take long since I had never

learned anything about demons, except that they were in Africa. I wondered at the time, how had this one arrived in Canada and why was it in my small town? Becoming desperate, I then reviewed everything I had learned in Sunday School hoping that somehow my forty years of faithful attendance would be of greater value to me than all the attendance awards that I had earned. Into my mind popped the memory that Jesus had dealt with such a situation successfully. With a feeling of hope, I quickly recalled the incident and how Jesus solved the problem. My new found optimism and confidence quickly disappeared when I realized that I could never do what Jesus did. Where would I get that many pigs and on such short notice?

After the longest minute of my life, with my heart pounding and every hair on end, I did recall that there was something about the name of Jesus that had power. I guess a missionary must have mentioned it during a slide presentation. Since that was the only weapon I could come up with, I decided to use it. With the most confidence that I could pretend to have, I said to the voice 'In the name of Jesus I command you to be silent!' Well, the voice thought that was ridiculous. It responded that I had no right to tell them anything and they had no intention of obeying.

Things were not going according to plan and my confidence level was finding new lows. Perhaps, I thought, the pigs would still be a good idea. Since I only had one weapon with one bullet, I was unable to try a different counter-offensive. I wisely refused the opportunity to debate with the voice its right to remain. I didn't want to demonstrate an even greater degree of incompetence by entering into a discussion. I returned to my one weapon and continued to slowly repeat my previous command over and over again. After the longest ninety seconds of my life, the voice said, 'Okay, okay, we're going.' At that moment the patient became alert again and asked me what had just happened, she had no awareness of the event. I of course, was totally exhausted and emotionally drained. At that moment, I probably needed a doctor more than she did. She was able to understand what had happened. After several more months of treatment and with the help of Neil Anderson's book *The Bondage Breaker*, she came to freedom and is now well and free of demonic attack.

What do you think was happening in the unseen world during this brief encounter of mine? I of course don't know but it probably was something like this.

The demons intended to scare me off, since they were aware how little I knew about my authority as a believer. I must have looked like a scared boy scout carrying a nuclear weapon on my back (my previously unused authority). They knew that as long as the weapon stayed on my back, I was no threat to them. During my encounter, as Jesus directed my thoughts to using His name, the weapon slowly came off my back and into my hands. I can imagine how nervous they became as I began to fumble with this nuclear weapon, not knowing which end to point away from myself and not knowing where the trigger was. They put up a brave intimidating face as they watched me reach for the trigger, not really knowing what I was doing. When the trigger was finally pulled, the authority of the name of Jesus was released, warring angels were dispatched and the demons had to retreat. I was the most surprised of anyone in the room, seen or unseen. The authority of the name and blood of Jesus worked, even though I had no experience nor confidence in using such a powerful weapon. We can all be effective warriors using our authority regardless of how confident we feel.

Later that same year, at the same hospital, I was interviewing a very depressed woman. As the conversation turned to more personal and spiritual matters, she suddenly developed double vision, became nauseated as one would have with motion sickness and was unable to continue the interview. I was very concerned with what was happening. I considered that it could be a drug side effect or in fact a small stroke. My hospital was too small to have a neurologist available so I returned to my office to consider transferring my patient to a larger city where a brain scan could be obtained.

In the subsequent hours, it dawned on me that this could be a spiritual attack to distract us both from the spiritual bondage that was magnifying her depression. Having had my previous experience using my authority as a believer, I had the confidence to return to the hospital and check out my theory. When I arrived she was still immobilized by the double vision which prevented her from safely getting out of bed. I asked her to close her eyes and repeat after me a prayer to bind any forces of darkness which could be interfering with her vision. She was a believer and had no objection to such a procedure. At the conclusion of the prayer, she opened her eyes and her vision was completely normal. This time I was not surprised. The authority of the believer was a very useful tool indeed! I however, did not attempt to explain to my medical colleagues that I had discovered a new faster treatment for double vision.

Clothes and skin

Many of you reading this chapter would agree with me that believers have authority but you are not convinced that you have authority and you hope you are never in a position to need it. That's exactly how I was too. There is a world of difference between head knowledge of authority and heart knowledge of authority. It is identical to the difference between clothes and skin.

Our clothes determine how others see us and how we want to see ourselves. They may be no reflection of our inner selves or character which is represented by our skin. Clothes are a convenient cover of our true hidden selves. Head knowledge is like our clothes. We can believe all the right things and look like we are competent while cowering with insecurity inside. All the right knowledge does not necessarily affect how we live and think, since that is the state of our character (skin).

To live and move in our proper authority, we need a change of character so that our head knowledge becomes our heart experience. When this happens, our clothes and skin become one. 'So how can this process happen?' you are surely wondering. This takes place through the renewing and refining power of the Holy Spirit who wants to transform your life and sweep away the lies that you have lived with that say you have no authority. As we are set free from the bag of lies and old nature that we have carried for so long, we come into a new relationship with God that carries with it the realization of who we are, seated with Christ in the throne room of God.

'And God raised us up with Christ and seated us with him in the heavenly realms in Christ Jesus, in order that in the coming ages he might show the incomparable riches of his grace, expressed in his kindness to us in Christ Jesus.'

(Ephesians 2:6)

When we realize where we are seated, it's easy to walk in power, authority and joy. Our walk with God is no longer a continuous struggle. Authority then becomes who we are, not just what we know.

The keys to authority

There are three keys to the character transformation required to walk in authority. The first key is that you must be a Christian who has made Jesus Lord of your life. You must be within the kingdom of God to escape from Satan's authority. If you have not yet asked Jesus to enter your heart and to forgive you from your sinful and rebellious past, then I suggest you do so right now. Everything that follows in this book presumes that you are a believer. You will not be able to experience any of the emotional freedom I'm describing unless you have taken this key initial step.

The second key to authority is to repent of sins that you are involved in. You cannot use your authority if you are involved in secret sin. Your sin gives Satan a foothold in your life and it gives him legal grounds to attack you. If there are darkened areas in your life where you have habits that you can't break, shameful activities that you can't stop, then you need to bring them before God and repent of your actions. You can be free today through repentance.

The third key is forgiveness. As long as we harbour unforgiveness, we allow Satan to fuel the fires of bitterness and resentment. This too gives Satan legal rights to attack and chain you. We must be willing to forgive those who have hurt us. Yes, it's a gift that they may not deserve but God forgave us and we certainly did not deserve it. By forgiving, we set ourselves free of the chain of bitterness. We forgive for our own freedom, not to 'let them off the hook.' John Arnott has written a powerful little book on forgiveness which has helped many come to freedom and even physical healings. The reference is found at the end of this book.

Neil Anderson has printed 'The seven steps to freedom' in most of his books. These steps will systematically walk you through the process of repentance and forgiveness to remove the hooks that Satan wants to leave embedded in you. The 'steps' are very powerful tools as I have mentioned before in reference to Anderson's books.

There is another source of bondage which Satan wants to use against you to keep you from walking freely in authority. It is the power of generational sin. This subject is dealt with very thoroughly by Peter Horrobin in his books *Healing through Deliverance* which are listed in the 'Recommended reading' section.

When our ancestors have been involved in sinful practices, their sin can invite Satan to attack, harass or attach to our family lines. This is particularly true with occult activities like witchcraft, shamanism, native 'medicine,' fortune telling or any other activity where contact with the spirit realm is sought. Watch for patterns of sinful behavior that keep reappearing in each generation, like adultery, alcoholism or violence. We can come under the attack of Satan because of the sins of our ancestors which gave Satan the right to attack us. We don't have to live with this situation though. By using the authority that you have as a believer, you can break this curse upon you and your family. The following is the sequence of prayers that we use to lead people to freedom from generational curses. There are many such prayers and I would refer you to Peter Horrobin's book for more detailed information.

1.   You must repent for the sins of your family which invited darkness into your blood line. They worshipped other gods and that has brought evil into the family.

2.   Forgive your ancestors since they usually didn't realize the danger of what they were doing. We must honour our ancestors as the Bible teaches, for the good things they did for our families and forgive them for their

wrongdoing. We must repent for any hatred that we have held against them for their sinful behavior. = Lostness

3. Ask Jesus to place His Cross between you and your ancestors so that any curses upon them would be blocked by the Cross from reaching you. The authority of the Cross and the blood of Jesus will protect you from what is moving down the family line. Thank Jesus for His sacrifice which has set you free from this bondage.

4. Ask Jesus to wash the blood lines of your family with His cleansing blood to break the curses and free them from bondage. Ask to be washed free of the tendency to serve other gods. A: you must died 2B born New, in Jesus Life; Way

5. Thank Jesus for breaking the curses off you and your family, for binding all the spirits that were assigned and attached to your family. Ask Jesus to release angels to come and protect you and your family from the attack of Satan.

6. Pray that a new blessing would be released by God upon you and your family to replace the curses that you have lived under for so long.

I have seen many come to a new level of emotional freedom after these prayers, they are very powerful. Expect your life to change as you walk in a new level of authority.

In the final section of this book we will learn more of the process of coming free from the third link in the chain of emotional bondage – woundedness.

my faith in Jesus' Work 4
my place of Helpless is
Acknowledging
Leaning on the Everlasting
Arm
Alter Native
Current

SECTION 3

Woundedness

Chapter 17

Who needs inner healing?

'For I am poor and needy, and my heart is wounded within me.'   (Psalm 109:22)

This last section of the book will deal with the third link in the chain of emotional bondage – **woundedness**. This section is the largest, since it is a huge problem that affects every one of us. We have all been damaged emotionally by the actions of others through abuse or neglect. It happens because we are members of a fallen race and we are all raised by wounded people.

The chapters that follow discuss the most important and disabling wounds that I have witnessed or experienced myself. These chapters in many ways reflect my own journey to emotional freedom. I would never have known about woundedness and inner healing had God not exposed my own wounds and then walked me through the healing process.

My wife has written one of the chapters on marriage. She describes the slow painful process of having our marriage dysfunctions exposed by God and then the victory that God brought us to.

To answer the question, 'Who needs inner healing?' – everyone who is wounded needs inner healing. God has made healing available for everyone. Unhealed emotions disrupt every part of your life. Relationships are damaged, your body suffers from stress-related pain and even your Christian ministry is contaminated by your sinful attitudes. Your godly character is handicapped when you have unhealed wounds.

So many people I know (usually men), consider counseling and inner healing to be an endless time-waster where 'the past is continually dredged up and returned to its place and nothing ever changes.' They feel that the past should be forgotten since 'it's under the blood' and people should just 'get on with life and stop whining.' They feel that those pursuing emotional wholeness are just introspective, navel-gazing, self-absorbed people trying to avoid their responsibilities.

I must admit that I shared some of those opinions until God showed me my own wounds and the long painful path to freedom. My attitude quickly changed when I experienced emotional pain and wanted to find the fastest way out of it. Suddenly, inner healing and counseling became my lifeline. I experienced the power of the Holy Spirit to heal my emotions and to set me free.

The life and death of Diana

There are many who would argue that emotional wounds are not as common as I have described here. They would say that I have exaggerated the problem and that most people are just fine and getting on with their lives. These critics assume that if a person is functioning, then they must be emotionally well. This of course is not so and I feel that this position is illustrated by the life and tragic death of Diana, Princess of Wales.

Diana was a public example of one who had overcome a difficult childhood where she was deeply emotionally wounded. She then rose to international stardom in a marriage that many described as 'storybook.' This fairy-tale life then collapsed with a failed marriage and public humiliation as her personal emotional struggles became public knowledge. She then once again fought back to win the hearts of the people as a kind, attractive, sensitive, intelligent, compassionate international humanitarian and single parent.

She was not just a famous member of the Royal family but she came to represent the hopes and dreams of millions of similarly wounded people struggling with their emotions and relationships. She gave hope to the wounded that they too could succeed and overcome the odds. She was a study in contrasts, weak and strong, wounded but progressing, famous but with a common touch. There was something about her that everyone could identify with both in weakness and strength. Her example gave people permission to admit to emotional struggles with broken homes, failed marriages, rejection, humiliation, depression, and bulemia, even though they appeared to be successful.

When she died under such tragic unexpected circumstances, the bubble of hope for the millions of wounded people that she represented was burst. They could not believe that there was no happy ending for the 'fairy-tale' princess. The hopes and dreams for a happy ending for millions of struggling wounded people died with her. The unexpected outpouring of grief from around the world shocked everyone. It even shocked those who grieved and were unable to understand why they felt the loss so personally. The answer, in my opinion, is clear.

They were grieving for themselves, their own loss of hope that they could have a happy ending for all their struggles. Life really did appear to be unfair. The woundedness that usually remained hidden in people's lives spilled out onto the streets during that unforgettable week of global mourning. It was an uneasy reminder of the degree of unexpressed sadness and loss that exists in the lives of millions.

Why is there so much emphasis on 'inner healing?'

There is no question that in the Christian and even in the secular world there is a much greater interest in emotional wholeness. One only has to look in secular bookstores and television programs to see how preoccupied Western society is with emotional recovery. There are several reasons why this is so in the secular world. The first is that there is built into every human the drive to find personal peace. We will discuss that drive in greater detail in the next chapter. Mankind is searching for a spiritual answer to their existence which will give them peace. This explains the explosion in

Our society is preoccupied with self-help methods.

self-help groups, new-age therapies and renewed interest in Eastern religions. Another reason for this drive for peace is that to a great extent, in Western society, personal peace is the only challenge left to conquer. Western man has conquered his environment, improved his health and safety, totally embraced materialism and yet he is still unhappy. He now has more leisure time to explore spiritual themes.

In the Christian world too, there is an explosion of interest in emotional recovery. This in my opinion, is God's divine direction to His children. In recent years, I have observed an unprecedented outpouring of the Holy Spirit which has resulted in widespread emotional transformation. In all my years in mental health, I have never before seen such rapid recoveries in those who have emotional illnesses after being touched by the power of the Holy Spirit. Many have commented and I have wondered myself, why God has chosen to make emotional recovery such a high priority.

It seems to me that God has chosen to touch His children's emotions, since the Western church has been so paralyzed by believers who were in emotional bondage. Through this bondage, Satan has been able to influence or even control the lives of many believers. God wants to put an end to this enslavement and to bring His children into freedom. One could say that this outpouring of emotional healing is for the rehabilitation of Christians. The Western church has not been ready for a great harvest of new believers since it has been limping along in bondage. We've seen very little supernatural power or growth and the church has had bad relationships between members and between denominations. We have not been very attractive to the world so it's no wonder that they have not been knocking down our doors trying to get in.

The emotional bondage of Christians has made us vulnerable to Satan's attack and we have been distracted from the primary goals of the church while we were nursing our wounds. We have developed an intellectual relationship with God instead of a full heart relationship. I will discuss this particular problem in Chapter 20. We have kept God in too small a box where our expectations of Him were very low and where we could attempt to control His activities. It's easy to see that the believers and churches need to be healed first, then they will be ready to receive a greater anointing for evangelism and discipleship of new believers.

I hope in this book to help you understand the emotional bondage that you have been living with your whole life. Then I hope you will see the path of recovery that God has placed before you to walk out of your chains. For some it will involve medications or deliverance but for all it will involve the healing of your wounds. This healing will often require the help of a trained counselor. Don't be afraid or ashamed to go and be helped. We must break the stigma and shame that we have attached to seeing a counselor. I can't imagine the state that I and my marriage would be in today if God had not directed me to a counselor who could hear from God, make sense of my emotional pain and guide me to freedom. I was also greatly blessed by the writings of Leanne Payne and John Sandford. Their books opened my mind and spirit to what God was saying and doing with me. I cannot recommend them highly enough. Most of what you read in this book and particularly in this section has been greatly influenced by the writings of these authors and others whom I'll refer to as we go along. In these pages you will recognize many concepts that come directly from those authors, since my thinking has become so intertwined with theirs.

The shame that we have felt is a result of a lie that Satan has planted in us to keep us from recovery. It is working very well. In my opinion, the greatest shame is to remain in emotional bondage while God is handing you the keys to unlock your prison cell. My view is that there are only two kinds of Christians, those in recovery and those in denial. Which kind are you?

Here is the story of one of my patients who chose to recover.

The story of Mr P

I am tired.

Tired of being depressed. Tired of trying to 'get happy.' Tired of feeling guilty. Tired of crying inside. Tired of the mask that I put on every day when I say, 'Oh fine and how are you?' Will this day ever end? Is there hope for tomorrow? When will sleep's sweet escape come? I just want the smile on my face to be real. I want to be joyful. I want to feel at peace with God and people. I want the freedom to discover who I am and why I am here. I want to love, live and embrace life with a heart full of passionate peace. I want to stop running and expecting. These days are dark. Everyone seems so happy, healthy, rushing this way and that. They are finishing school, working, meeting, playing, falling in love, having children and aging gracefully through the stages of life. All the while, here I sit, motionless, slow, tired and missing everything. I always feel on the outside, alone, watching, feeling the cold dreadful pangs of doubt and fear. I do not know God. I do not know myself. I am a child with my arms wrapped tight around my drawn up legs. Only my eyes protect me. Eyes that prevent, avoid, defend and keep the world out. No one can hurt or touch me here. I am still that child inside though, alone and terrified.

I wrote that only six weeks ago while in the throes of incredible pain and confusion. I am a committed Christian with ministerial credentials with my denomination. I had just finished a masters degree in clinical psychology. My potential as a therapist was highly regarded by my supervisors and peers. In the middle of setting up my own practice, my world fell apart. The pressure I put on myself to succeed created such anxiety that it simply broke me.

Many of you reading this are walking in the valley described above or you know a friend or family member who is. I'm sure you ask yourself, 'Is there a future for me? Will I ever recover?' These were the very questions I asked myself, my family and my God many times each day. I only heard one answer and this is my answer for you, 'Yes, Yes, Yes!' There is hope for you. The fact that you are reading this book means that you are taking the first crucial steps toward getting the help you need.

The journey is not easy but the alternative, as you already know, is to have more of the same pain that you are now experiencing. From my personal experience, I feel that the most powerful treatment for depression encompasses the three basic components of your humanity: physiological, emotional and spiritual.

First, if you are suffering from depression you may have a chemical imbalance that triggers the unwanted thoughts. It is crucial to understand that this physical imbalance must be treated if you are ever going to make progress with emotional and spiritual issues.

A medication prescription may be helpful but it is by no means the complete solution. The emotional and spiritual issues need to be addressed with the help of a counselor. They will help you identify and resolve deeply rooted issues that have contributed to your depression. It is much easier to address these issues however, when your concentration and thought control is being restored through medications.

These are the steps that I have taken myself. I am taking an antidepressant daily. Does it make me happy? No. It does however, reduce the anxious and depressing thoughts to the point where I can control and cope with them. It gives me the ability to shut off my irrational guilt feelings and negative thoughts about myself which have controlled me for so long.

My journey is not complete but by the grace of God I am growing each day toward a health that I have never known.

Are you feeling too weak to do something about your depression? I became so sick and tired of living in despair that I resolved to do whatever was necessary to break free of my emotional chains. I no longer cared who I had to see, what I had to reveal or how painful it would be. I resolved to get out of bed and try, or die in the attempt. Even though I didn't feel it, I had the strength to reach out for help. You do too, even though it seems like such an overwhelming task. Begin today to take even baby steps to recovery. Pick up the phone, make the necessary appointments. Get the help you need. There is an end to your suffering when you reach the light at the end of the tunnel. You are not alone. Jesus wants to take your hand and escort you to freedom. Have the courage to walk out of your prison with Him.

If you choose to be in recovery, then the following chapters will help unlock your prison's doors.

Chapter 18

The quest for peace

'Peace I leave with you; my peace I give you. I do not give to you as the world gives. Do not let your hearts be troubled and do not be afraid.' (John 14:27)

Through the years of being a mental health physician, an elder in my church and just a human being, it has been my observation that the number one pursuit of man (if we exclude the desire to feed oneself) is to have personal peace. It seems that man will do anything to find peace, its draw is so powerful. It is the most sought after and perhaps the most elusive of all mental states. I didn't realize how little I knew about it.

As I have mentioned before, in 1994 I was touched by an historic outpouring of the Holy Spirit that flowed out of Toronto, Canada. A new and more intimate relationship with God started to grow in my heart at that time. Over the next year I began to notice occasional brief episodes of a peace and contentment that I had never known before. They didn't last long but they lasted long enough for me to note that my thinking and emotions were distinctly different during those times. These episodes taught me two very humbling lessons. The first was that having had a taste of peace, I realized that I was usually not living in peace at all. The second was that I had been a Christian my whole life and had never been at peace. I didn't realize that such a state of peace was even possible until I experienced it for the first time in 1994.

So here I was an elder in my church, a mental health professional, a public speaker on the benefits of Christianity and I didn't even know what peace was. To make things even worse, I realized that if I didn't know peace, then likely a large percentage of Christians didn't know peace either.

Once I had tasted briefly of this new peace from God, I desperately wanted it again. I began to be more aware of how unhappy and unsettled my thinking had always been. I didn't of course realize how bound my thinking was until I had a brief taste of mental and emotional freedom. I, like every other human, then began my pursuit for peace. God gave me a taste of it and then led me into the healing process so that I could obtain His lasting peace. My journey to freedom is the substance of this book. Each chapter in some way reflects my path to emotional wholeness. God has shown me that the key to peace is to break free of the three links in the chain of emotional bondage. That's the path I hope you too will take.

What is peace?

I always thought that peace was the absence of war or the absence of interpersonal conflict. As long as I wasn't fighting with someone, then I thought I had peace. This is likely a distinctly male perspective. Women usually have more insight and don't fall for such over-simplifications. Men love over-simplifications.

Peace to many of us is a sense of survival, that we are keeping everything under control. It is a feeling that we are successfully and perhaps frantically keeping the lids on all the boiling pots of stress in our lives. This of course, is not peace at all. It is control, a dangerous defence mechanism that we develop to cope with our lack of peace. God does not want you to confuse peace and control. Now that I have had more experience with peace, I have come up with a possible definition, as least from my perspective as both a physician and a Christian.

In my opinion, to be at peace is to be relaxed, content, able to concentrate, having a clear quiet mind, in control of your thoughts and behavior, coping with circumstances, free of anxiety and with complete confidence in God's love, closeness and care for you.

Control doesn't give peace.

'Wow, some definition' I'm sure you are thinking as you descend into hopelessness at the thought of ever attaining such a state. You're right, there are very few people who could meet these criteria. This however, is what God is calling us to. I challenge you to set your sights higher. I like you, thought this to be impossible and settled for much less, thinking that my present reality was as good as things could get. God deliberately gave me a taste of His peace to shake me out of my complacency so that I would pursue that which He wants for all believers. Once again, let me remind you that the key to this kind of peace is to break the chains of emotional bondage.

God wants you to live this way all the time. Listen to what He has told us.

> *'You will keep in perfect peace him whose mind is steadfast, because he trusts in you.'*   (Isaiah 26:3)

> *'Peace I leave with you; my peace I give you. I do not give to you as the world gives. Do not let your hearts be troubled and do not be afraid.'*   (John 14:27)

'*And the peace of God, which transcends all understanding,
will guard your hearts and your minds in Christ Jesus.*'

(Philippians 4:7)

'*Therefore, since we have been justified through faith, we
have peace with God through our Lord Jesus Christ.*'

(Romans 5:1)

Remember that Jesus was called the 'Prince of Peace' and
His birth was announced with the declaration 'peace on
earth.'

As you can easily see from these verses, peace is a high
priority with God. It is a *'fruit of the spirit'* (Galatians 5:22). In
other words, peace should be a direct result of walking with
God and living in the kingdom which He sets up in our
hearts.

Why does everyone want peace?

God has placed inside every human spirit the desire for
peace. This peace however, is the kind of peace that can only

The path to destruction pretends to be the path to peace.

come through such an intimate relationship with God, that the Holy Spirit controls all our thoughts. This is basically an internal spiritual drive in every person to have a relationship with God. Another author described it as 'the God-shaped void in every man.' This drive compels man to search for peace until he finds it. It could also be thought of as an automatic 'homing' device that draws man to God. In other words, man will never stop searching until he finds true peace. When Christians find emotional freedom, they can at last rest from their search. For those who never enter the Kingdom, their search will be endless.

It is absolutely essential for Christians to find true peace. We are best able to hear God's voice, obey Him and withstand the attacks of the enemy when we are at peace.

Why is peace so hard to find?

Satan is well aware that man is driven to search for peace which should ultimately lead him to God. Satan cannot change that basic characteristic of man so he has put all his skill and cunning into diverting man's search into endless dead end traps and futile pursuits which will exhaust man and keep him from ever finding God. Satan creates an unending series of blocks in the path to peace so that man remains in his kingdom and under his control. Satan has convinced man that he can find peace by satisfying human desires like money, fame, relationships and an unlimited number of alternatives. He entices man to use the familiar phrase, 'If only I could have ... I would be happy.' Others are trapped into using chemicals like illegal drugs and alcohol to find a temporary imitation of peace. Many are led into false religions that promise peace but offer emptiness or the bondage of demonic attachment. Some even enter the occult spiritual world thinking that if they connect directly with Satan he can offer them peace.

These counterfeits are all dead-end streets designed to trap, confuse and exhaust the victim so he gives up looking for peace and falls into hopelessness. Unfortunately this is the state of the world, endlessly chasing Satan's lies for a lifetime. The Bible describes this state quite accurately:

'*All his days his work is pain and grief; even at night his mind does not rest. This too is meaningless.*'

(Ecclesiastes 2:23)

'"*There is no peace,*" *says the* Lord, "*for the wicked.*"'

(Isaiah 48:22)

It's easy to see how Satan ensnares those in his kingdom but why do Christians have so much difficulty finding peace? There are many influences that interfere with the pursuit of peace even in Christians. Anything that affects our thoughts will interfere with our ability to find peace. The state of our emotions is the most significant influence on our thoughts.

As we mentioned earlier, there are three links in the chain of emotional bondage. If we, even as Christians have any trace of emotional bondage, we will not attain the full peace that God intends for us. If we have a medical condition like depression, this physical illness will rob us of peace. When we are harassed by Satan, it will take our peace. The unhealed wounds of our past will continue to hurt us and destroy our peace. This whole book is intended to show you how to break free of your chains and come to emotional freedom which will release you into peace.

Everyone is searching for peace.

A different view of life

When you have experienced emotional freedom, you will look at life from a totally new perspective. I was greatly assisted in my understanding of this perspective by Francis Frangipane's book *The Three Battlegrounds*. I highly recommend it.

There are two ways to look at any situation in life, the natural and the supernatural. When you are in emotional bondage, you will usually use the natural view which sees the circumstances around us as threatening. Your response will be worry, sadness, anger or any other negative emotion since you are believing only what is visible. This is the view that Satan wants you to have since in this state he can best influence your thoughts, attitudes and behavior. He will continue to feed you lies and misunderstandings which will disturb your thoughts and rob your peace. With this perspective, you are always the victim of your circumstances.

The other way to look at circumstances is to take God's view of reality. Peace can only be found with this viewpoint. Once again, the key is to recognize that the unseen world is more real than the seen world. It is the unseen realm that influences everything that happens on earth. You must remember that God is in control of the unseen world and that He is continually working on your behalf regardless of the circumstances that you can see. God is never worried, upset, intimidated, defeated, threatened or in a hurry. As His sons and heirs, we are entitled to have the exact same view of reality. Look at the description of what it's like around God's throne:

> *'At once I was in the Spirit, and there before me was a throne in heaven with someone sitting on it. And the one who sat there had the appearance of jasper and carnelian. A rainbow, resembling an emerald, encircled the throne. ... Also before the throne there was what looked like a sea of glass, clear as crystal.'*   (Revelation 4:2–3, 6)

> *'As I looked, thrones were set in place, and the Ancient of Days took his seat. His clothing was as white as snow; the hair of his head was white like wool. His throne was flaming with fire, and its wheels were all ablaze. A river of fire*

*was flowing, coming out from before him. Thousands upon
thousands attended him; ten thousand times ten thousand
stood before him.'* (Daniel 7:9)

Our God has total authority, surrounded by worshipers
and a sea that is at total peace. How you may ask, can that
help us while we are still on earth. You must realize where
your spirit is even while your body is here on earth.

*'That power is like the working of his mighty strength, which
he exerted in Christ when he raised him from the dead and
seated him at his right hand in the heavenly realms, far above
all rule and authority, power and dominion, and every title
that can be given, not only in the present age but also in the
one to come.'* (Ephesians 1:19–21)

*'And God raised us up with Christ and seated us with him in
the heavenly realms in Christ Jesus, in order that in the
coming ages he might show the incomparable riches of his
grace, expressed in his kindness to us in Christ Jesus.'*
(Ephesians 2:6)

At this moment, your spirit is seated with Christ in the
throne room that Daniel described, surrounded by absolute

At this moment your spirit is seated with Christ.

authority and peace. This of course is very hard to absorb. It is far beyond the limits of human understanding, but it is nonetheless true according to the Bible. If we can shift our focus and always look at life using the 'view from the throne,' then our lives will be transformed. We will only be able to do this however, if we have emotional freedom from Satan's lies. We no longer need to be threatened by circumstances. If God is not upset or worried, neither do we have to be, since we are sitting right beside Him.

Satan will do everything he can to prevent you from seeing reality in this way. When Christians see spiritual reality correctly, Satan is totally disarmed and he can no longer intimidate and frighten us. He runs when he sees Christ's peace and authority shining through us. Jesus was never upset or worried over any circumstance since He was continually aware of the spiritual reality of who He was and where He was seated. Jesus was always in control and at peace. We can share in that same reality. Remember what it says in the following verses:

> *'Let the peace of Christ rule in your hearts, since as members of one body you were called to peace.'*   (Colossians 3:15)

> *'I have told you these things, so that in me you may have peace. In this world you will have trouble. But take heart! I have overcome the world.'*   (John 16:33)

Our level of peace will be determined by the reality that we choose to accept. When our peace is challenged by disturbing circumstances, we must run into God's lap and remember where we are seated and accept His viewpoint of reality. A radiant peace will be one of the most effective evangelistic tools to attract the lost and searching world to the only source of true peace.

In the remaining chapters of this book, we will examine how God wants to free you of your emotional chains so that the peace of the Holy Spirit can control your life. Emotional freedom is the key to walking in God's peace. God wants to set you free.

Keep reading.

Chapter 19

How to find your true Father

'Though my father and mother forsake me, the Lord *will receive me.'* (Psalm 27:10)

'A father to the fatherless, a defender of widows, is God in his holy dwelling.' (Psalm 68:5)

Open-pit mining

I have already mentioned that we appear to be in a time of unprecedented visitation by the the Holy Spirit for emotional healing and inner transformation. It has been my observation that the healing process often comes in two phases. There is an initial touch of the Holy Spirit when the power of God's personal love for you is realized and you draw closer to God than you've ever been before. At this time there are often rapid, profound changes in personal emotional characteristics which, for example, give a person the freedom to forgive or to stop worrying.

I distinctly remember enjoying this initial healing experience. There were times when I experienced significant changes in my emotional responses and thinking after times of special prayer. One evening, the improvement in my thinking pattern was so profound after prayer, that I came home from a service and mentioned to my wife that I felt so different, it was like having brain surgery at church. The parts of my mind that had been irritating me with worry and discouraging thoughts became silent as if they had been removed. My spiritually sensitive and empathetic wife was pleased to hear the good news but wondered if there was anything left inside after the 'operation!'

Many have likened this touch of God to a gentle rain which softens the soil of our hearts to allow the Holy Spirit to transform our emotions in areas where we never thought we could change. It is the 'opening of the door' to be changed more quickly into God's image. At these times we are reassured of God's personal, intimate and unending love for us. This, in my observation, is only the first step in the process of emotional transformation.

So many of the people that I know who have been through this 'gentle rain,' have some time later been plunged into the greatest emotional pain that they have ever experienced. This came as quite a shock to them after having had such a significant healing experience. I too couldn't understand why this was happening until God took me through the same experience. I then realized that the 'gentle rain' was the prelude to what I call 'open-pit mining.' In the 'rain' stage, we learned to trust God and experience His love in a new and more intimate way. We needed this degree of reassurance to prepare us for the radical surgery which was required to transform the bedrock of our character into His image.

Open-pit mining is God's way of changing our character.

If we are serious about serving God, then He will transform us. The 'mining' phase is the next logical step in emotional healing. In this step our pain is exposed so that God can heal it since we can never be healed from what we are unaware of. As long as we remain in denial, we will stay in emotional bondage. When we are in pain we can receive from God in a way that we never could while in denial. If you examine the lives of many of the most anointed ministers of our time, you will find that they each had an experience of brokenness that transformed their lives and prepared them for greater service in the Kingdom. Remember that the 'alabaster box' in Mark 14:3, had to be broken for the fragrance to be enjoyed by those around.

It is my observation that the path to greatest ministry effectiveness and anointing is through brokenness. This is when we get to know God in a way that we would never have experienced otherwise. As our emotional wounds are healed, we will emerge ready to carry a greater anointing, and be far less vulnerable to Satan's attacks.

Many of you who have had this experience will sympathize with those who have responded to open-pit mining with the cry 'take us back to Egypt!' Like the Israelites, we have felt such pain during the surgery that we have been tempted to return to our old dysfunctional state to avoid the pain of transformation. Even though in 'Egypt' we were bitter, angry and fearful, at least it was familiar and predictable. The process of healing is unpredictable, uncomfortable and requires us to trust the loving hand of God to lead us to freedom. There have been times when we have all felt that God had abandoned us in this process. Quite the contrary, He is walking with us closer than ever as He leads us 'through the valley of the shadow of death.' It is at these times that we must remind ourselves of the love and closeness of God that we experienced during the 'gentle rain.'

The reason why this mining experience is so difficult is because it breaks open all our defences and exposes our emotional wounds and pain. God does this of course, so that He can heal us and reduce our vulnerability to Satan's attack. We have often spent our lifetimes avoiding and covering our pain with thick defensive walls so we wouldn't be reminded of it. God must come and break these walls much like the shell of a walnut must be broken to get at the nut. It is through these experiences that head knowledge is transformed into heart experience.

What happened to me

As I have already mentioned, God started the process of healing in me with a 'gentle rain' when I was able to experience profound changes in my thinking and feeling. I of course, had not realized that I needed any repairs, since being a man, I was proud, rigid, intolerant, critical and totally in denial of any emotional need. In my opinion, my emotional responses were totally justified and reasonable. The 'gentle rain' was a surprise when I found myself thinking differently and enjoying a change of attitude when I had not felt any changes were necessary.

Within a year of this experience I took my family to a developing world country to visit and minister to the people there. It was an exciting opportunity and I asked God to show me new things about ministry so that I would return home changed. God took me at my word that I wanted to change but His list of necessary changes were far different from mine.

The trip went very well but upon our return my normally strong, capable, confident, unflappable wife Kathy collapsed emotionally. The journey had exposed areas of unresolved emotional pain in her life that overwhelmed her usually strong defenses. She will describe her experience more completely in her own chapter later in the book where we discuss marriage.

Kathy's collapse so was shattering to me that I quickly followed her into emotional turmoil. I had not realized how emotionally dependent I was on my wife and that we had been living in a state of codependency our whole married life. This was another situation that God wanted to correct and I will discuss it in greater detail later.

We both sank into an emotional abyss since our usual support systems (each other) were shattered. We wondered what had happened to us and why. Was this judgment or an attack by Satan? Having experienced the 'gentle rain' we knew that neither was true. We were then left with no option but to turn to God with an intensity we had not previously known. This of course, was exactly God's plan so that He could lead us through our own 'valley of the shadow of death.' For Kathy and I, this was to be the most difficult thirteen months of our lives.

As we entered this time of transformation, it soon became clear that God wanted to change both of us in such a profound way that we had to be stopped cold in our tracks. As a man, I would have found every way possible to squirm out of this experience and consider it all to be Kathy's problem. God prevented this, by having me experience the same level of brokenness and vulnerability that Kathy felt.

I was forced to face my own negative emotions and wounds. It was humbling and I was shaken by the experience. I began to see my own emotional dysfunction which made me so critical and impatient. My life had become so busy and unsatisfying since I like so many others, had been caught in the 'performance trap' where I needed to attract the approval of others through my performance. I felt that I could only feel good about myself through overwhelming busyness. This very common trap has been thoroughly described in Robert McGee's excellent book, *The Search for Significance*.

God had to take me out of my comfort zone to expose my own emotional deficiencies and need for healing. God will do whatever it takes to get your attention and shake whatever you have been emotionally dependent on. I couldn't use my religious credentials or previous experience with the 'gentle rain' to escape from this transformation process.

The box of pain

While I was in this 'valley,' I felt that I was slowly being squeezed into a box of pain. This box was like something from a nightmare. There were no windows, doors nor ways of escape. It hurt to touch any of the walls or floor. It was totally dark and seemingly hopeless. The walls slowly came closer together and the floor rose to squeeze my very life out of me. This was where I lived for months on end.

As I slowly proceeded through the healing process with the help of a counselor who understood the ways of God in these matters, I eventually noticed something about the box that I had never seen before.

There was no lid.

I had been spending all my time looking for a familiar escape route through a door or window which didn't exist. I was relying on my previous methods to run from emotional pain. In this box however, all my usual escape routes were blocked and God forced me to look elsewhere for a solution.

As the walls and floor closed in on me, when out of sheer desperation I finally had the courage to look up, I had one of the greatest surprises of my life. There looking down at me was the smiling, loving face of my heavenly Father, God. He had been patiently observing all my struggles to free myself, knowing that I would eventually see the open lid when the walls were nearly touching. When I finally made eye contact with God, it was as if He said to me 'I was wondering how tight the box would have to get for you to notice Me.' I then realized that the only route out of the box of pain was up and into God's loving arms which were reaching out to me.

'I didn't know the only way out of the box was up.'

This box was not a form of punishment but the most effective way of getting my attention off myself and my usual coping methods which didn't work and onto God, the only solution to my struggle. These verses were such a comfort to me when I was proceeding through this dark valley:

> *'The LORD is close to the brokenhearted and saves those who are crushed in spirit.'* (Psalm 34:18)

> *'So do not fear, for I am with you; do not be dismayed, for I am your God. I will strengthen you and help you; I will uphold you with my righteous right hand.'* (Isaiah 41:10)

> *'And I pray that you, being rooted and established in love, may have power, together with all the saints, to grasp how wide and long and high and deep is the love of Christ.'*
> (Ephesians 3:17)

My new Father

Through this experience I began to know God as my best friend and true Father. It's embarrassing to admit that though I had been a Christian my whole life and I thought I knew all about God, I had never experienced Him in this personal intimate way. I felt that in comparison, my previous understanding of God was merely 'head knowledge' but now I was getting to know a real person who cared for me more deeply than I could ever imagine. I also then realized that if I, having been a Christian for so many years didn't know the true fatherly love of God, then there were likely a very large number of Christians who had a similar misunderstanding.

At this point in my journey God led me to a very helpful book which I highly recommend, Floyd McClung's *The Father Heart of God*. This book introduced me to my real heavenly Father whom I barely knew. I began to see that God wanted to have a 'daddy' relationship with me rather than the distant authoritarian 'association' that I imposed on Him for so many years. I was shocked to discover that God wanted to be closer and more available to me than my natural parents. I had never thought of God in the way that He described Himself in Isaiah 66:13:

> *'As a mother comforts her child, so will I comfort you.'*

I hate to admit it but even though I was a 'know it all' Christian, I was quite unfamiliar with the book of Zephaniah (and all the other minor prophets and several of the major ones too). When I was directed to Zephaniah 3:17:

> *'The Lord your God is with you, He is mighty to save. He will take great delight in you, He will quiet you with his love, He will rejoice over you with singing,'*

I was amazed to think that the almighty Creator was that interested and excited about me. God began to give me pictures in my mind of Jesus dancing and celebrating over me with a clear message that He wanted me to celebrate and dance with Him too. This didn't sound particularly reverent or religious.

I started to see a slight contradiction in the way we have related to God. Most Christians try very hard to be solemn, reverent, orderly and perhaps even fearful during worship services since that is how we envision God to be. It was hard for me to imagine that all the while Jesus was dancing and rejoicing and inviting us to join in the celebration. Jesus wants us to be as emotionally free as young children in our relationship to Him. He wants to release us from our emotional prisons so like a five-year-old child we can crawl up onto His lap and enjoy the security of a Father–child relationship.

When Jesus was on earth He demonstrated all the kind, compassionate attributes of God. Jesus had time for everyone, young, old, rich, poor, religious, pagan, sick, well, men, women and all races. He broke whatever social custom that was necessary to reach people with His love. No man-made rules could hold Him back from extending His love. Jesus did not wait for people to come to Him, He went out of His way to find them. He was never distracted by image, status or facade, He saw right through people and loved them at their point of need. I was so relieved when I realized that *'Anyone who has seen me has seen the Father'* (John 14:9) so that all these characteristics of Jesus were also those of the Father. Now that was a God I could love and relate to!

Why is this so difficult to accept?

I had always assumed that God was a somber, remote, benevolent father figure who was busy being saviour of the world in a place far away from me (likely some exciting mission field). I knew that God had given us the Bible to be our guidebook and operating manual. I felt that God had just left us with it and gave us an address where He could be reached if we needed help and that occasionally He would look in on us and see how we were doing. I mistakenly thought that it was a virtue to be able to use the Bible effectively and not need any divine intervention to assist me. I became an independent, intellectual Christian, knowing all about God but not knowing Him in a personal intimate way. We had more of a business relationship than family intimacy.

The reason why I and so many of you had this impression of God is because we have assumed that God was like a

Human fathers often seem distant.

human father. Human fathers expected us to become increasingly self-reliant and independent based on previous family experiences. If we remained dependent on our fathers it was a sign of immaturity. It is very difficult for intelligent, mature, independent (especially male) Christians to realize that God is totally different. As we mature in faith, He wants us to become increasingly childlike and dependent on Him. Many Christians reject this and continue to live in emotional poverty without the relationship that God wants so much to have with them.

Our love deficit

Every human has been created with an enormous need for love. I call it our 'love deficit.' It resembles a huge cistern that holds millions of litres. No human is emotionally complete until this cistern is filled. As long as the deficit remains, we are unhappy, restlessly searching for the love that will bring us peace and contentment. Satan takes advantage of our quest for love and offers us counterfeits so that we search for love in all the wrong places and only receive a few drops that barely wet the cistern. There is only one source of love that can fill the tank to overflowing and that is the love of our Father God. The good news is that God has an unlimited supply and wants to generously give His love to us all so we can become emotionally free. We must come to Him regularly however, as hungry dependent children to see our tanks filled.

God wants to be our daddy and our friend. Unlike human parents, He loves to hear our thoughts, opinions and cries for help, twenty-four hours a day. Jesus knows how we hurt. He sees all our emotional scars, our emptiness and need for love. He is the only one qualified to heal us and meet our emotional needs and He desperately wants to. You don't have to convince God to care about you or your needs. He is interested in you, pleased with you and wants to chat with you forever.

A friend of mine, Rev. Todd Pratt once told me that God had showed him this profound truth:

> 'We will be emotionally free and healed to the degree that we know that we are loved.'

Only Jesus can totally fill our deficit. Satan only offers a few drops.

As our love deficit is filled, freedom will come.

What keeps us from an intimate relationship with God?

Our own personal emotional bondage will prevent us from having the full emotionally free relationship with God that He desires. As you will recall, there are three links in the chain of emotional bondage. We must be healed in all three areas if we are to become emotionally free.

If you are suffering with a chemical imbalance mood disorder (the first link), it will be very hard to pray, worship, read the Bible or stop worrying. When one is bombarded with depressing thoughts it will be very difficult to relax in God's arms of love and enjoy a relationship with Him or anyone else for that matter. If you have an untreated mood disorder you will have great difficulty coming to emotional freedom. Please go and get treated and pray for healing so you can proceed through the healing steps of this book.

The second link is the direct harassment by Satan. He loves to attack, discourage, distract and take advantage of our emotional bondage. He will exploit every chemical imbalance and unhealed area of our personality or old nature by filling our minds with lies so we will find it very difficult to receive the love that God so willingly offers us. Know your authority and use it!

The third link is of course comprised of the wounds of our soul or personality. These are the biggest chains that block us from a full relationship with God. All humans have been wounded through damaging relationships with other wounded humans. As we have more and more unsuccessful relationships we begin to expect failure. This expectation is projected onto God so we then presume that He will hurt and reject us like everyone else. Satan uses this to distract us from God and he uses the lies he implants to mold us into his image. In this way Satan disrupts our relationships with God, others and ourselves, which are our three most vital relationships. God wants to heal those wounds and restore our relationships.

How did we get wounded? rewound in church traditions

It was God's original plan that His complete loving nature was to be communicated to children through the godly love which was transmitted by their parents. In this way parents were to become a mirror that reflected God's nature to children. Parents were to demonstrate and make visible, God's invisible characteristics to the children so that they could easily understand and come to know God.

As a result of the Fall, sin entered the heart of man and the 'mirror' cracked. Sin wounded mankind and contaminated our natures so that we could no longer accurately reflect the nature of God. Parents then taught children out of their woundedness so that they too would become sinful, wounded, with dysfunctional relationships and difficulty relating to God. Through varying degrees of abuse or neglect we have all been raised to be emotionally handicapped by imperfect parents. We have all fallen short of God's plan of emotional freedom for us.

Our view of God's love will always be distorted by our view of our parent's love. We can never fully imagine the full extent of God's love for us since we have an imperfect human frame of reference as we look into a cracked mirror. Wounding experiences in our childhood, damage our understanding and reduce our expectations of love. If for example, we have had a broken or damaging relationship with a father, not only will we have difficulty trusting human authority figures but we will assume that God is as untrustworthy and damaging as our parent. This becomes a deep inner belief based on the lie that Satan plants at the time of the initial wounding that convinces us that God is no better than a human parent. We then will have great difficulty trusting or becoming close to God or anyone else. When through this process, we are unable to come emotionally close to God, then our relationship to Him becomes solely intellectual and protective walls go up around our hearts. This becomes a serious emotional handicap that God wants to heal so that you can be set free.

I, like many of you, became an intellectual Christian through this same process. The walls were so high around my heart that I never felt anything in my relationship with God or with anyone else. I was emotionally frozen and couldn't understand those who 'felt' God or who could get excited during a worship service. I kept a formal emotional distance from God and considered Him to be more of an institution than a daddy.

You don't have to live this way

It was very difficult for me to accept that my perception and understanding of God was incomplete. I was, remember, an intellectual Christian who thought he knew all about God. I had to learn that we have an emotional God. I had never thought of God as being anything but an efficient, kind administrator. How can we know that God is emotional? There are many references to God's emotions in the Bible but the most convincing evidence to me is the fact that humans are emotional. Where did we get emotions from? They have clearly come from God since they are meant to enrich our lives. Emotions are an attribute of God that was given to us as a gift when we were made in God's image. We have become suspicious of emotions only because like every other gift from God, Satan has contaminated them and used them to hurt us. We need to bless and encourage our emotions rather than curse and flee from them which is our usual practice (especially with men).

God wants to heal our emotions and bring us to freedom from our wounds and chains. We each must be healed individually, just like we came into God's kingdom individually. The hard reality is that emotional healing does not happen automatically at the time of salvation. We must choose to come free of our chains after we enter the Kingdom.

Remember the walled city illustration from the beginning of this book. After we enter the Kingdom we are given a choice to either remain in our chains huddled by the gate or to proceed to the throne room and be transformed into the emotionally free bride of Christ. The choice is ours. I hope that this book will encourage you to choose freedom and to get help from the many resource people that God has provided to His children.

This process of transformation is as important to God as the end result. It is through the process that God shapes us into His image and sets us free. It is never too late to start down the path to freedom and meet your real 'Daddy' for the first time. God is waiting for you now, He's calling to you, inviting you to crawl up into His lap and begin a new relationship with Him of emotional freedom. In my view, we are all five years old before God. All he expects from us is what we would expect from a five-year-old, to obey and love Him back. Stop trying to be a sophisticated intellectual Christian and just be His child.

Jesus was wounded on the Cross for us. He was wounded to take our wounds from us. He paid the price so that we could walk free. We must continually give Him our wounds and corrupted thoughts so that He can take them from us and replace them with His thoughts of love and acceptance. The first step is to forgive your parents and all those in authority who wounded you. Of course they don't deserve to be forgiven but we didn't deserve God's forgiveness either. We forgive to set ourselves free not to 'let them off the hook.'

Then repent for hating them for what they did. We sinned in our response to their wounding. We must repent for believing the lies that were planted in us at the time of our wounding and ask Jesus to show us the truth so that we can trust and become vulnerable again.

Having done that, now ask Jesus to come and heal your wounds, fill you with truth that will push out the lies and crawl up into the lap of an approachable, warm, loving and friendly God who is very interested in you. Then begin your new relationship of emotional closeness with your heavenly Father. Let Him fill your love cistern to overflowing for the first time in your life.

Some of you just can't do what I have just suggested. Your heart is still frozen and cold. That's a very common state so we deal with you in the next chapter.

What is forgiveness?

Dialogue with an angel

What is forgiveness?
My heart wants to know,
Does it come all at once, ☆✓ yes.
Or does it slowly grow? ✗ no

It can come in all forms
From the intense to the soft,
And already you've pardoned
More often than not.

I say 'I don't' care,
To me no difference it makes'
Yet I am so angry
And how my heart aches.

We feel hate and anger,
Which are love's flip side,
When we hurt the most,
They mask love deep inside.

But the anger I feel
Is so deep in my heart,
And I fear that without it,
I'd just fall apart.

Child, you need to let go,
Let the Lord do his part, all,
He can then take away,
All the pain in your heart.

Well, I'm tired of anger,
I'm weary from hate,
I want to forgive now,
Before it's too late.

I know it feels scary,
To let anger go,
What will come in its place?
Soon you will know.

Where once I felt hate,
Again I feel love,
This new peace drifted in,
On the wing of a dove.

Forgiveness will has happen,
When we learn to let go, A NEW
Then the love in our hearts,
Will be whiter than snow.

(Diana L. Tiessen)

GOD gave us a New Heart, at New Birth and a New Spirit that agrees with HIS HOLY SPIRIT WAY

Chapter 20

Now my Head can be ReNewable, informed BY HIS TRUTH.

Reconnecting our head and our heart

'I will give them an undivided heart and put a new spirit in them; I will remove from them their heart of stone and give them a heart of flesh.' (Ezekiel 11:19)

In the last chapter I described how God took Kathy and me into the painful process of inner healing by exposing our pain and wounds. This opened the doors of my heart to discover God as my true Father for the first time. A new more intimate and enjoyable relationship with God was born.

As God walked me through the healing process I was able to look inside myself and see how emotionally frozen I was because of past wounding. My frozen heart interfered with all relationships including those with my wife, children and with God. After reading the works of John Sandford, I realized that I had 'a heart of stone,' and that God wanted to heal it. I became so grateful for the verses in Ezekiel that offered me hope:

'I will give you a new heart and put a new spirit in you; I will remove from you your heart of stone and give you a heart of flesh. And I will put my Spirit in you and move you to follow my decrees and be careful to keep my laws.'
(Ezekiel 36:26–27)

How did I freeze up?

I came from a very logical, methodical Christian home. Everything we did seemed well thought out, balanced, reasonable and never on a whim or impulse. When I became a Christian as a child, it just seemed like the logical thing to do based on what I observed in my home and church. As a teenager I decided to remain a Christian since that seemed like a more reasonable lifestyle than that of the secular world. I never felt anything in my faith since it was just a series of logical decisions. I always marveled at those who had so many 'feelings' at the time of conversion or in their walk with God. I couldn't imagine what they were talking about.

In university I chose to study science since it was logical, predictable and profitable. Like most science students, we had only contempt for those in the 'arts and humanities' courses. We just couldn't understand why people would waste time studying things that led nowhere but to more educated-sounding 'party chatter.' In those years I couldn't understand students who had a passion for literature, art, learning or anything for that matter. I thought the only reason to be at university was to graduate as soon as possible and get a job. I wasn't a lot of fun to be around because my pursuit of grades (not knowledge) pushed out every other activity of life. I could talk myself out of every leisure activity that would keep me from my work.

My relationships were mostly cold and logical. I was unfeeling except when I felt bitter, angry, cynical or worried, which was quite often. I married Kathy who, you guessed it, was also a science graduate, very logical, rational and who came from a family of logical science graduates.

My faith was logical, reasonable and unfeeling. I became a rigid, proud, intolerant legalist. My walk with God relied on rules more than it did on relationship. I felt that I was above feelings since they were undependable, illogical and often led people into unwise decisions and actions. It seemed logical that I could please God by doing religious things that would attract His attention.

Throughout my education and working years I had learned that I could please men and earn great praise by performing well and surpassing their expectations for me. This worked both in medicine and at church. The harder I worked the greater was the praise and the better I felt. It soon became an addiction.

When our hearts are frozen, we lose the ability to feel.

I assumed that 'being' meant 'doing.' There was no time to relax or have fun since that didn't generate any praise. I became caught in the 'performance trap' as a 'performance addict.' I didn't enjoy relationships because they wasted time. I never felt close to God, I just hoped that He was pleased with me because of how hard I was working for Him.

Due to the orientation of our society, my dysfunctional attitudes and lifestyle not only fit in well but I was greatly rewarded for it. In non-Western societies I would have more correctly been considered an eccentric, unbalanced misfit.

The head–heart split

Like many of you, my attitude was a product of the mind-set of our society but how did Western society get that way?

Since the time of the renaissance, science, logic and reason have been elevated to be the highest virtues of Western society. These virtues were the domain of the most élite minds and have become idolized as the gods of our society. The goal of human mental development was to become rational, logical and scientific. Other virtues like feeling and faith have been greatly devalued and felt to be the domain of lesser minds and lower classes.

In this way our society has made a false separation between thinking and feeling and between reason and faith. We have lost the ability to use all these virtues to explore the same subject. Faith, feelings, creativity and intuition are considered to be unscientific and illogical. Spirituality is based on the creative, intuitive, emotional and feeling mind which is the part of us that has been so devalued by society. Faith is no longer seen as an essential part of human existence but a crutch for the uneducated masses. It's easy to see why Satan has encouraged this separation since it drives people away from the pursuit of God and it becomes more difficult to discuss spiritual issues.

The Western medical profession has been thoroughly contaminated by this attitude. I was trained to consider a human to be merely a machine that could be treated through logic and reason. Feelings, faith and all that makes up the human spirit were ignored as unmeasurable, untreatable and therefore unimportant. We were trained to shut off our feelings and perform our tasks during outrageously long working hours. We became finely tuned and very unhappy medical machines working on human bodies. I learned to perform well in this dysfunctional environment but like many physicians, I had difficulty relating to people in a personal way.

As Leanne Payne has said at her conferences, 'When the rational mind replaces the feeling mind then our souls are devalued.' We then lose our emotional, feeling, creative intuitive nature which is the part of us that can hear and experience God. This process is much like turning a satellite receiver dish so it points to the ground and then wondering why it is no longer picking up the signal. Our ability to sense and communicate with God is damaged. When we lose this part of our nature, we also lose the capacity for intimacy since close relationships require the ability to feel and become vulnerable. Domination by the rational mind will interfere with all significant relationships, especially with spouse and children. Communication becomes one-dimensional, filled with words but without feelings. This defective communication style is best illustrated by the difference between a telegraph message and a personal visit. Which would you choose to transmit – a message, or love and compassion? The telegram could accurately transmit the words but the true message would be lost. We were not designed to relate to people or to God on a purely intellectual level. The separation of thinking and feeling is a major handicap to relationships, spirituality and to our society.

Christianity has also been contaminated with this false separation since the church is filled with people like me who worship logic and reason. We have elevated the intellectual side of faith to avoid criticism from a society that devalues feelings and experience. The church has substituted head knowledge about God for true walking with God. We can talk about it better than we can experience or live it. Working for God has become our substitute for receiving God's love because we have lost the emotional capacity to experience anything supernatural.

When God chooses to touch His people in a supernatural way, the church becomes very confused since it doesn't know how to receive anything that does not come via logic and reason. The antenna for supernatural reception is pointing at the ground. The ability to feel and hear God has so shriveled up from lack of use that when God moves supernaturally, the church often just rationalizes the event and explains it away. I have seen churches label supernatural acts of God as occult, rather than accept the uncomfortable reality that God is trying to touch His people using routes that have long been closed by the church. In my observation, there seems to be a very old tradition that states, 'What the church doesn't understand, it will criticize.' This keeps slamming the door on God's attempt to reach His people to transform their hearts. Christians have become suspicious and afraid of those who can feel or hear God or those who respond in creative, prophetic ways. The manifestations of the power of the Holy Spirit are beyond logic and reason so they cause great

A frozen heart is a spiritual handicap.

difficulty in the church. These same manifestations invite fascination and wonder from those outside Christianity looking in at churches that have finally come alive.

My observations of the way the church has been contaminated by this false separation of reason and faith only applies to Western churches. I have many times visited churches in the non-Western world and they have no such separation. Is it any wonder that they are the churches reporting the fastest growth and the greatest number of miracles?

I was guilty

You can imagine that with my lifelong pursuit of logic and reason, I was not a good influence on the church. I elevated logic and reason above feelings and faith so my head was totally split from my heart. I was the worst offender when it came to condemning emotionalism in the church. My faith needed to be logical, filled with facts that could easily be explained to someone else.

In this handicapped state, I was unable to hear God, sense His presence or have an intimate 'Daddy' relationship with Him. As I mentioned in the last chapter, I had to try and win the approval of man and God through religious activity that I hoped would please both. Man was easy to please but I was never sure if I was pleasing God because I was unable to hear or feel Him. I just kept striving.

This continuous performance trap never satisfies and it actually breeds restlessness. Many people after years of unsatisfying performance addiction just wear out and give up. They then become very passive, cynical, apathetic and do the minimum required of them as they lower their expectations. This leads to a greatly devalued life and unsatisfying Christianity. They know the truth in their minds but they have long lost the ability to feel and enjoy it.

My dysfunctional intellectual Christianity seemed to work very well until God visited my church in an unprecedented way. This visitation was documented in Guy Chevreau's book, *Catch the Fire* on pages 182–188, within the testimony of my pastor Rev. Terry Bone. I would have normally been a vocal critic of such unusual supernatural events but this time I had to hold my tongue because it was happening to my best friends and even to my wife and brother. As I began to open my mind and heart to what God was doing, I started to feel things that I never felt before. I began to sense God's presence and was able to enter into worship more. I was thawing out from a lifetime of emotional freeze-up. I didn't understand what was going on but I knew it was good.

How do we get frozen?

During this time of emotional transformation I came across John Sandford's book, *Waking the Slumbering Spirit*. This book along with the books by Leanne Payne explained what had happened to me and how God was leading me out of my bondage. I will explain it here so you too can be free.

We of course, are all eternal spirit beings who are temporarily resident in human bodies. As spirits, we are influenced by spiritual forces both good and bad. It is our spirit that God wants to indwell and bring into His Kingdom so we can live eternally with Him. The condition of our spirit determines how we relate to God, Satan and other humans. It also influences our personality or soul.

Our spirits enter our bodies at the time of conception. From that point on the infant spirit is susceptible to spiritual influences. In God's original plan, every spirit was to be born healthy, vibrant and ready to relate to others. We were then to be nurtured, trained, molded and encouraged by emotionally healthy parents who modeled God's love. The growing child would then have healthy relationships with both God and man.

You will remember from the last chapter that as a result of the Fall, sin entered into man and he was no longer able to properly reflect or model God's nature to children. Sin contaminated our spirits and wounded our souls so that we all became dysfunctional. The wounding can take place at any time after conception usually through abuse or neglect and it leaves us emotionally handicapped and not fully functional. It's almost like we wither emotionally in the areas where we have been wounded. After being hurt we will always pull back from any risk of further injury. We then build walls around our hearts and emotions to protect us. This damages our ability to have healthy intimate relationships including those with others, God and with oneself.

When we have been so wounded, our relationships become only superficial and intellectual since our emotional walls block our ability to feel or relate to anyone emotionally. Intimacy is difficult because it requires vulnerability which is impossible when you live behind high emotional walls. You can never feel close to someone due to the thickness of the walls protecting your wounded soul. This situation is clearly a major handicap to marriage, child rearing and walking with God. You will be too hardened to give or receive love.

This was me. I believed all the right things but felt nothing. I served God with my mind but my heart was not responding. I just kept busy doing religious things hoping that I was pleasing God. I substituted activity for my lack of relationship. All my relationships were distant and intellectual but I felt this was just me, I wasn't the emotional type. I didn't know that there was any alternative so I resigned myself to this lifestyle.

This problem of wounding, leading to emotional freeze-up, which leads to intellectual relationships and the splitting of the head from the heart is so common, it's almost universal. It is particularly common in men since we have made it socially desirable to be the 'strong silent type,' when in fact, it's a disability. These wounded people become emotionally disabled spouses, parents and Christians.

We have large numbers of Christians who through this process are isolated, lonely, unable to respond to God or feel close to Him, incapable of true intimacy, unable to worship and have one-dimensional intellectual lives. They become dependent on rules and procedures in their churches and have cold, loveless families. When churches are filled with these wounded people, the assembly will become rigid and lifeless. This then breeds cynicism in the church youth who hear about faith but see only emptiness with nothing to feed their starving emotions. A dead church is no threat to Satan so he loves to encourage this situation. If a church can't keep its youth then it soon becomes extinct and Satan is delighted.

The slumbering spirit

We all have parts of our spirit that are functioning better than other areas. This is because we are all wounded in different ways and at different times. On page 115 of *Waking the Slumbering Spirit* (referenced at the end of this book) John Sandford gives a list of symptoms of slumbering that will help you determine in what areas you may be frozen, handicapped and split off from your heart. The checklist is printed below. If you see yourself strongly in the list I suggest you read John's book.

1. In worship, can you feel and enjoy God's presence or is it a mechanical or intellectual exercise?
2. In your prayer and devotional time do you sense God's love and presence or is it mechanical and intellectual?

3. Do you always feel that God is far away and hard to reach?
4. Do you ever feel creative or is life a monotonous bore?
5. Are your relationships cold or mechanical? Can you ever sense or feel what another is communicating or do you only hear words? Do you enjoy being with people or ever feel lifted by being with them?
6. Is sexuality in marriage a fulfilling intimate spiritual experience that draws you closer together or is it a mechanical, boring or even exploitative event?
7. Do you have a functioning conscience that prevents you from sinning or do you just feel badly when you're caught?

God wants to draw so close to us during worship and devotions that we can sense His presence. The Holy Spirit is the most creative force in the universe and He wants to inspire you in creativity. God wants you to have warm satisfying relationships with Him and with others so that you can communicate with your spirit, not just with words. Sexuality is dependent on emotional health and is very vulnerable to wounding. If your sexuality is not what it should be then ask God to show you how your wounds have caused this situation. Go for help from a trusted counselor. God doesn't want you to put up with emotional handicaps.

The healing of our will

Our emotional freeze-up is a direct result of emotional bondage which began at our first wound after conception. To come free of our slumbering and the splitting of our head from our heart we must be set free from emotional bondage. As you recall, there are three links in the chain of emotional bondage and each link must be addressed. If you have read this far, you are already familiar with the first two links. The third link of woundedness is the subject of this entire section. God wants you to be free in all three areas. The overwhelming power and authority of the love of God can break your chains. There is one very powerful obstacle however, that must first be overcome.

You must want to be set free.

You don't have to change. You can remain by the entrance gate of the Kingdom and stay in your chains. Recovery requires a deliberate act of taking action to put an end to your enslavement. You must choose to ask Jesus to begin the healing process which will involve 'open-pit mining.' You may need to go to a counselor or physician. You must do it! Don't let Satan convince you that nothing can ever change or that it's not worth the bother. That's a lie.

We must use our will to walk to freedom but for many, this is a very difficult step. When we have been wounded in the past, our wills were often the first part of our soul to wither and die. Our wills were broken by being put down so often by authority figures or they shrank when we finally gave up the performance treadmill and fell into passivity. When we live with a broken will, we resign ourselves to hopelessness, frustration, emotional suffocation and we remain very susceptible to Satan's temptations and lies.

God wants to heal and strengthen your will to walk to freedom and serve Him. As we draw closer to God, His will fills and strengthens our will so that we will naturally desire to do the things that He puts in our hearts to do. As Leanne Payne put it so clearly in her PCM conferences,

> 'God becomes like a hand that is inserted into the empty glove which is our will.'

From that point on His hand moves your glove and your wills become one. You will just naturally want to do His will.

Moses and Peter

Let's look at two Bible characters who suffered from many of the problems discussed in this book. We'll start with Moses.

Moses likely had a confusing upbringing. He started life in a very unconventional way which must have left a significant mark on his soul when he found himself abandoned on the Nile. Some have referred to Moses as the original 'basket case.' He had two families, Hebrew and pagan which must have caused some identity confusion. As a young man we see him fall into the performance trap when he kills the Egyptian to try and win the approval of the Hebrews. He was obviously

Moses recoiled from the supernatural assignment.

struggling with his identity. Was he going to identify with the slaves or rulers?

When his plan collapsed and he was pursued as a murderer, he fell into passivity and brokenness as he fled to the wilderness for forty years of obscurity. We can tell how broken he was by his response to God's message in the burning bush. If I was visited by God in such a dramatic way, I think I would be quite excited about the prospect of working with God using signs and wonders. Moses though, recoiled from the challenge. He was so broken and lacking in confidence that he could not even get excited after such a supernatural display. God in his mercy knew that Moses had been broken and humbled enough that he was now usable. Quickly Moses came alive and God healed his will and heart so that he rose to become the prophet leader of the nation. He had a rough start, many wounds, a criminal record, total obscurity and God used him mightily.

We don't know anything of Peter's upbringing but he clearly demonstrated performance addiction and approval seeking. Who was the first one out of the boat to walk on the water so that all would see him? On the Mount of Transfiguration he wanted to build three buildings to please everyone. When Jesus was arrested he cut off the ear of the servant in what was an impulsive and futile attempt to resist overwhelming force. He did it to demonstrate his loyalty to onlookers. During Jesus' trial Peter wanted so much to be approved of by the servants at the fire that he denied Jesus three times right after cutting off the ear to prove his loyalty. He then fell into brokenness and passivity. We know how deep this was since it was recorded that he 'wept bitterly' and that he was the one who suggested that they return to fishing in John 21:3. In my opinion, Peter was saying that he was returning to his old career now that Jesus was dead and that phase of his life was over. After the miraculous catch of fish Jesus reinstates Peter and his will is healed to become a powerful apostle who preached the Day of Pentecost message.

There is no one who is so damaged that God cannot heal and empower them to serve Him. God wants to heal your will by healing the wounds of the past that broke your will so that you can choose to walk to freedom. My wife Kathy describes the healing of her will in Chapter 23.

Jesus will fill you with His will when you draw closer to him as it says in Philippians 2:13:

> '*For it is God who works in you to will and to act according to his good purpose.*'

Then He will give you the strength to walk to freedom and become the victor rather than the victim.

If you want to start the process of healing your will, you must first forgive those who wounded you and caused your will to be broken. Then repent for hating and judging them for what they did even though you feel justified. Ask Jesus to come and reactivate your will so that you begin to think His thoughts. Ask Him to heal your wounds and give you a new heart of flesh so that your head and heart can be joined again.

After my will was healed, God walked me through a healing process which has transformed my heart from the frozen, logical, emotionless and wounded heart of stone, to the heart of flesh that beats with feeling, intimacy, joy, creativity and love. My relationships and walk with God were transformed. Kathy will tell you that I'm not perfect yet but there's been a big improvement. I now serve God out of joy not obligation nor to attract His attention and approval. I now walk with God and relate to others with my head and heart. I'm still logical but I know now when to push it aside to hear from my heart and from God.

Some of you are now realizing that you were wounded as young teenagers and from that point on you froze up and even began to hate yourself. The next chapter is for you.

Chapter 21

Finding self-acceptance

'He heals the brokenhearted and binds up their wounds.'
(Psalm 147:3)

Emotions grow too

Everyone knows that as the human body grows, it must pass through certain developmental phases to reach maturity. There are no shortcuts around these milestones and if you don't pass through them you will not mature. As physicians, we watch for these milestones to tell if a child is growing correctly. If a person is developmentally delayed, it is usually quite obvious that they have not reached their milestones.

Emotional maturity is much the same. There are stages of emotional maturation that everyone must pass through if they are going to successfully reach maturity. The big difference is that if someone is not reaching their emotional milestones, it is much more difficult to detect than if they miss a physical milestone. It is possible for someone to be in emotional childhood yet look fully mature in an adult body. In this chapter we will discuss the emotional developmental stage of adolescence and the consequences of not passing through it correctly.

At puberty, everyone becomes self-conscious about their physical development and acceptability to others. We all ask ourselves, 'Do I fit in, do I look and act right?' If our emotional maturation process proceeds correctly, we will pass from a very inward looking, self-conscious stage, to an outward looking, self-confident stage where we feel secure in our identity and self-worth. To successfully pass through emotional adolescence we must come to the place of self-acceptance. To reach this milestone, we need to have godly parents who themselves have come to emotional maturity so that they can guide us through these stormy waters.

What if we get stuck?

If a person does not pass through this stage successfully, they will become stuck in the self-centered, self-conscious, insecure emotional state of adolescence regardless of their biological age. When this happens a person is unable to accept themselves or to find their own identities as individuals. This is a very painful place to be.

God designed us to pass quickly through this very awkward and uncomfortable yet important stage. If development stops at this point, a person will be continually driven by the emotional pain of insecurity, self-consciousness and inadequacy to search for an identity. This state is that of being in perpetual emotional adolescence regardless of age.

The pain of this search drives people into compulsive activities and performance addictions to try to attract

We can be stuck in adolescence regardless of our age.

enough attention to make them feel secure and worthwhile. This never works of course, because the feeling of satisfaction that we get while others are approving of us only lasts until they stop patting us on the back. As soon as they raise their hands off our backs we're craving more and devising a plan to arrange it. It also fails because a person can never find self-acceptance from the approval of others. People caught in this trap will for their whole lives be introspective, insecure, self-critical, anxious and unsure of themselves, just like a young teen, always trying to find an answer to the emotional pain and emptiness of not having accepted themselves.

The shocking reality is that very few of us ever complete this process of self-acceptance and release from emotional adolescence since we don't have parents, particularly fathers, who have accepted themselves. An insecure father is unable to lead his child to self-acceptance. This means that many are emotionally fatherless even though their father was present in the home. Being fatherless leaves large gaps in our emotional development and deficiencies in our personalities where we didn't receive enough love or nurture. God is very sensitive to this common situation and in Psalms 68:5 it says:

> *'A father to the fatherless, a defender of widows, is God in His holy dwelling.'*

He cares very deeply for us and wants to heal us from this state. Remember in a previous chapter I explained the love deficit in every human? When God is allowed to fill that cistern, there is enough of God's love to more than make up for any deficiency left over from poor fathering.

The volcanoes

When this emotional adolescence remains unhealed, people hate themselves and become preoccupied with their own sense of emptiness, guilt, shame and inadequacy. Unfortunately, most of us are still struggling with this phase and these unhealed immature emotions keep breaking through our adult facade to shock and embarrass us.

This state is like living on top of a volcano. The mountain is filled with our unhealed emotions from childhood and adolescence even though we are now adults. It continues to grumble, shake and give off steam or fumes if we come under any kind of stress which reminds us of our past. These tremors can even give us stress-induced physical symptoms like fatigue, muscle pain, headaches, stomach-aches and itching.

We all make the top of the mountain look very pleasant and mature. We plant a garden and a grass lawn with a beautiful cottage and a picket fence. Everything looks perfect and serene. Your neighbour is also sitting on a grumbling, smelly volcano and he too has created a mature, serene adult facade where he lives. You very maturely and serenely wave at each other in friendship and agree not to notice that you are both living on active shaking volcanoes.

Satan knows that you are sitting on a volcano waiting to erupt. He knows how to trigger an eruption since he was the one who put all those unhealed painful memories and emotions in your mountain as he was trying to mold you into his image. He knows where your huge red button is

Satan knows how to trigger our volcanoes.

located which will trigger an eruption. When you least expect it and when you are feeling like you have everything under control, he will hit your button so you explode over some circumstance. The top of your volcano blows off along with your house and garden. Your rage and fear comes spewing out for all to see. You become horribly embarrassed that you could act in such an immature way when you are really such a mature adult. You lose confidence in yourself and in your faith which didn't protect you from the eruption.

You quickly tidy up, replant the garden, replace the fence and house and then wave over to your neighbour as if nothing happened. He waves politely back as if he hadn't noticed anything so that when he erupts you won't admit to noticing it either.

Some men have a slightly different fence on their volcano. They realize that they erupt occasionally but they think that it's an acceptable manly thing to do and is in no way immature nor childish how and when they erupt. They are not ashamed of it since being men, they are always in control of their behavior and their eruptions. They demand the right to 'let off steam' occasionally. To show how in control they are, they don't use the useless picket fence, they put up much stronger steel diversion fence with a sign that says, 'Lava flows this way.' They then sit confidently in their castle at the top and wave in a serene way to the neighbours. When Satan hits their button and all their unhealed childhood emotions explode, they don't look any different than the picket fence crowd. Everything is blown to bits in the usual way. Lava is no respecter of fences.

There is no way to control unhealed emotions. Satan will always use them against you and they will rise up and bite you at very inconvenient times. We become a slave to these emotions since they can't be controlled and that's why we can't be at peace with ourselves or others. 'Walking in the Spirit' becomes a difficult struggle. As years pass, the pain of this insecurity and lack of self-acceptance just builds and explodes regularly. I suspect that this is one of the causes of the so-called 'mid-life crisis.'

The traps

This lack of self-acceptance and self-hatred is a very danger-ous and powerful foothold for Satan. He will continually attack us with temptations to try his counterfeit methods to find self-acceptance and worth. He wants to lure us into sin and a return to our old nature.

Let's first look at the example of an adolescent girl who has never had a father who made her feel worthwhile or who gave her confidence as a developing woman. She has what we will call a 'father wound,' which means a deficit of father love and affirmation. She never feels that she has the approval of her father, so for the rest of her life she will be seeking for male acceptance to try to fill the father love deficit.

Satan loves this situation since her pain is so great that she will try anything to fill her emptiness. He comes to her and offers her all the male approval that she could want if she sexualizes her need and becomes promiscuous. Her desire for male approval is so great that she falls for the lie and is ensnared in even greater bondage through sexual sin. Her need was for parental love not sexual love. Satan tricked her into believing that all male love is the same and can be bought with sex. This commonly happens even to Christians who know better than to get involved in sexual sin. She may intellectually want to obey God but the emotional pain overwhelms her when Satan triggers the volcano and she easily jumps at counterfeit love.

An adolescent boy who didn't get enough love and affirmation from his father will also have a male love deficit and a father wound. Satan may tempt him to become a workaholic and idolize money to make himself feel worth-while and to try and get the approval of his father. He could then become a performance addict to get enough praise to accept himself. When this inevitably fails, hopelessness and passivity fill his mind and he becomes easy prey for the temptation of alcohol. He becomes another statistic in the epidemic of men with passive broken wills because they could not perform their way to self-acceptance.

Let's look at another possible outcome for a boy with a father wound and a male love deficit. Satan comes to him and offers him all the male love he could want if he sexualizes his need and becomes homosexual. His need for male love and approval may be so intense that when Satan triggers his volcano he is lured by his emotional pain into sexual sin and greater bondage. Once again the victim has fallen for the lie that sexual love can fill a parental love deficit. Yes, this can happen to Christians since when the volcano blows, the pain is so intense that a person is easy prey to temptation and the pain overwhelms our intellectual rules. Exploding lava cannot be controlled by intellectual fences.

I remember a twenty-five-year-old Christian man who came to me wondering if he was homosexual. He was struggling with an attraction to men and a desire to be hugged by them. He however, was repulsed by the sexual advances that were made at him when they sensed his attraction. He couldn't understand why he was attracted to men and if he was gay, why did he run from their sexuality?

This situation was very easy to explain. He had a poor relationship with his father and felt that he could never please or get close to him. This young man had an obvious father love deficit which he was searching to fill with the hugs of men. He craved father love, not sexual love. When Satan offered him sexual love as a substitute, he knew it was not what he was looking for and was repulsed. When I explained this to him he saw clearly that he was not gay but had a father wound. The answer was for him to find his real father in God who would fill his love deficit to overflowing. I realize that this does not explain all same sex attraction situations and the answers are rarely this simple but he serves as a real life example of a father wound leading towards homosexuality.

These wounds are very common so our churches are full of people struggling with emotional adolescence and father wounds. This also means that there are many in our congregations who are struggling with same sex attraction as a result of this wound. The church generally does not know how to help someone with this kind of sexual struggle. Too often the response has been that of shame and condemnation because of the church's anger over the politics of homosexuality. The wounded person gets trampled by the church's stand against that lifestyle. When the person senses the shame and rejection, Satan steps right in and offers them total acceptance if they will join the homosexual community. When the person realizes that the church is not going to help him, Satan's temptation looks quite attractive. There are many whom the church has driven into a homosexual lifestyle when they were in fact crying out for father love. We must repent for how we as Christians have treated those who are struggling with this kind of wounding. While we were hating the sin, we lost track of the wounded person inside, whom God wants to rescue. We must ask God for a heart of compassion to reach out to those who are struggling with same sex attraction and lead them to the love of their real father, God. This particular struggle is thoroughly described in Mario Bergner's book, *Setting Love in Order* where he describes his own journey out of homosexuality and into full-time ministry through the process of emotional healing. There are many helpful ministries that assist people struggling with same sex attraction. One such international ministry is Exodus International. I have listed several of their offices at the end of this book.

The father wound epidemic

Even the secular world recognizes the serious consequences of the lack of father love. In the November 1997 edition of *Canadian Living* magazine, John Keating stated the following: CRIME = NOT WANTING GOD

> 'Now a growing body of evidence is showing that the involvement of fathers has a greater influence on the way our children turn out than we ever imagined. An involved father increases a child's chances of academic success, social development and sense of self-worth. A 1993 study conducted by researchers at the City University of New York shows that the likelihood that a young male will become involved in crime doubles if he is raised without a father. A 1995 study showed that high

school students from single parent households were 1.7 times more likely to drop out than students with two parents.

One study found that girls who had warm relationships with their fathers tend to be more competent in mathematics. They also tend to have more confidence in their femininity. A girl's relationship with males seems to be based on how well she gets along with the first male in her life, her dad. What daughters learn from their fathers is their own love worthiness. Girls whose fathers left the family tended to behave in an inappropriately forward and sexually flirtatious way. Often these girls go on to have a series of stormy, short-lived sexual relationships, a sort of fruitless quest for male approval, says David Blankenhorn the author of *Fatherless America* (HarperCollins 1996).

This same author stated at a Toronto conference in May 1997 that, "The role of a father in rearing his children has more influence on their future than socio-economic factors such as income, education and neighbourhood. None of these things matters as much as whether or not there is a father in the home. The presence or absence of a father in the life of a young man is the single most important predictor of outcome regarding the likelihood of being arrested and ending up in prison." '

Many researchers are now suspecting that there have never before been so many fatherless children in our society. This of course means that we are in an epidemic of father wounding and the emotional damage that always results.

Ouch, that feels like my wound too

I of course, was a confident, know-it-all Christian who never had any of these problems with self-acceptance. You already know however, that I was caught in the trap of performance addiction. I compulsively did religious things to please my church and medical things to please my profession and patients. My family was always left out. I hoped I was pleasing God but I really couldn't tell. I needed and enjoyed the praise so it drove me on.

I noticed that I was never content with the present, I was always living in the future of what things could be like. I was always in a hurry to get things done for the future because I had set for myself endless exhausting goals. Relationships weren't important since they got in the way of my goals. I became bored very quickly if I wasn't working on or talking about my goals. I couldn't cope with being idle or delayed since then I would notice my personal emptiness. If I stopped working, no one would approve of me, they would forget about me and then I'd feel worthless. I was a prisoner of my emotions which drove me and I was showing signs of lack of self-acceptance.

When you can't accept yourself, you will always be depending on others for approval. You then become a slave to those you seek approval from, a man-pleaser rather than a God-pleaser. Satan loves this condition since he can lead us into all his traps as we seek approval from men.

When these wounds remain unhealed, it will always block your spiritual progress and emotional freedom. If we continue to hate ourselves, we will never have a secure identity and we will be robbed of the joy and love that is ours in Christ. It will force us to live in our old nature which makes us very vulnerable to sin in an attempt to meet our emotional needs. Why do you think Christian leaders sometimes have moral failures? As you have already seen, when Satan hits the 'erupt' button and our volcano of emotional pain explodes, we will be very vulnerable to any suggestion that Satan makes that offers us relief from the pain. Satan knows where our weaknesses are and he will attack them to remove anyone from ministry. God wants us to be healed from our emotional pain so that we will no longer be vulnerable to Satan's attacks and so that we can carry a greater anointing in our ministries.

When people minister with unhealed emotions, their wounds distort God's message. It is very difficult to pastor if you struggle with self-hatred and are always evaluating yourself through the eyes of others while trying to win their approval. We must learn to see ourselves though the eyes of Jesus who loves and approves of us.

Dying to self

We have all been taught that we were to 'die to self.' Most of us interpreted that to mean that our wills were to be crushed. I always felt that anything I really wanted to do must be wrong since it was my idea and my will was sinful and had to be died to. Others felt that death to self meant to always be self-critical and never to accept a compliment.

This is wrong. The self we are to die to is our old self from our old nature. We are to celebrate and enjoy our new nature and it's desires since it is the Holy Spirit living in us to bring creativity and freshness. Unfortunately, many Christians are dying to their new selves and putting down their new identities and gifting because they can't accept themselves. Instead of being God-conscious and looking to Him for acceptance, we are self-conscious, focusing on our inadequacies and our wounds.

Christian women seem to have a particular problem with self-acceptance. Due to misleading teaching which we will discuss later in the marriage chapter, many women feel that their identity comes from their role as submitted wife and mother. When they are looking for identity in a role, they become dependent on man's approval rather than God's. Their lives then become an empty role of servitude. Christian men have taken full advantage of this problem and encouraged women to submit and be slaves to their approval so that their needs would be met.

We must release women to find their identity in Christ and to serve Jesus first. Jesus always related to women as people not as roles. He even rebuked Martha for putting her role ahead of her worship. Men must repent for expecting women to meet their needs and for encouraging them to find their identity in their role. Women must repent for being man-pleasers rather than God-pleasers. Both spouses must repent for trying to control the other to meet each other's needs. As we will discuss in the marriage chapter, our needs can only be met by Jesus so stop trying to force your spouse to do something they can't.

The way out

Remember the love deficit I explained earlier and the cistern that can only be filled by God's love? As we are filled with His love, we begin to feel His approval of us so that we can accept ourselves as we see God accept us. As God's love pours in, He fills the gaps left by our natural fathers so the father wound is healed by the love of our heavenly Father. We can then accept that our new Father is not looking for ways to criticize or punish us. God wants to encourage, love and empower us. As our cistern fills we will no longer be preoccupied with our wounds since they will melt away. The recurring thoughts of self-condemnation and hatred will fade.

Jesus was wounded for us. He wants to take our wounds from us so that we can be free. Remember,

> *'He heals the brokenhearted and binds up their wounds.'*
> (Psalm 147:3)

We must learn to continuously give to Jesus our thoughts from our old nature and exchange them for His thoughts of peace, love and hope. We then can evaluate ourselves through the eyes of Jesus. We are His bride, wrapped in the robe of righteousness, seated with Him in the throne room with God looking upon us approvingly since He sees Jesus in us.

> *'I delight greatly in the LORD; my soul rejoices in my God. For he has clothed me with garments of salvation and arrayed me in a robe of righteousness, as a bridegroom adorns his head like a priest, and as a bride adorns herself with her jewels.'*
> (Isaiah 61:10)

We can accept ourselves because we accept our new selves which is Jesus living in and through us. We can then live out of our new man, walking confidently in the Spirit with peace and joy. We can listen to God instead of the cries of our old wounded nature. I have learned that there is only one thing a Christian has to do to earn God's approval. We must be breathing. If we are alive, He approves of us, if we aren't, we're in His presence.

This will transform our ministries. As we know God and His love, approval and security, it will radiate out of us in every activity. We will no longer be performing trying to win approval. It will be enough that we are approved by our Father. We will then minister like Jesus, out of the relationship that we have with God.

So now I no longer moan about my inadequacies, I in fact celebrate them since they remind me of my total dependency on God. I enjoy being dependent since before God we're all really just five years old sitting on His lap. He only expects us to love Him and obey. We can give up trying to impress Him with our performance. I love the feeling that He is carrying me and hugging me. In the past, I would squirm out of his embrace to demonstrate what a great Christian worker I was, to win His approval. I've learned that if I stay in His lap, more gets done as He works through me and it is far more relaxing. I can now accept myself since the real me is in fact Christ living in me.

To enter this healing process yourself, you must first forgive your parents and particularly your father for not

'With Jesus, I'm always five years old.'

nurturing you enough. We recognize that all our fathers were wounded and likely no one nurtured them either. We must repent for hating those who hurt us and repent for hating ourselves. Ask Jesus to take all these wounds and damaged emotions upon Himself and onto the Cross so that they can be taken from us. Then He will replace them with words of love, comfort, reassurance and acceptance and your life will be changed.

God cares very deeply about our most significant human relationship, our marriage. Kathy and I learned some hard lessons that may help you. Stay tuned.

Chapter 22

What's gone wrong with our marriages?

'... This is a profound mystery.'   (Ephesians 5:32)

In my opinion, the most significant emotionally-based decision that we make in our lives is to get married. This decision and the relationship that follows is greatly influenced by the state of our emotions. If we are suffering emotionally, then our marriage will be greatly affected. The condition of our marriage will reflect the state of our emotions because they are so intertwined. Since this book is about emotional recovery, then we should look at least briefly at marriage and how our emotions help or hinder it.

There are many very helpful books on marriage and I don't want to pretend to be a marriage expert. This is a huge subject and no one can give you all the tools you need for a successful, godly marriage. I am however, experienced at marriage and have learned some important lessons the hard way. In this chapter we will look at some foundational problems in our relationships that disrupt marriage. In the next chapter, my wife Kathy will explain our personal journey through emotional and marital healing. We hope that these chapters will encourage you to believe that God is able to improve your marriage.

The most familiar and controversial passage in the Bible on marriage is in Ephesians 5:21–33:

> *'Submit to one another out of reverence for Christ. Wives, submit to your husbands as to the Lord. For the husband is the head of the wife as Christ is the head of the church ... Now as the church submits to Christ, so also wives should*

*submit to their husbands in everything. Husbands, love your
wives, just as Christ loved the church and gave himself up for
her ... In this same way, husbands ought to love their wives
as their own bodies. He who loves his wife loves himself ...
For this reason a man will leave his father and mother and be
united to his wife, and the two will become one flesh. This is a
profound mystery – but I am talking about Christ and the
church. However, each one of you also must love his wife as
he loves himself, and the wife must respect her husband.'*

The phrase out of this passage that best describes how two
people of different temperaments and from different back-
grounds can live together and get along is Ephesians 5:32,
'*This is a profound mystery.*' I think it's a miracle that anyone
can live so closely together in peace.

Marriage is very important to God. He created man to love
relationships and want to be with others. God knew that
Adam could not be happy alone so He created Eve. This was
the first perfect marriage where two adults related perfectly
to each other and to God. There was full and complete
communication between all three.

God used marriage as the model of the relationship between
Christ and His bride, the Church. This is the most powerful
and enduring relationship on earth. God also chose marriage
to be the environment to raise children where parents would
model the love of God. The healthy love and security of
marriage was to communicate God's love to children.

The Fall of man allowed sin to contaminate and disrupt all
relationships so marriage fell short of God's original plan.
God wants to heal our hearts so that our marriages can be
restored and we can once again enter into the relationships
that man had in Eden.

You will recall from previous chapters that because I was a
man, I felt that everything was fine in my work, home,
church and marriage. I knew it all. When God took Kathy
and me through 'open-pit mining,' I was forced into an
accelerated course in emotional brokenness. God exposed
our wounds and weaknesses and at times it was overwhelming. I was so grateful to those who directed us to the books of
Leanne Payne and John Sandford. Those books helped us

make sense of our pain and point us in the direction of recovery. This chapter on marriage is a summary of what I learned from these authors. I encourage you to go and read them for yourselves.

In the Garden

Before the Fall, Adam and Eve walked and talked with God no differently than they talked with each other. They both had complete access to God, full communication, companionship and reassurance in God's presence. They were totally secure, fulfilled and loved. They were complete.

When man fell, it was because he believed the lie of a creature more than he believed God. Adam instantly went from being God-conscious to self-conscious. He immediately became ashamed, embarrassed and afraid of God. Adam was guilty and became separated from God by his sin. This separation caused him to become emotionally incomplete since the necessary relationship with God for personal wholeness was removed. Adam then discovered loneliness since he was separated from his source of life, being and meaning.

As a result of the Fall, all humans are born into this state of incompleteness and separation from God, it is a consequence of sin. We all have a loneliness and longing for completion which can only be satisfied with a restored relationship with God. This longing for completeness and relief from loneliness drives all humans their whole lives until they find wholeness and healing in Christ.

When man fell, he lost God consciousness and began to look to created things to fill the void in his life that was previously filled by his relationship with God. This search has been exploited by Satan ever since and he provides every possible lie and counterfeit to distract man from finding completeness in God. He has kept man blinded from accepting God's offer of reconciliation through Jesus.

How does man try to fill the void?

Loneliness and emptiness are so painful to man that it drives him to search for anything and anyone who will fill this void and end the pain. Man is looking desperately for fulfillment, meaning, purpose and identity. Whatever we find that seems to help becomes incredibly important to us and we quickly become dependent on it for emotional satisfaction. This is the root cause of addictions. As soon as we find something that eases the pain of emptiness, we become addicted to it as an escape from our pain. We can be addicted to anything, though the most common are materialism, fame, chemicals, false religions and relationships. They become our idols which replace God whom we turned away from. These idols are the counterfeits that Satan offers man to substitute for a relationship with God, the only true source of completeness.

One of the most common idols is relationships. Through relating to others, we are searching for their approval which will make us feel accepted and worthwhile. We will do anything to get this approval. First, we will desperately and selfishly search for the perfect relationship which will fill our emptiness. This, of course, can never be found. Then we will try to win the approval of the people we have found by performing for them. When this doesn't work we will try to dominate, manipulate, control and exploit people to meet our insatiable needs. The alternative is to allow ourselves to be manipulated and controlled to please others and win their approval. This is a cruel trap that Satan leads us into. It always leaves us chronically unhappy, bitter, lonely, rejected, unsatisfied and deeply wounded. Satan loves it.

This addiction to people and relationships which I have just described makes us dependent on them. Since they are also dependent on us for the same reasons, this is referred to as codependency. Like all addictions, there is no end and no achieving of satisfaction. No one can ever get enough approval to fill their emotional needs since the emptiness can only be filled with the love of God, which man turned away from. As we spend our lives in this futile search, Satan leads us into greater idolatry, sin and bondage.

In this state, man is self-conscious rather than God-conscious. He will always be looking inside himself in a futile search for answers. When you are incomplete and self-conscious, you will always be listening to negative thoughts of inadequacy, low self-esteem, self-hatred, jealousy, rejection, bitterness and anger. These are the thoughts of our wounded inner child and our old nature.

Can this happen to Christians?

In theory, Christians shouldn't have to struggle with the emptiness and incompleteness that I've just described because they have a relationship with God which should make them complete. The truth is however, that Christians do struggle with all these issues since they have not received healing of their emotions. They have not experienced the completeness that comes when the love of God fills their emptiness. Remember that emotional healing does not automatically occur at the moment of salvation. It is optional and must be chosen by each believer individually. It is quite common for Christians to refuse God's offer of emotional recovery and to remain huddled at the gate of the Kingdom in their pain.

This situation is like having a membership card in the Kingdom but not enjoying the benefits of membership. Christians in this state continue to struggle with the negative thoughts, lies and behaviors from the unhealed old nature which keep rising up to overcome their new nature. We remain focused on our inadequacies, self-condemnation, wounds and pain and we don't see our true selves in Christ.

How does this affect marriage?

Most of us marry hoping to find the perfect relationship that will fill our emotional void that only Jesus can fill. We hope to find the person who will give us meaning, identity, unconditional love and acceptance. This of course, is impossible so we never find such a person. We all enter marriage carrying the baggage of our past. We all have dysfunctional ways of relating to others that we learned as children. We of course presume that our way is the right way and that our spouse just isn't normal. Christian marriage can be just as turbulent as secular marriage.

In the last chapter I explained how Christian women often accept the lie that their identity and self-worth comes from their role as submitted wife and mother. This misunderstanding has come from an incorrect interpretation of Genesis 3:16:

> 'To the woman he said, "I will greatly increase your pains in childbearing; with pain you will give birth to children. Your desire will be for your husband, and he will rule over you." '

They feel that it is correct for the husband to rule and for them to submit since Ephesians 5:21 tells them to. This makes women man-pleasers rather than God-pleasers and they make idols of their husbands and children. When they eventually realize that they can't be perfect in this role, their self-worth and identity is threatened and they begin to fear rejection by family, friends and even God. To avoid this fear they become slaves to their roles in an attempt to cover up the emotional emptiness they feel. They may even become so afraid of displeasing their husbands that they don't obey God to avoid any conflict with their husband's will or their role. When they become emotionally dependent on their husbands for identity, they really devalue themselves. They may even become manipulators to force their husbands to say and do things to meet their emotional needs and give them identity. This of course, never works. Controlling and manipulating behavior is discussed in a later chapter. To make matters worse, Christian men encourage this unhealthy situation since it caters to their unhealed emotions. The end result is an unhappy, turbulent marriage relationship.

This misunderstanding has arisen because Christian women have assumed that the description of women being ruled by their husbands is to be understood as a command. It is really a description of the fallen state of women whom Jesus came to liberate.

At the time of the Fall, God said to Adam in Genesis 3:19:

> 'By the sweat of your brow you will eat your food until you return to the ground.'

We expect our spouses to meet all our emotional needs.

This meant that man was to be a worker and initiator. When a man has unhealed emotions he may be driven to find his identity in his work and become a performance addict. As I have described previously, this will make him idolize success, money, fame, power, status, influence and materialism. When he has not had the necessary affirmation from his parents, he may be in emotional adolescence and be struggling with emptiness, self-hatred and inferiority. All these unhealthy feelings may drive him to dominate, manipulate and control his wife to meet his unmet needs. She of course, submits to him to keep him happy and earn his approval. It is easy to see how two wounded spouses can reinforce each other's wounds, bondage and get caught in an endless cycle that never satisfies their real need for completion that can only be found in Christ. They never develop a proper relationship with each other, with God or with their children who learn the same dysfunctional behavior.

A message to singles

There is a very strong message here for singles. Don't fall into
the trap of marrying someone to meet your own emotional
needs for meaning, purpose or affirmation. It will never work
and you will have an unhappy marriage, always feeling
rejected by the spouse who can't possibly meet your needs.

To have a successful, healthy marriage, you need to come
to emotional healing and completeness in Christ before
choosing a spouse. It's better to remain single than to be
caught in a trap of emotional codependency.

How can we get out of this mess?

The cause of all these dysfunctional relationships is once
again, emotional bondage. There are three links of course, in
the chain of emotional bondage. All three must be healed if
we are going to be emotionally free with healthy relationships. If you are struggling with a chemical imbalance like
depression, it will greatly disrupt all relationships. When you
are hearing the voice of darkness filling your mind with lies
or you have unhealed wounds from the past, your life will be
a struggle. Don't hesitate to go to a physician or counselor to
get these chains broken.

To set our relationships free, we must first recognize that
we have created idols that we have looked to for identity and
self-esteem. The idols may actually be good things like
spouses, roles or even your church but they have taken the
place of God as your source of identity. Ask God to show
you where your idols are. Then repent for trusting in them
rather than the finished work of Jesus to give us emotional
wholeness.

We must refocus on God as our only true source of meaning, purpose, identity, self-esteem and approval. As Jesus lives
in and through us, He gives us all we need to be emotionally
complete. We no longer then have to be man-pleasers and
slaves to the opinion of others. We are able to turn from self-
consciousness back to God-consciousness and reverse the
effect of Adam's sin. We no longer have to work for acceptance or approval, it's ours as a free gift from God because we

are His cherished, worthy children. We can feel relaxed and complete, free of the insecurity of Satan's lies. We are no longer dependent on our spouse for acceptance or approval and we aren't angry with them for not meeting our needs.

Ephesians 4:22 says:

> *'You were taught, with regard to your former way of life, to put off your old self, which is being corrupted by its deceitful desires, to be made new in the attitude of your minds.'*

We must allow Jesus to come and dispose of our old selves and accept that our new selves are in Christ, totally complete. Jesus lives in and through us so that our once severed relationship with God is now restored. We can return to the state of walking close to God, free of fear or shame, enjoying God's love and friendship. We no longer have to seek for identity or completeness since we are continually receiving it from Jesus living in us.

True headship in a home is when the husband continuously receives his identity, reassurance, security and confidence from Jesus. He is then a humble yet confident leader who releases his wife to receive her identity from God and participate in shared leadership. He will earn the respect of his wife so that it will be easy for her to submit to him. When a man is a balanced leader, he needs the gifting that a woman contributes and he isn't threatened by her. When a marriage is following God's pattern, both spouses are emotionally whole, receiving their identities from Christ, submitting to each other in love and reflecting the nature of Jesus to their children.

To start the journey out of marriage codependency, men must first repent for controlling women by misusing Ephesians 5:21 and expecting them to meet their needs. We repent as men for encouraging women to wrongly find identity in their role. We repent for abdicating the spiritual leadership role in our homes and for making success and performance our idol. We now release women from the chains that we have placed on them and see them rise up to find their identity in Christ.

Women must repent for seeking their identities in their roles as wife, mother and daughter. They must accept that

Jesus is the only source of identity and forgive men for controlling them. Women must also repent for controlling men to meet their needs.

As we repent, forgive and turn from our idols, Jesus will heal our relationships.

I know I have made this sound too easy to be possible. In the next chapter my wife Kathy will describe how God exposed the codependency in our marriage and how He walked us to freedom. You're right, it was not easy, it was in fact the most painful journey of our lives.

Chapter 23

What really happened to us

by Kathryn Mullen

*'Your whole head is injured, your whole heart afflicted.
From the sole of your foot to the top of your head there is
no soundness – only wounds and welts and open sores,
not cleansed or bandaged or soothed with oil.'*

(Isaiah 1:5–6)

I appreciate the opportunity to explain how God healed our marriage relationship over these past few years. We too went through the 'open-pit mining' experience because God did not want us to live any longer in the dysfunctional patterns that we had developed. The assurance that God had brought us together in marriage helped us to cope with the pain of emotional transformation. I hope that this chapter will give you confidence and comfort that God is at work in your life to change you and reshape your relationships.

Our perfectly dysfunctional marriage

We had been married about thirteen years at the time. Having come from stable Christian families and being Christians our whole life, we didn't seem to have any overt problems that we were aware of until Christ began this work in us in 1995.

When we were engaged and going through the pre-marital questionnaires and counseling, we found that our approach to critical issues was much the same. Even though I felt that Grant didn't do things the 'normal' way at times, when it came down to the essential areas of money management and child rearing, we approached things basically the same way. We seemed to have a pretty solid base from which to start a marriage. After the honeymoon there were the odd bumps here and there where things had to be worked out but most of the time life seemed smooth.

As Grant already mentioned, in May 1994 our church was turned upside down by an unexpected outpouring of the power of the Holy Spirit. This outpouring started one evening at the end of a Sunday School picnic planning meeting. After the picnic business was completed, the pastor began to close in prayer but during this prayer the power of God came on all those who were there. For an hour-and-a-half people were laughing, some were worshiping on the floor and others were dancing! We had never attended a picnic planning meeting like this before. This event was documented in the book *Catch the Fire* as Grant previously mentioned.

Grant was at home so he wasn't involved in the meeting. I sort of stumbled in the door and said, 'You won't believe what just happened!' From that day forward our church was changed as we witnessed the transforming power of the Holy Spirit in action. Grant was not directly involved in these events and he remained on the periphery for several months, evaluating what was going on in keeping with his intellectually-based faith.

One Sunday evening he was staying home with the kids. I was leaving for church when God showed him an attitude in his life that was affecting our relationship and that needed repentance. He mentioned it to me as I went off to church. The kids were outside so he started praying and repenting in our bedroom. Within a few minutes he felt the presence of God so strongly in the room that he became unsteady on his feet and needed to lie down for safety reasons. Once he was on the floor he began to shake, which was certainly a new experience for him.

We found out how connected we were in our spirits because during that same evening the power of God came on me at church and I too found myself on the floor shaking. I was trembling so severely that I couldn't drive myself home. This was a powerful illustration that when things happened in Grant's spirit, my spirit was affected too. We were as the Bible says, of one spirit.

Along with the positive connection, we also noticed that there were negative ones too. If Grant was under a spiritual cloud, I was also negatively affected. I was under him as my spiritual head, not that I had to go through him to God but he was my spiritual covering. We were spiritually connected for better or for worse.

We were unaware how dependent we were on each other. We thought we were normal. If you had identified us as codependent or dysfunctional we would have denied it absolutely. We just didn't realize that it was dangerous to depend on a spouse to make us feel right. If I didn't feel good, I would go to him and expect him to make me feel better. We assumed that was normal.

I was very good at finding significance in my role as wife, mother, daughter, ladies' Bible study leader, women's ministries leader, nursery worker, children's church teacher and anything else I was asked to do. I was very busy and very efficient at doing a good job and that was how I found my significance. It was a difficult pattern to unlearn.

In the summer of 1995 we began our period of discontent. Grant was entering a time when he became dissatisfied with life because God was 'stirring the pot.' We went away on an extended overseas trip and on our return I fell apart. I just knew things couldn't continue the way they had been. I didn't know why, I didn't know what was going on. On the inside of me things were starting to erode. I still maintained my roles on the outside. Most of the people in the church did not have a clue what was going on. It was so hard to continue to lead a Bible study when I was in the middle of such a mess. I did spend a lot of time in prayer. I took advantage of every opportunity my church offered for prayer ministry but I was just not coping on the inside. Things got so bad that we had to get help from a counselor. That was a big step for me because I had felt that counseling was not an acceptable option. Only people that were really messed up needed counseling so it was a major change for me to agree to it. In hindsight, it was that abrupt 'in your face' kind of pain which was necessary to bring us to a stop in the direction we were going. God could then turn us around and do something in our lives. We were so oblivious to how dysfunctional we really were that God had to literally stop us cold and turn us around.

Bent over spouses

When we were created, God designed us to stand tall in a 'vertical' relationship with Him whereby we would receive all our love requirements and emotional satisfaction directly from Him. I learned about this relationship and how man fell from it from the books by Leanne Payne which are listed later on.

In our marriage, I was always looking to Grant to meet my needs, expecting things from him, demanding things from him and likewise he from me. This was the state of being 'bent' towards each other as we lived in codependency. We tried to force each other to meet the needs that could only be met by God in a vertical relationship. Our bent relationship always seemed to overpower our vertical one.

I unknowingly made Grant into an idol, since I sought his approval more than God's. I was basically unaware that God had any opinion of me. I knew He loved me because the song said 'Jesus loves me this I know' but I felt nothing. I wanted Grant to affirm me even when I didn't think I deserved it. If I knew I wasn't quite meeting all his needs, I still hoped he would tell me I was okay. The fact was however, that when I wasn't meeting his needs, he didn't reassure me so I felt the pain of rejection.

The problem went both ways because I couldn't always affirm Grant and he would then walk away rejected, like a wounded puppy with his tail between his legs. We were feeling this rejection going back and forth without being able to put a label on it. The feeling was there subconsciously but we couldn't identify what was wrong. We were just never able to measure up to each other's expectations.

Straightening up

The process of becoming 'unbent' towards each other and becoming vertical to God was extremely difficult. We did not enter into it voluntarily. As I mentioned, when we came back from this trip, I was forced into it. I just could not relate to Grant any longer in the way that I had been. I could no longer cope with life as it was. When I fell apart I found it very difficult to be married to a doctor who specialized in mental health. Grant slipped into his 'analysis mode.' He tried to figure me out by asking me clinical diagnostic questions, 'Is it this or is it that?' and 'How do you feel about this and how do you feel about that?' He had trained me well after so many years of marriage to answer his questions and to tell him everything. It was something that I had to learn because I wasn't a good communicator at the beginning of our marriage. Over time I learned to be able to report things as they happened, when they happened, how they happened. It was like giving a medical history every time I saw him.

We were good communicators but that was part of our dependency. He needed to know everything that went on in my life and he would likewise report everything that went on in his. We needed to be in each others lives. When I would share a painful feeling with Grant, I would then look to him for affirmation and reassurance. One step in our healing process required that we not communicate in that dependent way any longer. As a result, a major binding force in our marriage was taken out from under us. That level of verbal intimacy and codependency was removed. This was a very painful experience for both of us because we were then plunged into continuous feelings of mutual rejection. Neither of us were able to meet any of our emotional needs. Grant could have shifted his desires and his craving for affirmation to someone else. Our pastor, when he realized what we had been through, felt it could have been so easy for Grant to have had an extramarital affair. He could have shifted his desire for affirmation to his work or to anything else but instead he began to look to God.

There was a very painful time when even though I had stopped being dependent on Grant, I had not yet become vertical to receive my affirmation from God. I felt lost since I wasn't having my emotional needs met by anyone. It was only our deep commitment to God and to each other during this difficult phase in our lives that saw us through.

After seven months of pain, the first ray of hope came when Grant's relationship to God came alive in unprecedented ways. He began to have a vertical relationship with God which satisfied his emotional needs so that he was no longer dependent on me. While away on a trip, he read two books that changed his life, *Waking the Slumbering Spirit* by John and Paula Sandford, and *The Father Heart of God* by Floyd McClung. When he came home he said, 'My spirit is waking up, I'm starting to have a relationship with my Father.' He was beginning to receive his affirmation directly from God.

The problem with passivity

After ten months of feeling down and defeated, Grant and the counselor worried that I had become medically depressed. My mood had been down for months and I wasn't able to get out of this low state. On evaluation though, I didn't have any of the racing thoughts or poor concentration that are listed on Grant's checklist. I was just very, very low. Psalm 23 spoke about the 'valley of the shadow of death'. Well I felt like I was walking through a really deep valley. It was very dark, lonely and difficult. The verse also talked about a rod and a staff. I was learning that the rod and the staff were picking my chin up and pushing me a little bit this way and a little bit that way. The rod and staff were correcting me and straightening me up so I would stop looking to Grant and start looking in the right direction.

About this time I began to recognize that I was a passive person. I had been passive in our marriage, looking to Grant for affirmation and I was just going through life letting things happen to me and taking whatever came my way. This pattern worsened during my downward slide. I also realized that I was very afraid to move out of that passive state. I was believing lies the enemy was feeding me that I shouldn't leave that state of passivity because nothing would change. I wasn't sure that I could trust Grant to remain changed if I improved. I was seeing good things happening in him but I thought they were just to get me better and as soon as I was better, he would go right back to his old ways. That's a codependent thinking pattern right there. I also wasn't sure if I could trust God to catch me if I jumped into the unknown world of recovery. My relationship with Him as Father was really weak. I had to repent for this lack of trust and ask Him for help to renew my mind so I could stop believing all of these lies. This was a process that took time.

During this time in the 'valley', my counselor had a prophetic picture of me. I was in a dungeon and was plastered against a wall feeling like there were manacles around my neck, wrists and ankles. My body was really wasted indicating that I had obviously been there for some time. The interesting thing about this picture was that there was actually nothing binding me at all. I was standing in prison believing that I was held there against my will and unable to move. All I needed to do was to look around and see that there were no chains and I could walk out. I was just too weak to actually move out even if I did stop believing those lies.

When I finally understood that I was free to go, I said 'God, would you carry me out of here? I don't want to be in here anymore, I want out.' I asked Him if He would pick me up and take me out of the prison and make me all better. To my surprise the answer was simply, 'No.' He would not take me out of that prison. I was devastated! That meant I would have to do something on my own and I didn't feel I could because I was still extremely fearful and not strong enough in my spirit to walk out. My passivity won out and I remained stuck.

A secular prescription

We went off on our summer vacation that year which meant I wouldn't see my counselor for six weeks. He was probably relieved but I panicked over how I was going to survive with Grant. As we prepared to go camping, Grant gave me the books that he felt I needed to read to make me better. He suggested the books *Waking the Slumbering Spirit*, and *The Father Heart of God*. He assumed that if they had worked for him they would work for me. He gave me the same prescription that had helped him. My choice of reading material for the holidays was my daughter's book *Anne of Green Gables* by Lucy Maude Montgomery. I had never read it when I was her age and I had always wanted to. I decided to read it after I had faithfully read through Grant's list.

I struggled through Grant's books and they didn't help me at all. Grant had to learn the lesson that emotional recovery was just like medical recovery. The treatment that cured one person didn't always help the next person with similar symptoms. When I finally got to my book, I was really attracted to 'Anne Shirley,' the main character. I remember sitting by the campfire thinking, 'Is she ever neat. I really like her. You know, she is a really interesting person.' God then put the thought into my mind, 'Anne has an awakened spirit, that is what it's like to be alive in Me.' This was my first glimpse of what an awake spirit was like. I became attracted to the idea of being 'awake' like the character 'Anne.' God used a secular book to motivate me to seek change. I thought that was really neat. He met me where I needed to be met.

The healing of my will

We returned from our holidays and began preparing to attend a Pastoral Care Ministries conference with Leanne Payne. We had heard that these meetings had helped bring healing to the emotionally broken. We were broken and we needed help. To prepare for this conference we read most of Payne's books and those of her co-workers. One of these books was Mario Bergner's *Setting Love in Order*. Mario was a former homosexual who wrote about his abusive relationship with his father. He described how he had progressed to a point in his life where he was emotionally stuck. Mario was passive in how he approached life, ministry and everything he did. I thought, 'That sounds familiar, I'm feeling just like he was, I'm passive, I'm going through life with no energy to change, I'm unable to will myself to do anything.'

Mario described how his abusive father had broken his will. I couldn't relate to that because I'm not from an abusive family. I felt very loved while I was growing up by both my parents and we had a good relationship. I did know however, that there were situations that had wounded me in my past and that my cries for help had not been attended to. My will had been ground down so I reached the point where I stopped asking for help when I was in pain. I wasn't even aware that I was hurting and that I was just going through the motions of life with no will to get better or change.

Mario recorded a prayer that he said to ask God to heal his will (reprinted below). This was strange to me because I had been raised with a theology that expected our wills to be broken. We were to submit to Christ and we didn't want our wills to be working in opposition. Mario explained that when our will was healed we could more easily work with God since His will would become our will. I decided that I too would pray specifically for the healing of my will using his recorded prayer. I asked God to heal my will where it was wounded and I asked Him to strengthen it so that I would let my will become one with His. I asked that He would empower me to obey and follow Him. I forgave those who had been in authority over me who had broken my will. I then began to take responsibility for my life instead of letting others influence me. It was at this point that I started to enter into a vertical relationship with God. When I asked Him to heal my will I became spiritually able to stand up and walk out of my prison.

The recovery

A month later I began to see results. There was a women's day at our church and something the speaker mentioned made me realize the change had started. My spirit jumped saying, 'Yes I am going to get better!' I started to walk with the assumption of improving. It was no longer 'Someday I hope.' It was 'Yes, I am going to get better.' A purpose had come into me and I was able to start implementing Philippians 2:12, 13 where it says:

> *'Continue to work out your salvation with fear and trembling for it is God who works in you to will and to act according to his purpose.'*

Up to that point I couldn't work with Him to work out what

He wanted to do in my life. I had been just a blob of gelatin that absorbed everything and couldn't move.

Grant prayed for the healing of his will about two months after I did and it caused a significant change in our marriage. That was another point where something happened in him spiritually and it affected me. His passivity decreased and all of a sudden I had hope for our marriage. There was something in my spirit that just responded because his spirit was taking charge. He began to pick up the proper headship because his will could now work with God in leading our family and my spirit sensed that immediately. I knew that I could follow him and that we could move together.

As I moved from that prison of lies I became a stronger individual. There's been more of a sense of purpose. I don't need to depend on Grant now to know who I am because I've settled that with God. I go to Him instead of Grant for affirmation. We're no longer threatened by each other. If Grant is changing something in his ministry or work it doesn't affect me the way it used to because now I have my feet on solid ground. I'm not shaken when something changes with him. He's not threatened now if I'm not always there to look after his needs, make the beds, do the laundry, vacuum the house, and shop.

Another blessing from my spirit coming alive is that I have a new sense of creativity and joy in worship that has never been there before. I've always been somewhat creative but I usually only made functional things. I sewed clothes and made drapes and other useful items. Now I enjoy making worship flags, banners and using them during services. My love of worship has increased and I can express myself in new creative ways. Best of all, I know God approves of me.

The healing in our relationship has had a tremendous affect on our children too. The year that we were going through our pain and were dealing with lies and sin in our relationship, the kids really suffered from the tension in our home. We were feeling rejection and anger under the surface, and they demonstrated it. As we broke the generational ties, released each other and came free ourselves, we saw our kids come free too.

'There was nothing actually holding me in prison.'

[handwritten: over 2000 years age Jesus died 2 bury our sins. Because "world"]

The Pastoral Care Ministry conference was a turning point in our lives. As Leanne Payne, Mario Bergner and others explained and prayed for emotional recovery, our chains fell off. We came home transformed people. The conference was the culmination of a long process of healing and at last our heads 'came above the water line.' What we learned and experienced there was so profound that it changed the course of Grant's ministry and you can see the influence of Leanne Payne throughout this book.

This whole process of strengthening my will and the healing of both of our emotions took over a year and it is still ongoing. It was a year of endless prayer times, pain and counseling appointments. There were times of deliverance, affirmation, repentance and forgiveness. The two major turning points for us were the forced breaking of our codependency through the process of me falling apart and the healing of our wills so that we could move ahead with God.

It has been a continuous process of 'straightening up' to a vertical relationship with God. You must remember to look up and receive your affirmation from the Lord. It's always a process of releasing judgments and constantly forgiving one another. If you stay in a vertical position and cultivate that relationship with God, your relationship with your spouse will be free to become what God wants it to be. You won't be craving and grasping affirmation from them like you used to.

If your will has been broken into passivity, you need to forgive those that contributed to its breaking. The following is the prayer which I prayed, taken from Mario Bergner's book page 108. Perhaps this will help you to be healed in this area of your life.

> 'Come, Holy Spirit. Even now, Lord Jesus, enable me to grab hold of Your outstretched hand. As I reach out my hands toward heaven and look up and out of myself, I cry out as St Paul did, "In my weakness, O Lord, You are strong." Now, Lord, enter into my will and heal it where it has been wounded. Reveal to me any person from the past who has exhausted my will, wounded my will, or even broken my will. [*Let the Holy Spirit speak to your heart about any person who so wounded you.*] Now Lord, give me the grace to choose to forgive that person for sinning against me. [*Name that person*], I choose to forgive you in Jesus' name for your sin against me. I look now to God to restore my will. Let Your divine power, O Lord, wrap itself around my weak, tired will; cause it to grow and to strengthen. Let my will be one with Your will, dear Heavenly Father. I thank You for doing that just now. I thank you for empowering me to obey You. I thank You, Lord, that from this day forward I will take responsibility for my life before You. Amen.'

I hope this chapter has encouraged you that there is hope for your emotions and your relationships. I'll let Grant continue now.

Chapter 24

I will trust and not be afraid

'Surely God is my salvation; I will trust and not be afraid. The Lord, is my strength and my song; he has become my salvation.' (Isaiah 12:2)

'God is our refuge and strength, an ever present help in trouble. Therefore we will not fear, though the earth give way and the mountains fall into the heart of the sea, though its waters roar and foam and the mountains quake with their surging.' (Psalm 46:1–3)

'Peace I leave with you; my peace I give you. I do not give to you as the world gives. Do not let your hearts be troubled and do not be afraid.' (John 14:27)

Fear is an obstacle that every human must deal with. God is very interested in how we deal with fear, so the Bible is filled with references to fear. Let's look at some of the greatest Bible characters and see how they handled fear.

Did the heroes of faith ever get nervous?

The first mention of fear was in the Garden of Eden in Genesis 3:10:

'He answered, "I heard you in the garden, and I was afraid because I was naked; so I hid."

The problem of fear obviously goes back a long way to the first man. Fear entered man's mind and heart as a direct result of sin. Adam sinned when he fell for the temptation to make knowledge more important than trusting God.

Abraham gives us an example of how a patriarch, hero of faith, father of nations, handled fear.

> *'Say you are my sister, so that I will be treated well for your sake and my life will be spared because of you.'*
>
> (Genesis 12:13)

When Abraham feared for his own life, he was quite willing to give up his wife to save his own skin. This blatant sin of overwhelming selfishness did not just happen once but twice and he was rebuked both times. This shows how even a man of faith can be so overcome with fear that he acts foolishly, knowing the consequences of his actions. He hadn't yet learned to trust God.

Jacob had a life-changing wrestle with an angel that confirmed his special relationship with God. Then the next day,

> *'In great fear and distress Jacob divided the people who were with him into two groups, and the flocks and herds and camels as well.'* (Genesis 32:7)

He was overwhelmed with fear even after a supernatural visitation and on the eve of a miraculous reconciliation. He hadn't yet learned to trust God.

Elijah had just called down fire from heaven, killed the prophets of Baal and the following happened:

> *'So Jezebel sent a messenger to Elijah to say, "May the gods deal with me, be it ever so severely, if by this time tomorrow I do not make your life like that of one of them." Elijah was afraid and ran for his life.'* (1 Kings 19:2–3)

Even after being part of such a supernatural demonstration of God's power, he was terrorized by the threat of the queen. There was still an area in Elijah's heart where he hadn't learned to trust God completely.

Peter was so afraid at Jesus' trial that he denied Jesus three times. He even swore and cursed himself. His fear overwhelmed his loyalty and trust in Jesus.

Abraham's fear overcame his trust.

It is quite plain to see that our Bible heroes often struggled with fear when their trust in God was weak. We are in good company when we are afraid, it's a common problem. After the Fall, fear became a normal part of life but God has given us a way to prevent it from controlling our lives.

Anxiety and fear

Anxiety isn't all bad. It is actually a gift from God designed to protect us from danger. Anxiety is a normal part of childhood as children confront new and potentially dangerous situations. It was God's original plan that anxiety was to be recognized and released as loving parents taught children how to avoid danger. In this way the anxiety would never become overwhelming and it would be channeled into learning experiences. Home would become a safe place to take risks and build confidence. Anxiety was meant to serve us, not to be our master. It was a safety guardrail not a roadblock. Like all other gifts, Satan found a way to use anxiety against us to hurt, paralyze and ultimately to control man. Fear is the term I use to describe the level of anxiety which is used by Satan as a weapon against us to disrupt our lives.

The three links in the chain of fear

As there are three links in the chain of emotional bondage, there are three links in the chain of fear which must be overcome if we are to be released from that prison.

1. Physical causes

The first link is again, chemical imbalances or physical causes of fear. In medicine we call these the anxiety disorders. They are a type of depressive illness where the repetitive unwanted thoughts are all fearful rather than the sad thoughts that characterize depression. In this disorder one can't shut off the fearful thoughts and they just keep racing through the mind like an audio tape that can't be stopped.

The symptoms may be mild in which case the person is chronically tense, afraid, easily threatened by unfamiliar circumstances, irritable and with poor concentration. They often have trouble sleeping since it is too difficult to shut off the anxious thoughts. In severe cases there can be panic attacks where a person is consumed by fear, loss of control, with pounding heart, sweating, shaking and felling like they're going out of their mind. This illness can magnify the other causes of fear or emotional bondage to overwhelming severity.

Like depression, these are inherited conditions which usually respond well to antidepressants. These medications correct the chemical imbalance and return thought control to normal. I have seen many complete recoveries in people suffering from this disorder after medical treatment. If you suspect that you may have such a condition, check yourself out in the first section of this book or the symptom checklists in Chapter 12. If you see yourself described there, take your list of symptoms to a physician to start treatment.

2. Demonic interference

The second link is the harassment of Satan. His weapons are lies, fear and intimidation. He loves to attack people with fearful thoughts which he inserts into their minds. Satan loves anxiety and depressive disorders since those conditions make people so vulnerable to his inserted thoughts. He does not want anyone to get treated for mood disorders since when a person recovers, they regain their thought control and slam the door on his lies. Satan will use many arguments to prevent you from getting treated. His favorite ones in my experience, are to tell a Christian that it's unspiritual to take medications for a thinking problem, that they should be ashamed of themselves for having this weakness, that they should never admit to feeling this way and if they had enough faith they would be well. Satan has kept many Christians away from effective treatment by using religious arguments which shame the depressed or anxious person.

Satan will take advantage of every anxious circumstance by planting a lie that makes you very fearful. He may create an illusion of risk and then place lies in your mind so that you feel threatened. Satan will encourage you to misinterpret events to increase your fears.

3. Woundedness

This is the most common cause of fear because all humans since Adam have been emotionally wounded by painful relationships.

Wounds can begin very early. Even a fetus can be wounded by fear that the mother may be feeling about her circumstances. Children may learn a lifestyle of fear if their parents themselves haven't mastered fear. Children can get stuck in childhood fears if their parents don't nurture and reassure them through this normal developmental phase. It's quite common for adults to be struggling with fears from childhood which become cruel masters. Satan loves these unhealed childhood emotions because he can manipulate and use them against people.

There are an unlimited number of ways that fear can express itself in adult behaviors. I'll illustrate a few.

Amniosis

People who have been wounded by fear as children are often very passive, avoiding any risks, decisions, new situations or change. New circumstances are interpreted as threatening and to be avoided. These people are very dependent on others to look after and make decisions for them. They crave security and unchanging routines. Intimacy or an open exchange of ideas is avoided since it requires vulnerability and can't be controlled. This of course is a major handicap in marriage. Spiritual growth is greatly limited because they recoil from change or challenge. Supernatural activity is too threatening and unfamiliar so it too is avoided. Due to their low self-confidence and self-esteem, they must be pushed or dragged into any new situation.

John Sandford calls this state **amniosis** because it represents the inability or reluctance to come out of the womb and be born. It is the desire to flee from reality and retreat to a womb of safety where all needs are met and there are no demands. Sandford's writings helped me understand these fearful characteristics.

Amniotic people cope with insecurity by trying to control and manipulate others to do their will and avoid change. A fearful mother, for example, will smother and overprotect her child to avoid any risk to the child. She also does this to avoid any risk to herself of having to cope with new situations that the child may have to confront. This type of mother may control and manipulate the family members to protect herself from change or risks. She may use passive control through inducing guilt and shame or by giving or withdrawing love. Active control uses anger to force obedience.

Over-protection breeds fear into the children so they too will fear change or risk. This deprives children of the necessary challenges to develop self-confidence and identity. They may remain emotionally childlike their whole lives.

A fearful father may fall into such passivity that he abdicates the leadership and parenting role in the home. He becomes an absent father though he is physically present. These men often retreat to their work, television or outside to their garage to 'tinker' with things as an escape from relationships, demands and vulnerability. Men love the TV since when they are holding the remote control they are at last in control of their world. If you ever want to test my theory that the remote control is a male addiction to cover up unhealed childhood emotions, just remove it from him and see what

How to trigger the volcano.

happens. This simple test will often demonstrate the volcano that I described previously.

When children have an amniotic fearful father, they never see boldness, initiative, courage or confidence so they grow up to be the same way. A fearful father may also show active control in which case he will be full of anger and rage to intimidate people to stay away from him so that he never has to face a challenge.

Amniotic families like this are very tense. They want peace at any cost, confrontations are forbidden and issues are never dealt with. All feelings and opinions have to be submerged because they would be perceived as a threat by the fearful parent. Everyone is trained 'not to rock the boat,' to keep that parent happy. This breeds chronic deep resentment in all family members. Children learn to fear, manipulate and avoid feelings or change to keep others happy. Under these circumstances the spirit of a child shrivels up, creativity is lost, spontaneity is crushed and joy is not worth the risk to pursue. These families carry heavy emotional chains that interfere with all relationships.

Fear can also trigger performance addiction when the approval of others is sought to overcome insecurity. In this state a person is emotionally dependent on the reactions of others. I have already described how dangerous it is to be caught in this addiction, evaluating yourself through the eyes of others.

Fear can be demonstrated by compulsive religious activity which is done to win the approval of man and God. Those who were afraid of their fathers will likely also be afraid of God, assuming that they both share the same characteristics.

Churches too, can be paralyzed by fear; it is a form of corporate bondage. Church leaders and members can be afraid of anything that is difficult to understand or is unfamiliar to them. This of course limits God and restricts the activity of the Holy Spirit since God is always trying to bring about growth, change and supernatural events. Some of these churches will judge an act of the Holy Spirit as wrong or even occult merely because they don't understand it or can't explain it. In these churches, comfort and conformity must be maintained at all costs. Jesus was however, always making people uncomfortable as He urged them to change. He was not afraid to disrupt religious life by clearing the temple and making the religious officials angry at Him. Change is a natural part of walking in the Spirit. The underlying problem in these churches is that they are afraid of God and what He may do to challenge them. To manage their fears, it's easier to keep God confined inside a box with walls made of their expectations. By not allowing God outside of their boundaries, their fears can be lessened.

How did we get this way?

> ' "You will not surely die," the serpent said to the woman. "For God knows that when you eat of it your eyes will be opened, and you will be like God, knowing good and evil." '
> (Genesis 3:4–5)

In the Garden, Satan convinced Adam and Eve to believe
the lie that God could not be trusted and that He was
deliberately hiding information from them that they needed
to look after their own best interests. Satan convinced them
that they needed more knowledge and that God was keeping
it from them. Adam then began to doubt God's word and
accept Satan's view of rebellion as clever and wise.

After he sinned, Adam immediately became ashamed
of his nakedness and afraid of God. Adam illustrated that
when trust was lost, fear replaced it. Adam turned from
trusting God to trusting knowledge which led him into sin.
From this point forward fear, lack of trust (and even perhaps
the tendency to blame our wives) became entrenched in
man.

When we are wounded by damaging relationships, especially as children, it causes emotional pain and leaves an
emotional scar. At the time of the injury Satan sees that in
our pain we are vulnerable to attack so he comes and plants a
lie in our souls that is related to the wounding event. The lie
is meant to shape your way of thinking for the rest of your
life. One common lie that gets planted at the time of
wounding is to be afraid of all relationships in the future
since they might hurt you. Since the lie is based in a true
historical event, we accept it as true even though the
conclusion is false. Fearful emotions then build around the
lie which increases the pain of the old wound and disrupts
relationships and attitudes. The lie stays with you and
distorts your life until you are healed of the wound where it
was planted.

Satan may assign an evil spirit to reinforce the lie and
intensify the negative emotions that go with it. This spirit
will try to trigger the pain as often as possible and create
a stronghold of lies which is designed to control your
thoughts and emotions. In this way you can be kept in
emotional bondage. To cope with the pain, you create thick
walls to protect you from further injury. These walls
however, keep people isolated and they destroy relationships
with families and with God. When we continue to live
behind emotional walls we will spend our lives running from
our fears.

What is the way out?

*'The L*ORD *is my light and my salvation – whom shall I fear?*
*The L*ORD *is the stronghold of my life, of whom shall I be*
afraid?'   (Psalm 27:1)

'Cast your cares on the Lord and he will sustain you; He will
never let the righteous fall.'   (Psalm 55:22)

God wants you to be free from fear.

'Peace I leave with you; my peace I give you. I do not give to
you as the world gives. Do not let your hearts be troubled and
do not be afraid.'   (John 14:27)

'There is no fear in love. But perfect love drives out fear,
because fear has to do with punishment. The one who fears is
not made perfect in love.'   (1 John 4:18)

If we are not living in God's perfect love we will be
vulnerable to fear. God wants us to be so confident and
secure in His love that we fully trust Him and follow Him
fearlessly as a young child would trust their parent.

For those of you who recognize yourselves as amniotic,
Jesus now wants you to come out of the womb and be birthed
into a full, exciting life of confidently walking with Him.
Jesus will give us the courage to face reality with Him walking
at our side. He will make it safe for us to become vulnerable
and transparent in our intimate relationships. As Jesus fills
our love requirement, we no longer have to search for
humans to fill it. He was wounded so that He could take
our wounds from us and replace them with His love and
peace.

Fear entered mankind when Adam turned from trusting
God to trusting knowledge which caused him to sin. Jesus is
now reversing the process. As we return to trusting God and
away from the trust of knowledge, we are then covered
and filled with God's perfect love and our fear is taken away.

If you want to start the healing process, ask God to show
you the circumstances that wounded you as a child and
triggered your fear. As you see the event in your mind, look
around with the eyes of your spirit and see where Jesus is

standing in the picture and listen to what He is saying. Ask Jesus to tell you what lie Satan planted at the time of the wound and how that lie has disrupted your life and relationships ever since. Common lies that trigger fear are that you can't trust anyone, you mustn't take risks and that people will always hurt you.

Ask Jesus to tell you the truth about the event. When we hear His response to the lie, the power of the lie is broken. Listen to Jesus tell you of His unconditional love for you, how safe you are in His arms and that there is no need to fear. Let the comforting words of Jesus replace the fearful thoughts that resulted from the wounding event.

Forgive those who wounded you and taught you to be fearful (parents, teachers, pastors and anyone who was in authority). I know they don't deserve it but we didn't deserve to be forgiven either and God freely forgave us. We want to be free of the chains they put on us. Forgive yourself for believing Satan's lies and not trusting God.

Repent for hating those who wounded you since that was a sinful response to their sin against you. Repent for believing the lie that Satan planted at the time of your wounding which has kept you bound in fear. Repent for times that you have manipulated and controlled others to avoid change and protect yourself.

Give all your painful memories and lies to Jesus so that He can take them away from you and onto Himself on the Cross. Invite Jesus to pour His healing into your wounds and replace the tormenting thoughts with His thoughts. Let Jesus put you on His lap and be your Daddy as He wraps His arms around you and fills your love deficit.

Ask Jesus to break the power of lies off your mind and to banish any evil spirit that has been attached to those lies to cause fear.

You must choose to leave the security of the womb and be birthed into a vibrant life of walking with God. You may now walk out of your prison of fear and choose freedom from the lies.

If you want to learn more about the process of allowing Jesus to come and show you the wounds and lies from the past, I recommend the writings of Dr Ed Smith. You can find his address at the end of this book.

The story of Ms H

I thank God that now I'm beginning to understand the lies that have imprisoned me for my whole life.

I grew up in an alcoholic household. About ten years ago memories of sexual abuse by an uncle were made clear. I have also struggled with a weight problem most of my life. When I heard you explain how Satan will embed a lie at the time of wounding, it was like an arrow shot from a quiver that hit home in me. God took me back to the time of wounding and began to reveal the lies that I believed since that time. One of the major lies He revealed was about my sexual abuse at age two. I've always mourned my loss of innocence. As I was praying, Jesus scooped me up and carried me back to my time in the womb and showed me that the fear I felt from my father was his anxiety about adequately providing for mom.

Jesus broke the lie. He then carried me to my time of abuse. I said to Him, 'I lost my innocence here!' In a gentle but firm voice He said, 'But I always saw you as innocent!' The arrow hit its target and burst open the lie that I was defective and scarred. He is continuing to take me back to the lies and then showing me the truth.

Praise the Lord, I can now go forward, look someone in the eye and no longer believe the lies.

Have you ever felt like you didn't deserve to be born or that you don't belong on this planet? You're not alone as you'll see in the next chapter.

Chapter 25

Overcoming rejection

'As you come to him, the living Stone, rejected by men but chosen by God and precious to him, you also, like living stones, are being built into a spiritual house to be a holy priesthood, offering spiritual sacrifices acceptable to God through Jesus Christ. For in Scripture it says: "See, I lay a stone in Zion, a chosen and precious cornerstone, and the one who trusts in him will never be put to shame."' (1 Peter 2:4–6)

The faces of rejection

I want you to look at the descriptions of four fictitious individuals who represent many people you know and perhaps even yourself.

Barbara was an excellent homemaker and church worker but she was extremely sensitive. Her feelings were easily hurt by seemingly innocent remarks from people who loved her. She would need several days of constant reassurance from her husband to get over these events. She could never understand why she reacted this way.

Bob was a successful businessman who had many accomplishments to be proud of but he was always tense and defensive. He didn't tolerate criticism and expected everyone to always agree with him. He was very active in the church and sought out leadership positions. Unfortunately he was often demanding and impatient on church committees. He felt he had a more complete understanding of Scripture than most people and certainly more than other denominations. If everything didn't go his way, he was very tense and angry.

People were very intimidated around him so they usually gave in to his demands.

Evelyn was a classic wallflower. She was always in hiding at her church and had to have personal and specific invitations to every activity. She never just came on her own initiative. She never volunteered for anything and usually said she was too dumb to do anything right, so someone else should be asked. She would never read or pray out loud in a small group and always felt her opinion was wrong or not worth wasting the group's time to listen to. She could never accept compliments, always deflecting them or explaining them away.

Bill was a wild and crazy guy. He was constantly trying to entertain others and keep them laughing by having a quick remark for every situation. He worked fourteen-hour days and would rarely take a vacation since he was always trying to beat his sales goals and advance his career. He was very active in the church and volunteered for everything he could. People felt exhausted just being around him.

These people seem so different yet they are all unknowingly suffering from rejection and are demonstrating the symptoms. God wants to heal us and set us free from the chains of this very common emotional disability.

The roots of rejection

God intended that every child was to be a wanted child and that they were to receive unconditional affection in all circumstances from emotionally healthy parents who reflected the parental nature of God to their children. In this ideal setting, children would feel accepted, failure would never be a threat and love would be unconditional. They would grow to accept themselves and have a healthy self-confidence. As teens and adults they would be able to handle rejection or negative circumstances without feeling personal injury. They would respond to criticism constructively, keep an optimistic outlook and never feel threatened by others.

Sounds good, doesn't it? Of course this rarely happens since sin has so wounded us that we are never raised in such a perfect environment.

Everyone has a personal eternal spirit that enters your body at the time of conception. From that time on this spirit is sensitive and vulnerable to spiritual influences around it. Rejection, fear and other negative emotions can be sensed by the fetus and leave wounds. Positive emotions can also be sensed which gives the fetus security and peace.

Intrauterine fetal wounds are some of the most severe and long-lasting injuries that a person can have. As we will see, a child who has survived a failed abortion attempt may struggle for their whole lives with the feeling that they have no right to be alive and that they should die. An unwanted pregnancy and the negative emotions that are displayed in the parents towards the fetus can leave the child feeling rejected. Children may even reject themselves because they don't believe they have any right to be alive. This always leads to emotional and behavioral problems which continue to hurt the person until they are healed.

I have always had trouble understanding or believing how a fetus could be wounded or even aware of what was going on around it. The Bible actually proves that a fetus is spiritually responsive in Luke 1:41:

> *'When Elizabeth heard Mary's greeting, the baby leaped in her womb, and Elizabeth was filled with the Holy Spirit.'*

The fetus sensed the Spirit of Jesus in Mary and responded.

I had a very cute four-year-old patient that helped me understand this phenomenon. His parents brought him to my clinic due to his extreme violence at home. His older sister and parents were actually afraid of him since in his rage he could turn anything into a weapon. There did not seem to be any abuse experiences. He came from a loving, stable home without any obvious problems. They felt that he had been violent and angry from birth, so I asked about the pregnancy. He had been a wanted child and there had been no illnesses or injuries to the mother while she carried the child. When I asked about the mother's emotions, she said everything had been fine except for some difficulties with her mother-in-law during the pregnancy. These 'difficulties' turned out to be a series of fist fights between the two of them. The situation then became very easy to understand.

This child had been wounded by rage, hate and violence as a fetus and he just continued to act it out after birth.

I was recently teaching this at a conference and the following note was handed to me.

> I am fifty-five years old and from the time of conception my single mother and her family wanted to get rid of me. An illegal abortion was scheduled but on that day a snowstorm caused the procedure to be canceled. After my birth I was given up for adoption but somehow I never bonded there. I have always felt that I didn't deserve to live so I always kept in the background away from people. I tend to fear intimate relationships since I feel that if they get too close, they may want to get rid of me. I then withdraw from people so no one gets too close. I realize that I was wounded in the womb but God showed me during prayer that He had reached down and protected me in that helpless state.

What a clear example of the long-term effects of intra-uterine wounding and of how God wants to heal that wound.

After a child is born, the baby can feel rejected if the mother is unable to bond for whatever reason. If parents are too busy, the child may interpret this as rejection. Many parents are disappointed with the sex of their baby, this can be sensed by the baby and may be interpreted as rejection. How many of you were born only because your last sibling was the wrong sex and they were trying again? Some of you know that you were the wrong sex too and it has left you wounded. In extreme cases, this wound can lead a child to reject their own sex because they had sensed the parental rejection. This of course leads to severe emotional problems in later life.

When children are physically awkward they may not be accepted by other children and this commonly leaves wounds of rejection. They may then become self-critical with low self-esteem and resentment. Teenagers are very sensitive to how they are being accepted. They are very self-conscious of their appearance or behavior and can easily feel the wound of rejection if they 'don't fit in.'

Rejection can even be felt by children of well-meaning parents who fail to hug, touch or express affection. This creates an environment of emotional neglect. When a sibling dies or parents separate, a vulnerable child may feel rejected by the departing family member and may even feel responsible for the loss which then triggers self-rejection. Children who have never met their father or who were abandoned by him suffer from a very deep wound of rejection.

All forms of abuse are types of rejection. During the abuse, the body is used while the spirit and soul of the victim is being rejected and devalued.

Childhood and adolescence are the times of greatest vulnerability to rejection since it is the time when people need repetitive reassurance to build confidence and a healthy self-image. The more cold and rigid a family is, the more fear and rejection the members will experience.

Childhood rejection leaves very deep and lasting wounds which make children very vulnerable to Satan's lies. These lies can control a person's behavior for life, as was illustrated in the woman's letter above. Common tormenting lies from rejection are that you have no right to be alive, that you will have to earn love because you don't deserve it, you're ugly, stupid and deserve to be rejected, it's your fault that you were treated that way and you got what you deserved, you will never deserve anyone's love or God's blessing. These lies may cause people to reject themselves, fear further rejection and develop a defensive attitude to protect themselves from further rejection. This attitude causes them to be rejected again which reinforces the fear of rejection. Rejection becomes a cycle of self-fulfilling prophecy that torments people their whole life until it is healed. Satan loves this cycle and will do anything to promote it.

Adult rejection

There are many circumstances in adult life which can trigger feelings of rejection. Divorce is likely the most severe rejection experience in adulthood. The death of a spouse can cause the surviving spouse to feel rejected. As I pointed out in the chapters on marriage, when spouses are emotionally dependent on each other, they will feel rejected when the other spouse fails to meet all their emotional needs.

Many of you are asking yourselves why some people feel rejection and others don't, after the same negative event. The reason is simple. The people who feel the most rejection are the ones who were previously rejected as children and the adult event brings back all their unhealed childhood emotions. These surfacing emotions can often drive a person to overreact in very childish ways since their origin was in childhood. Many adults are still children emotionally since their development stopped at the time of childhood wounding.

As I pointed out at the beginning of this chapter, feelings of rejection can trigger a wide variety of behaviors in adults. All four scenarios were behaviors resulting from the wounds of rejection.

Barbara, the overly sensitive housewife who needed constant reassurance was rejecting herself and protecting herself from further rejection. She had no self-confidence and was showing a passive response to rejection.

Bob, the tense, demanding, aggressive, impatient business-man was showing chronic anger as a response to his feelings of rejection. He couldn't tolerate criticism since it reminded him of the rejection in his past. Through anger, he actively responded to rejection and intimidated those around him.

Evelyn, the wallflower who never showed any initiative, was passively rejecting herself and living in the fear of failure which caused others to reject her. This then confirmed her fears so she withdrew even more.

Bill, the wild and crazy workaholic was a performance addict. He craved the constant approval of his friends and superiors to fill his emptiness. He would do anything to get their attention and impress them. This was his method of compensating for the rejection he felt in his childhood where he never thought he belonged in his family. He was always trying to earn a place in his family, office and church. Bill rejected his true self and he was trying to create a new self and then convince himself that it was his real self. He craved the approval of others to help him feel accepted and was dependent on their reactions for his security.

man was made 2B a dependant Being
34.7 man must choose Light or the
we must be darkness 261 *'cause*
ependant on/for men love 2 stay in
Wisdom or Know- hiding from Love
Ledge of _ or _ that frees, Light

Many adults are still wounded children inside. **BeCauSe,**
we are alway **CONTROLLED BY the Devil or GOD.**

Generational rejection is another kind of bondage that can happen to any persecuted minority group. If there has been a history of rejection in an identifiable group, then they all may suffer from a wound of rejection and develop a defensive attitude to protect themselves from further rejection. This attitude causes them to be rejected again which reinforces their perception and creates a stronghold which Satan protects. God wants to set you free from such bondage.

What is going on?

You will recall from the last chapter that when we have been wounded, it leaves an emotional scar and causes emotional pain. Satan then plants a lie about the event while we are vulnerable and in pain. Typical lies after being rejected are that you're worthless, no one wants you, you deserve to be rejected, you will always be rejected, you should reject yourself, you will always be a failure, no one will ever love you, you will always be criticized and will never be understood.

Since there was a real wounding event that hurt you, the lie is accepted as fact and it is cemented into place within the memory of the event. You can't be talked out of it because the event really happened and you presume the lie is also true. This lie stays with you and hurts you for life until you are healed of the wound where the lie is embedded. You will suffer with recurring emotional pain whenever the memory of the event is triggered.

This recurring emotional pain causes us to build thick defensive walls around ourselves to protect our feelings from vulnerability to further injury. We harden our hearts and refuse to let anyone close to us for fear of being rejected again. We rigidly try to stay in control of every situation to prevent anything from triggering our pain. We avoid intimate relationships or anything that demands vulnerability. This destroys marriages and parental relationships since it is impossible to be intimate across thick protective emotional walls. Even our relationship with God will remain distant and intellectual when we are hidden behind our walls. In this situation we prefer the pain of loneliness and isolation rather than the risk of further injury.

Satan knows that people stay in emotional bondage as long as he can keep the lies active which will always cause pain. He makes sure that your life events are always reminding you of the lie and the wound where it was planted so that your pain is continuous. An evil spirit may be assigned to the lie to keep your mind filled with tormenting thoughts based on the lie. Occasionally, spirits of infirmity will be attached to the lies to cause physical illness along with the emotional bondage. It is easy to see how emotional wounds are such a point of vulnerability for demonic harassment.

As long as your wounds remain unhealed, you will be vulnerable to the lies and the pain that results from them. Our response to the pain can hurt others and increase our own pain and isolation. There are two general ways that people respond to emotional pain. Some respond passively through emotional withdrawal, giving or withholding love, shame and manipulation. Others respond actively through rage, anger, revenge, bitterness and hate to dominate and control. These are all sinful responses which increase our own bondage by giving Satan more legal grounds to harass us.

The pain of rejection causes people to be tense, expecting to be rejected and acting in such a way to cause people to reject them, which proves they were right in their expectation. This attitude damages all relationships including that with yourself through self-rejection, with others who you expect to reject you and with God whom you can't trust since you expect Him to reject you also. Your spiritual, family and social life is paralyzed. How effective is a church full of emotionally bound people? You're right, it's no threat to Satan at all, so he loves it and does everything he can to keep it that way. He will resist every attempt you make to break free of the three links in the chain of emotional bondage. The good news is that as you come free, you will be able to move in a higher level of anointing and be a severe threat to Satan's kingdom.

What's the way out?

We have to first accept that regardless how good our upbringing was, we all have a love deficit that is so large, no human love can fill it. It can only be filled with God's love. We have all been wounded and have areas of emotional bondage. The good news is that God totally accepts us the way we are and that each of us are unique and special to Him. Jesus loved us when we were at our worst. He didn't reject us then and He doesn't reject us now. If we don't accept ourselves, we imply that God made a mistake with us. This is a terrible wound that many of us carry. Jesus never rejects His children and we never have to perform to win His approval. He approves of us because He bought us and there is nothing we have to do but accept it. Jesus wants you to relax in His presence and love.

Jesus knows what it's like to suffer the pain of rejection and abandonment and He cares for those of us who are experiencing it. Let's look at how Jesus was described in Isaiah 53:

> *'He grew up before him like a tender shoot, and like a root out of dry ground. He had no beauty or majesty to attract us to him, nothing in his appearance that we should desire him.'*
>
> (Isaiah 53:2)

Jesus knows what it's like to be physically unappealing.

'He was despised and rejected by men, a man of sorrows, and familiar with suffering. Like one from whom men hide their faces he was despised, and we esteemed him not.'

(Isaiah 53:3)

Jesus was not exempt from emotional pain that humans experience. He knew the pain of total rejection and public humiliation.

'Surely he took up our infirmities and carried our sorrows, yet we considered him stricken by God, smitten by him, and afflicted. But he was pierced for our transgressions, he was crushed for our iniquities; the punishment that brought us peace was upon him, and by his wounds we are healed.'

(Isaiah 53:4–5)

Jesus took our illnesses, emotional pain, sins and wounds upon Himself so that we would no longer have to carry them. The message of the resurrection is not just that we can have eternal life in the future but that Jesus wants us to be set free now!

To come to freedom, we have to recognize our wounds and pain so that we can bring them to the Cross. As Leanne Payne so often says at her conferences,

'God wants us to feel free to come before the Cross and hurt.'

We can be totally honest with God about our feelings and brokenness. He knows what it's like to hurt. He wants to carry your wounds for you. When Satan was defeated by the Cross, Jesus broke the power of lies so that we could be free of our emotional bondage. We must give Him our tormenting thoughts, wounds, sins and lies so He can dispose of them on the Cross. Allow Him to fill your mind with new thoughts of peace, joy and full acceptance.

To begin your walk to freedom, you can repeat the prayer sequence that I introduced in the last chapter. First, ask God to show you the memories of the wounds that caused you to feel rejected. Then look for Jesus in the memory and listen

We must bring our contaminated thoughts to the Cross for disposal.

to Him tell you what lie you believed as a result of the wound. Common lies are that you are worthless, you deserve to be rejected, you will always be rejected and that you should reject yourself.

He will then tell you the truth that will replace the lie. The truth that you are totally loved, accepted and beautiful in His sight. You were not a mistake, Jesus knew you in the uterus, He did plan your birth and celebrated your arrival. Listen to His healing and comforting words that He is speaking to you now which will replace all the tormenting thoughts from your wounded, angry inner child.

You must again remember to forgive all those who wounded you including parents, teachers, pastors, employers, spouses and former spouses. Repent for hating them and for believing Satan's lie which has tormented you ever since. Repent for hating and rejecting yourself and for your behavior to others as a result of your pain.

Now have the courage to walk to freedom and out of your prison and realize that you are totally accepted by your Daddy, God. Feel His arms around you.

Do you ever feel that you are being smothered or controlled by someone else? You may as well break free of that chain too while you're reading this.

Chapter 26

Breaking the ungodly ties that bind

' "Then you will know the truth, and the truth will set you free." They answered him, "We are Abraham's descendants and have never been slaves of anyone. How can you say that we shall be set free?" Jesus replied, "I tell you the truth, everyone who sins is a slave to sin. Now a slave has no permanent place in the family, but a son belongs to it forever. So if the Son sets you free, you will be free indeed." ' (John 8:32–36)

Do you recognize this couple?

Bill and Sue wondered what had gone wrong in their marriage. Bill was well liked at work but he was usually irritable, angry and impatient at home with his family. Everyone was very cautious with what they said and did when he was around. He spent as much time as he could watching TV or out in the garage tinkering with things but never doing the tasks that Sue needed him to help with around the house. If Bill's mother called and wanted help, he would respond immediately, though grudgingly and drop everything he was doing especially if it was for Sue. This infuriated his wife.

Sue gave up trying to be a perfect wife and would go for days frustrated and deliberately not speaking to Bill. She was always trying to be a perfect mother by running the lives of her teenagers. Their two teens weren't doing well. One was angry and rebellious always defying the household rules.

The other would just stay in his room and listen to music and rarely speak to anyone but his school friends. Neither ever went to church.

What do you think is wrong with this family?

They are suffering from the chains of emotional bondage and Satan is using those chains to destroy their relationships. God wants to set us free from this common bondage.

Peter Horrobin has described this type of bondage very clearly in his books which I have listed in the 'Recommended reading' section. The following explanation has been greatly influenced by his writings.

Godly soul ties

The desire for relationships is one of the most fundamental characteristics of being human. It's part of God's nature that He imparted to us when we were made in His image. God loves relationships and He has given that same love to us to draw us together with each other and with Him. Unfortunately, like every other gift that God has given us, Satan has done everything possible to distort and destroy these characteristics and he has used them to hurt us. Relationships were intended to be mutually beneficial and nurturing but as a result of the Fall, sin has caused human relationships to become unpredictable and often dangerous.

Whenever we are involved in a significant emotional relationship where we become vulnerable and share parts of our soul, we develop what has been called by many authors, a **soul tie**. Peter Horrobin describes a soul tie as a tube through which spiritual influence flows. There are basically two kinds of relationships and two kinds of soul ties. Healthy, wholesome, nurturing relationships create a healthy bond and a godly soul tie. Unhealthy, damaging relationships create bondage and an ungodly soul tie.

A good example in the Bible of a godly soul tie was the healthy relationship between David and Jonathan. They loved, respected and helped each other. This brought blessing to both of them. Godly relationships and soul ties are meant to create healthy nurturing environments for marriages, child rearing and friendships so that all involved will be strengthened.

Our first soul ties are with parents and family. God's original plan was for parents to have a proper relationship with Him, then with each other, so that a godly marriage soul tie would be formed that would build up both spouses. This healthy marriage would then reflect God's love to the children and create a godly soul tie with them through which proper nurturing would flow. This kind of parenting relationship would strengthen the child. In this way there would be a series of godly soul ties or tubes of blessing, starting with God, flowing to the parents and on to the children. Each tie would be secure, loving and emotionally liberating. As a godly soul tie matured, it would allow children to be released into adulthood with freedom of choice and with respect and appreciation for their parents. They would then be free to establish a godly soul tie with their spouse.

When a child is so surrounded by godly models of wholesome relationships, it's easy to relate to God and know His love. One of the greatest gifts that God has given to man is freewill. He wants everyone to be nurtured in such a way that freewill is preserved as we are instructed in how to make good decisions. The presence of God always brings freedom:

> 'Now the Lord is the Spirit, and where the Spirit of the Lord is, there is freedom.'   (2 Corinthians 3:17)

Any relationship that interferes with your freedom and controls you is contrary to God's plan.

Ungodly soul ties

Saul and David were a good biblical example of two people with ungodly soul ties because they had a very unhealthy relationship. Saul was so jealous that he tried to dominate, control and kill David. This was a good picture of how the emotional bondage of Saul led to a damaging relationship with David which then created the ungodly tie.

Ungodly soul ties and damaging relationships are all the result of the sin that Adam introduced into our race. Satan was then given access to our relationships so that they were no longer the healthy, nurturing godly soul ties which were to be channels of blessing. Relationships have all too often now become sources of bondage, pain and channels of evil.

What has happened to our families?

Everyone has been raised by parents who were struggling with their own emotional wounds. Parents then were often immature, selfish, domineering and controlling, depending on their own degree of wounding. This interfered with their ability to nurture children correctly and their emotional bondage was then passed onto the next generation through abuse or neglect. It is easy to understand how the parental soul tie became ungodly because it caused wounding and pain which often involved domination and control. When these children couldn't relate correctly to their parents, then they couldn't relate well to anyone, including God. They just assumed that God was no different from their parents who may have been controlling, abusive and untrustworthy.

When parents are codependent upon each other for emotional needs, they will usually try to dominate, manipulate and control the other to get their needs met. This creates ungodly ties within their marriage which naturally lead to ungodly ties with their children. Domination and control will appear at every level of relationship. Emotional emptiness in a marriage will often cause a parent to try to fill their void by seeking satisfaction in their role as parent. They may even try to find meaning or significance for their own life in what the children are accomplishing. This is a very unhealthy and damaging situation which can easily be demonstrated by the following example.

In Canada we have a place where adults come on a regular basis to publicly demonstrate their emotional health as parents. We call it the hockey arena. Any children's sports facility would serve the same purpose as long as there are parents watching a team competition. In my observation the most accurate psychiatric assessments can be made in these facilities when the children playing are male and there are

Parents may become emotionally dependent on their children.

male parents watching. During the games, I watch how emotionally involved parents become in these events. They often show extreme reactions to minor negative events in the game that happen to their team or child. This indicates to me that the parent feels personally threatened by the call of the referee or the event on the ice. The obvious conclusion is that the parent has become emotionally dependent on their child's success in sports for their own identity. They are unable to separate their own worth from the child's accomplishments. They are living through their children and so become dependent on the child's successes for emotional well-being. This drives them to dominate, manipulate and control the child so that he or she performs to the standard that gives the parent significance. This can be quite suffocating for the child who is continually pushed to meet the parent's need.

The next time you are at such a sporting event, watch for the parents who become irritating in the way they are demonstrating their emotional dependency on their children. Rather than joining the other parents and shouting at them the usual cry of 'get a life,' it would be more accurate and perhaps therapeutic to call out 'get your own identity.'

A parent with this kind of emptiness and emotional dependency on their children will suffer greatly from the **empty nest syndrome** after the children grow up and leave home. Their identity and purpose is threatened if they are no longer a parent and they can't cope emotionally if they are not being needed. Often these parents will try to keep their children dependent on them by controlling and manipulating them through guilt, shame, anger and the giving or withholding of love or approval. They may even offer financial loans to control the child and keep them dependent. These manipulated and suffocated children are deprived of free will and independence as they struggle against the ungodly soul tie with the parent.

When these children are grown, they make poor spouses since they remain controlled emotionally by the parent and are unable to 'cleave' to their spouse. These marriages are severely strained and the other spouse is always frustrated. Children living in these dysfunctional suffocating situations are likely to try to escape or rebel. It is usually done through either passive withdrawal from the family, even though they are boiling inside with frustration, or through overt rebellion and antisocial behavior to break every rule that the parent creates.

Satan loves these kinds of families because he can always keep the pot of emotional pain boiling in every family member. Satan wants to encourage us to use domination, manipulation and control to try to get our needs met since these are the tools of witchcraft. The purpose of witchcraft is to use occult power to control another person. When we use Satan's sinful tools, it gives him greater legal grounds to torment us.

What has happened to our marriages?

When most of us marry, we are basically emotionally wounded children in adult bodies. As I pointed out in a previous chapter, we usually marry to find someone to meet all our emotional needs. This of course, is not possible because only God can meet our needs and fill our love deficit. When a couple is codependent on each other in this way, it guarantees that they will be continually frustrated and angry with the other spouse.

To properly bond to a spouse with a godly soul tie, you need to be selfless, vulnerable, trusting and emotionally free. When you are emotionally empty and wounded, you will be selfish, protecting yourself from vulnerability, always feeling threatened and demanding what your spouse can't give you. In this circumstance you learn to keep your defensive walls high and thick to protect you from further injury. These walls of course, isolate you from proper intimate relationships with spouse, children or God.

To try and force our family to meet our emotional needs left over from childhood and to protect us from further injury, we use manipulation and control games. Once again control can be done passively through guilt and shame or actively through anger and rage. These of course are the characteristics of ungodly soul ties. This pattern creates rigid, emotionally frozen homes and marriages since everyone is carefully avoiding conflict and the emotional outbursts that would result. These homes are boiling cauldrons of anger, bitterness and resentment waiting to blow but no one is allowed to acknowledge it so that appearances can be maintained. The greater the manipulation and control, the stronger the ungodly soul tie and the greater rights Satan has to harass you.

Sexuality

Sexuality is another gift from God which was intended for our good but because of Adam's sin, Satan has used it as a weapon against us. Sex is primarily a spiritual act of oneness symbolized with a physical act. For it to be a blessing in marriage, there needs to be emotional and spiritual wholeness, free of domination, manipulation and control from either spouse. Emotional wounding or bondage in either person will damage and distort sexual intimacy. To have a healthy sexuality, you need complete trust, mutual respect and appreciation of each other which leads to oneness of body, soul and spirit. This creates a godly sexual soul tie.

An ungodly sexual soul tie occurs when sexuality becomes a tool of control. Yes, there can be an ungodly sexual soul tie even in Christian marriage. There can even be sexual abuse in Christian marriage which gets covered up by insisting on the scriptural submission of a woman to the will of the male. It is a sin to dominate, manipulate or control a spouse in any way, including sexually. It shows disrespect and treats the person as an object to meet the emotional needs of the other. Sexuality can be used as a tool of punishment or reward to control the other spouse. When it is used as a way of reassuring yourself of worth or acceptance, it can easily become an addiction that drives you for more. A very simple test of sexuality is to ask yourself this question, during sex are you lovingly giving yourself to your spouse or taking what you believe to be rightfully yours? If you are taking then you are on dangerous ground!

In my observation, most sexual problems are emotional and spiritual, not physical. The solution is the healing of our wounds.

Sexual sin will always create an ungodly soul tie, inside or outside of marriage. Sex is a spiritual event so sexual sin is a sinful spiritual act which makes one very vulnerable to the demonic, no differently than involvement in the occult. Satan has once again used our natural drives and attractions to lead us into sin and greater bondage. Ungodly soul ties are his route of oppression in relationships.

Back to Bill and Sue

Remember the troubled marriage of Bill and Sue? Bill was still being controlled by his mother and this frustrated Sue. His emotional wounds from childhood made him need to control his world so that he wouldn't feel any more pain. By being irritable and angry it intimidated the family not to do anything that would threaten his defensive walls. He escaped to the garage or TV as often as possible since there he could be in total control of his environment and not be threatened.

Sue had an emotionally empty marriage so she tried to find her identity in motherhood. She retaliated passively against

Bill's aggression by not speaking to him as a way to control and manipulate him. They both felt rejected by each other since they were codependent emotionally.

The teenagers were both in rebellion against the emotional pain and control in the home. One was passively rebellious through emotional and physical withdrawal, the other was aggressively rebellious through breaking all the family rules. Neither had any interest in church. They had become cynical since they saw no example of godliness in their parents. They lost respect for their parents' values so church represented just another form of bondage. This dysfunctional family had ungodly soul ties between Bill and his mother, Bill and Sue and between the parents and teens. The family was in severe emotional bondage, Satan loved it and made good use of it.

Many authors have noted that most marriage conflicts are caused by unhealed childhood emotions being triggered by a spouse. The relationship is poisoned by the unresolved past which causes couples to attack each other. The controlling relationships and ungodly soul ties of the past will disrupt the relationships in the present. God doesn't want you to live this way any longer. Recognize your wounds and pain and choose to begin the recovery process.

Could this happen in a church?

Churches are often referred to as big families because we are bonded to each other by our common interests and beliefs. As families, churches are then susceptible to all the relationship problems that families experience. Wherever you have people in emotional relationships you will find godly and ungodly soul ties. Yes, churches can be filled with ungodly soul ties whenever there are damaging relationships. Have you ever seen domination, manipulation and control in action in the church? Of course you have. It is not uncommon for there to be controlling behavior at every level of the church from layman, to deacon, to pastor. This gives Satan legal grounds to attack the church family since sin has contaminated these relationships. A church like this will be spiritually paralyzed and full of dissent. Satan loves these churches because they are never a threat to him.

How we get hurt

When we have been wounded by a damaging controlling relationship, it leaves an emotional scar and causes emotional pain. As I have mentioned before, when Satan sees our pain, he knows we are vulnerable. He then comes and plants a lie in our hearts that is related to the wounding event like, 'You must never trust them again,' or 'Never lose control of a relationship or you'll be hurt.' When there has been a church relationship wound, the lie may be 'Churches are dangerous places, never trust anyone, including God.'

Since there was a true historical event of wounding, the lie is accepted as fact and is again cemented into our hearts. This lie continues to disrupt our lives until we are healed of the wound. The pain of the lie causes us to build walls to protect our feelings but the walls harden our hearts and isolate us from people. When we live behind walls, we refuse to let anyone close to us for fear that we will be hurt again if we lose control of a relationship. This fear of vulnerability and the resulting walls, destroys our capacity for intimacy and becomes a major handicap in marriage, parenting and spiritual life. Again in this situation we choose the pain of loneliness and isolation rather than the risk of further injury.

Satan knows that he can keep people in emotional bondage as long as the lie and the ungodly soul tie is kept active. As we have seen before, he may assign an evil spirit to do just that. Emotional wounds and ungodly soul ties are points of great vulnerability to demonic attack. These wounds and ties must be healed if you are going to have godly healthy relationships, free of control and manipulation. God wants our freewill protected. We are not to be controlled or to control others. If you see yourself in this chapter it's time to break free from your bondage.

What's the way out?

Ask God to show you the ungodly soul ties that are controlling you or by which you control others. Prayerfully place the Cross between you and the ones who control you so that the channel of evil will be broken and you will be protected

The Cross can protect you from controlling influences.

from them. Ask God to expose and break the lies that have controlled you.

Forgive those who have controlled you, including parents, spouses and former spouses. Repent for hating them for what they did or are doing. Repent for controlling others to meet your needs. Then ask Jesus to set you free from the ungodly soul ties so that you can discover the liberty which comes in the presence of the Holy Spirit.

Well, it's time to wrap it up.

Conclusion

'Give thanks to the LORD, for his love endures forever.'
(2 Chronicles 20:21)

We have just completed a long journey together. We have
looked at the causes and solutions to the very common
problem of emotional bondage. You should now be able to
understand the balance between physical, personal and
spiritual factors that contribute to emotional instability. I
hope that God has spoken to you and revealed your areas of
emotional bondage. Most of all, I hope that you now realize
how much God loves you and wants to set you free. Now it's
up to you.

'What are you going to do now?'

Remember, the process of transformation is voluntary. You don't have to change. You can remain in your chains and still go to heaven. If God has exposed areas in your life where you need emotional healing, I encourage you to do something about it. Go and see a counselor. If you see yourself in the symptom checklist of chemical imbalances, take the list to your physician so you can start treatment. Don't be ashamed to walk down the path to freedom. Be brave enough to admit that you are tired of living the way you have been. It is God's will for you to be free. Take the risk of change.

Sometimes the changes come quickly and you will be greatly encouraged. At other times though, the process of change is painfully slow. Don't be discouraged, God is still leading you. To Jesus the process of transformation is just as important as the final goal. Be patient and never let go of His hand. You will never be the same again.

I would also encourage you to read the books listed in the 'Recommended reading' section. They will give you a great deal more information on many of the subjects that I have discussed.

Walk in freedom today.

I would like to close with a testimony from another one of my patients who made an amazing recovery and who was able to put it into words. I hope her story will encourage you to continue the journey that you began when you opened this book. May God bless and empower your walk to freedom.

Jesus came to release you from the power of sin, He also wants to set you free from the captivity of your mind.

The story of Mrs T

Ever since I can remember, I had nightmares and nagging feelings of self-doubt. I grew up in a very dysfunctional family and was the victim of emotional and sexual abuse. When I was a teenager, I contemplated suicide often and even wrote a suicide note on one occasion. Although I never acted on my thoughts, I had times of deep despair.

I had been raised a Christian but around the time of the worse sexual abuse I lost my faith in God. I always hoped something would happen so that I would get my faith back. I still believed Jesus was a very good man and I tried to live by His principles but I did not see Him as the Son of God or as any kind of personal redeemer.

I was plagued with very negative thought voices which said 'You are so useless, you are so stupid. The voices never said 'I am so stupid.' I did not realize the importance of this until I met Dr Mullen.

When I was twenty-two years old, I had open heart surgery to replace a damaged and infected mitral valve. The doctors could not adequately explain how I originally got the infection, why I deteriorated or how I could completely recover from the surgery. I took this as a sign that God wanted me alive and my faith in God began to grow again.

Almost two years later I was married and baptized along with my husband. Through these times I still had some very euphoric times and some very low times. I always felt I needed professional help. Since I always appeared to be so happy and relaxed, no one believed I needed help.

One day I almost exploded with rage and felt like punching someone in the face. I realized then that I had to get help. I entered into psychotherapy for the next several years. Although it was extremely hard work, it was by far the best thing I had ever done for myself. Even though it helped, I still felt there was a link missing in my healing. So I continued to search for inner peace.

I am a teacher and I had been studying about ADD to try to understand my students with learning disabilities. As I read more, I recognized myself and I wanted to get this confirmed and treated. It was at this time I met Dr Mullen.

How can I describe my first appointment with him other than to say that it was another major turning point in my life? As he took my history, my thoughts, my feelings, etc., he brought out things that I was not aware that I had been thinking. When he first started talking to me about demonic harassment, I thought he was nuts and I told him so. I had gone to see him for confirmation of my ADD and he told me that I was manic depressive with demonic harassment. The more we talked, the more it made sense and I was willing to try all that he suggested.

When I began lithium, I felt a new sense of calm in my mind and body that I had never experienced before. I was then able to read the book by Neil Anderson, *The Bondage Breaker* and went through the recommended spiritual cleansing. Once again this was a challenge for I had to be totally honest with myself and God. I learned how the abuse in my childhood allowed a foothold for Satan to get in and do his evil work. I also learned how other activities in my teen years also deepened the stronghold.

It was during this cleansing time that I began to gain an even deeper understanding and appreciation of what it meant to have Jesus as my Lord, Savior and protector. I only have to turn to Him in prayer for renewed strength, guidance and protection during times of temptation and harassment. Life is a journey and I feel much better equipped to handle the inevitable challenges life will have in store for me. My nightmares are virtually nonexistent and I am more focused. I have the mental and spiritual peace that I was searching for all my life.

I learned that complete healing was threefold:
1. Psychotherapy to heal the emotional scars left from years of abuse.
2. Medication to help me focus my mind for better thought control.

3. Spiritual cleansing and a deeper commitment to Jesus, made possible through the Holy Spirit who uses Neil Anderson's book.

If you feel you have any type of 'mental illness' I strongly encourage you to seek the professional help available. God wants us to be whole and happy people because it is then when we can do the best work for His Kingdom. I wish you God's richest blessing in your journey.

'May God himself, the God of peace, sanctify you through and through. May your whole spirit, soul and body be kept blameless at the coming of our Lord Jesus Christ. The one who calls you is faithful and he will do it.'

(1 Thessalonians 5:23–24)

Recommended reading

Most of the chapters in this book have been publicly presented by Dr Mullen and are available on audio or video for individual or group study. For more information contact:

Orchardview Medical Media
Box 395
Grimsby, Ontario
Canada L3M 4H8
Fax: 905-945-7770

or find a complete listing of Dr Mullen's material on the World Wide Web at:

www.orchardviewmedicalmedia.on.ca

or by searching for:

"why do I feel so down when my faith should lift me up?"

Books referred to in the text

Anderson, Neil, *The Bondage Breaker*. Harvest House, ISBN 0-89081-787-1

Arnott, John, *What Christians Should Know about the Importance of Forgiveness*. Sovereign World, ISBN 1-85240-215-6

Bergner, Mario, *Setting Love in Order*. Hamewith Books, Baker Publishing, ISBN 0-8010-5186-X

Chevreau, Guy, *Catch the Fire*. HarperCollins,
ISBN 0-551-02923-4

Eberle, Harold, *Spiritual Realities, Vol. 1, The Spiritual World
and How We Access It*. Winepress Publishing,
ISBN 1-882523-07-5

Frangipane, Francis, *The Three Battlegrounds*. Arrow
Publications, ISBN 0-9629049-0-2

Horrobin, Peter, *Healing through Deliverance, Vol. 1, The
Biblical Basis*. Sovereign World, ISBN 1-85240-052-8

Horrobin, Peter, *Healing through Deliverance, Vol. 2, The
Practical Ministry*. Sovereign World, ISBN 1-85240-039-0

Lowry, Mark, *Out of Control*. Nelson/Word,
ISBN 0-84991-300-4

McClung, Floyd, *The Father Heart of God*. Harvest House,
ISBN 0-89081-491-0

McGee, Robert, *The Search for Significance*. Rapha
Publishing, ISBN 0-945276-07-9

Montgomery, L.M., *Anne of Green Gables*. Seal Books,
McClelland-Bantam, ISBN 0-7704-2205-5

Mullen, Grant, *What Christians Should Know About
Depression, Anxiety, Mood Swings and Hyperactivity*. Sovereign
World, ISBN 1-85240-210-5

Payne, Leanne, *Crisis in Masculinity*. Hamewith Books, Baker
Publishing, ISBN 0-8010-5320-X

Payne, Leanne, *The Broken Image*. Hamewith Books, Baker
Publishing, ISBN 0-8010-5334-X

Payne, Leanne, *The Healing Presence*. Hamewith Books,
Baker Publishing, ISBN 0-8010-5348-X

Payne, Leanne, *Restoring the Christian Soul*. Hamewith
Books, Baker Publishing, ISBN 0-8010-5699-3

Payne, Leanne, *Pastoral Care Ministries (PCM) Conferences*.
Box 1313, Wheaton, Illinois, 60189-1313, USA

Sandford, John, *The Transformation of the Inner Man*. Victory House ISBN 0-932081-13-4

Sandford, John, *Healing the Wounded Spirit*. Victory House, ISBN 0-932081-14-2

Sandford, John, *Waking the Slumbering Spirit*. Clear Stream Publishing, ISBN 0-9637741-0-7

Sherman, Dean, *Spiritual Warfare for Every Christian*. Youth With A Mission Publishing, ISBN 0-92754-505-5

Smith, Dr Ed, *Alathia Equipping Centre*. Box 489, Campbellsville, KY 42719, USA

White, John, *The Masks of Melancholy*. Intervarsity Press, ISBN 0-87784-980-3

Exodus International

Exodus International is a ministry to help those struggling with same sex attraction and can be contacted at:

Exodus International Canada
PO Box 21039
Ajax, Ontario
Canada L1S 7H2

Tel: 905-686-7363
Fax: 905-686-1716

Exodus International Europe
PO Box 338
Watford, WD1 5HZ
England

Tel: 011-44-181-420-1066
Fax: 011-44-181-421-1692

Exodus International North America
PO Box 77652
Seattle, Washington
USA 98177

Tel: 206-784-7799
Fax: 206-784-7872

If you have enjoyed this book and would like to help us to send a copy of it and many other titles to needy pastors in the **Third World**, please write for further information or send your gift to:

Sovereign World Trust
PO Box 777, Tonbridge
Kent TN11 0ZS
United Kingdom

or to the **'Sovereign World'** distributor in your country.